Perspectives on Research Assessment in Architecture, Music and the Arts

Research in the creative fields of architecture, design, music and the arts has experienced dynamic development for over two decades. The research in these practice- and arts-based fields has become increasingly mature but has also led to various discussions on what constitutes doctoral proficiency in these fields. The term 'doctorateness' is often used when referring to the assessment of the production of doctoral research and the research competence of research students, but in architecture and the arts, the concept of doctorateness has not yet attained a clearly articulated definition. The assessment of quality has been *practiced* by way of supervising, mentoring and the evaluation of dissertations but much less *discussed*.

This book offers perspectives on how to qualify and assess research in architecture, music and the arts. It creates a broader arena for discussion on doctorateness by establishing a framework for its application to creative fields. The book is grouped into three sections and includes contributions from international experts in the various fields working in Australia, Belgium, Brazil, Canada, Norway, Sweden, Switzerland, Spain, the Netherlands and the UK. The first section offers general frameworks for further conceptualising doctorateness in the fields in question. It is followed by a section that describes and discusses various experiences, concerns and visions on the production and assessment of doctoral research reporting from doctoral programmes in different stages of development. The third section includes future-oriented perspectives on knowledge-building processes and asks how the ongoing, profound changes in academia could influence the concept of quality in both doctoral process and product.

The book presents different perspectives on research assessment practices and developments of relevant criteria in the practice-based and creative fields of architecture and the arts. The contributions propose ways of framing this issue conceptually, show the need for awareness of the specific context and tradition programmes develop and give proposals for various potential trajectories for the future.

Fredrik Nilsson is Professor of Architectural Theory and Head of the Department of Architecture at Chalmers University of Technology, Sweden.

Halina Dunin-Woyseth is Professor Emerita at the Oslo School of Architecture and Design, Norway, where she was the founding head of the doctoral programme.

Nel Janssens is Associate Professor in the Faculty of Architecture at KU Leuven, Campus Sint-Lucas, Brussels, Belgium, and visiting scholar in the Department of Architecture at Chalmers University of Technology, Sweden.

Routledge Research in Architecture

For a complete list of titles in this series, please visit www.routledge.com

The *Routledge Research in Architecture* series provides the reader with the latest scholarship in the field of architecture. The series publishes research from across the globe and covers areas as diverse as architectural history and theory, technology, digital architecture, structures, materials, details, design, monographs of architects, interior design and much more. By making these studies available to the worldwide academic community, the series aims to promote quality architectural research.

Cut and Paste Urban Landscape
The Work of Gordon Cullen
Mira Engler

Wooden Church Architecture of the Russian North
Regional Schools and Traditions (14th–19th centuries)
Evgeny Khodakovsky

Mid-Century Modernism in Turkey
Architecture Across Cultures in the 1950s and 1960s
Meltem Ö. Gürel

Bruno Taut's Design Inspiration for the Glashaus
David Nielsen

Conflicted Identities
Housing and the Politics of Cultural Representation
Alexandra Staub

Through the Healing Glass
Shaping the Modern Body through Glass Architecture, 1925–35
John Stanislav Sadar

Architecture as Cultural and Political Discourse
Case studies of conceptual norms and aesthetic practices
Daniel Grinceri

Sacred Architecture in a Secular Age
Anamnesis of Durham Cathedral
Marie Clausén

The Architecture of San Juan de Puerto Rico
Five centuries of urban and architectural experimentation
Arleen Pabón

Perspectives on Research Assessment in Architecture, Music and the Arts
Discussing Doctorateness
Fredrik Nilsson, Halina Dunin-Woyseth and Nel Janssens

Rethinking Basic Design in Architectural Education
Foundations Past and Future
Mine Özkar

Perspectives on Research Assessment in Architecture, Music and the Arts
Discussing Doctorateness

Edited by Fredrik Nilsson,
Halina Dunin-Woyseth
and Nel Janssens

LONDON AND NEW YORK

First published 2017
by Routledge
2 Park Square, Milton Park, Abingdon, Oxon OX14 4RN

and by Routledge
711 Third Avenue, New York, NY 10017

First issued in paperback 2018

Routledge is an imprint of the Taylor & Francis Group, an informa business

© 2017 selection and editorial matter, Fredrik Nilsson, Halina
Dunin-Woyseth and Nel Janssens; individual chapters, the
contributors

The right of Fredrik Nilsson, Halina Dunin-Woyseth and Nel
Janssens to be identified as the authors of the editorial material, and
of the authors for their individual chapters, has been asserted in
accordance with sections 77 and 78 of the Copyright, Designs and
Patents Act 1988.

All rights reserved. No part of this book may be reprinted or
reproduced or utilised in any form or by any electronic, mechanical,
or other means, now known or hereafter invented, including
photocopying and recording, or in any information storage or
retrieval system, without permission in writing from the publishers.

Trademark notice: Product or corporate names may be trademarks
or registered trademarks, and are used only for identification and
explanation without intent to infringe.

British Library Cataloguing-in-Publication Data
A catalogue record for this book is available from the British Library

Library of Congress Cataloging-in-Publication Data
Names: Nilsson, Fredrik, 1965– editor. | Dunin-Woyseth, Halina,
    editor. | Janssens, Nel, editor.
Title: Perspectives on research assessment in architecture, music and
    the arts : discussing doctorateness / edited by Fredrik Nilsson,
    Halina Dunin-Woyseth and Nel Janssens.
Description: New York : Routledge, 2017. | Includes bibliographical
    references and index.
Identifiers: LCCN 2016036573| ISBN 9781138695573 (hardback :
    alk. paper) | ISBN 9781315526652 (ebook)
Subjects: LCSH: Arts—Study and teaching (Graduate) | Arts—
    Research—Evaluation. | Doctor of arts degree.
Classification: LCC NX282 .P47 2017 | DDC 700.71—dc23
LC record available at https://lccn.loc.gov/2016036573

ISBN 13: 978-1-138-34220-0 (pbk)
ISBN 13: 978-1-138-69557-3 (hbk)

Typeset in Sabon
by Apex CoVantage, LLC

Contents

Acknowledgements	vii
Editorial: the art of assessment – focusing research *assessment from different perspectives*	ix
HALINA DUNIN-WOYSETH, NEL JANSSENS & FREDRIK NILSSON	
List of contributors	xxi

SECTION 1
Framing 'doctorateness'   1

1   Doctorateness: where should we look for evidence?   3
    MICHAEL BIGGS

2   Emerging epistemic communities and cultures of
    evidence: on the practice of assessment of
    research in the creative fields   15
    HALINA DUNIN-WOYSETH & FREDRIK NILSSON

3   Setting the scene: the development of formal
    frameworks for doctorates in Europe   33
    ANNE SOLBERG

SECTION 2
Various experiences, cases and concerns   49

4   Criteria for 'doctorateness' in the creative fields:
    a focus on architecture   51
    OYA ATALAY FRANCK

vi *Contents*

5 Preserving openness in design research in architecture 69
MURRAY FRASER

6 Design practice research in architecture and design at
RMIT University: discovery, reflection and assessment 85
COLIN FUDGE & ADRIANA PARTAL

7 Doctoral scholarship in popular music performance 101
TOR DYBO

8 Exploring, enhancing and evaluating musical
'doctorateness': perspectives on performance
and composition 114
KAREN BURLAND, MICHAEL SPENCER & LUKE WINDSOR

9 Constructing publics as a key to doctoral research:
a discussion of two PhD projects engaging in societal
issues with artistic and design-based methods 129
LIESBETH HUYBRECHTS & MARIJN VAN DE WEIJER

SECTION 3
Doctorateness to come? 145

10 Non-observational research: a possible future route for
knowledge acquisition in architecture and the arts 147
NEL JANSSENS & GERARD DE ZEEUW

11 When will it thunder? 159
ROLF HUGHES

12 Precision: the compositional accuracy of artistic
judgement 175
CATHARINA DYRSSEN

Index 190

Acknowledgements

The work with this book has engaged many people and entails, as with many book projects, a quite long process. The idea of the book originated, as it often happens, during academic discussions in a group consisting of several junior and senior scholars and which branches out in different contexts in the creative fields of architecture, design, the arts and art education.

The book frames within a larger research project entitled '"Doctorateness" in creative fields', which is part of the so-called strong research environment 'Architecture in the Making. Architecture as a Making Discipline and Material Practice' funded by the Swedish Research Council Formas. The aim of the program within the research environment is to develop architectural theories and methods to strengthen the field-specific research in architecture and has been done mainly from the perspective of the practices in the field. The aim of the specific project on assessment of research is to create a broader arena for discussion on doctorateness by establishing a framework for its application to creative fields.

The project on assessment of research in creative fields of architecture and the arts was initiated in discussions between Halina Dunin-Woyseth, Oslo School of Architecture and Design, and Fredrik Nilsson, Department of Architecture at Chalmers University of Technology, together with Laila Belinda Fauske and Anne Solberg at Telemark University College, which soon developed into the idea of this book. Soon Nel Janssens, KU Leuven and Chalmers, also joined the discussions. The book project woke interest also at the University of Agder, Norway, in the milieu of scholars in popular music, led by Professor Tor Dybo. The Norwegian and the Swedish participators of the project together provided funds for making the book. Since the beginning of the project, Anne Solberg has been an important driver in co-ordinating activities and securing extra funding, and she has made an invaluable contribution to the first stage of the book project. The editor team of the book highly appreciate her dedicated endeavours. We also thank Laila Belinda Fauske for her contributions in the early stage of the project.

As an important step in the process, an 'expert symposium' was arranged in May 2014 at Chalmers in Gothenburg, Sweden. Here the concept of the book was further defined in discussion among the editors, authors and a viii *Acknowledgements*

group of engaged scholars from the University of Agder, University of Southeast Norway (previously Telemark University College) and Chalmers, Department of Architecture, who engaged in constructive criticism of the draft chapters. We are grateful for the inspiring presentations by Michael Biggs, Oya Atalay Franck, Murray Fraser, Rolf Hughes, Tor Dybo and Catharina Dyrssen and the constructive criticism the presenters gave to each other and the valuable comments by Marte Gulliksen, Daniel Nordgård, Bjørn Ole Rasch, Laila Fauske, Anne Solberg and Marie Strid.

A special thanks to Michael Biggs, who has been an invaluable support to the editorial team through the process, with his sharp intellect and not least his excellent eye and skills for reviewing language. We would also like to thank Sade Lee, senior editorial assistant at Routledge and our main contact person, for all the support she provided.

We are grateful to the sponsors of the book, the University of Agder and University College of Southeast Norway, as well as for the financial support from Chalmers University of Technology and the Swedish Research Council Formas.

We would also like to thank our families for their constant support and patience during our academic endeavours and long exploration expeditions such as book projects.

Oslo, Brussels and Gothenburg, June 2016

Halina Dunin-Woyseth, Nel Janssens and Fredrik Nilsson

Editorial

The art of assessment – focusing research assessment from different perspectives

Halina Dunin-Woyseth, Nel Janssens &
Fredrik Nilsson

Over the past decades, the production of knowledge has become ever more recognised as being of central importance for our current society. The knowledge society therefore invests a lot in education and research, as can be noted from the relentless expansion of universities, both in number and in size, after 1970 and a similar evolution of large corporations with R&D departments and dedicated government scientific research institutions (Murphy 2013). In 1999 the Bologna Declaration was signed, and this was the start of major reformations in the European higher education institutions. In line with the increased demand for knowledge production, the Bologna process also brought about that areas that previously were not primarily driven by research, notably creative fields like architecture and the arts, now have to articulate how they produce knowledge and have to invest in developing genuine research communities.

The inclusion of the creative fields and their research culture in academia has a particular relevance in the dynamics of the Bologna process – a process that originated in a wish to strengthen openness, mobility, curiosity and creativity, inspired by medieval and Renaissance European culture (De Graeve 2010). Peter De Graeve points out the fundamental importance of architecture and the arts in this context and the central contributions made by Renaissance artists to the development of knowledge and scholarship. The same applies in the present-day situation. Current development in academia is obviously strongly connected with an economy driven by technology; but De Graeve argues that only if architecture and the arts are given – and take – a central place in the academic world will it be possible to attain the objectives of increased innovation, creativity and knowledge development.

Establishing a place in the academic world arguably involves to an important degree the development of research. This also implies the firm establishment of the doctoral level. In the Bologna-Berlin Communiqué of 2003 it was therefore stated that the ministers consider it necessary to go beyond the present focus on two main cycles of higher education to include the doctoral level as the third cycle in the Bologna Process (Bologna Process 2003, 7). It comes as no surprise, then, that research in creative fields has since been in dynamic and increased development. When using the term 'creative fields' in this book, we have in mind the fields of architecture, design, music and fine arts (cf. Frayling et al. 1997). Research in these practice- and arts-based fields has become increasingly mature in the past decade, yielding in various ways both field-specific knowledge and contributions to academic development in a broader perspective. This has happened thanks both to a well-developed but more traditional dialogue with established academic disciplines and to experimental and new forms and modes of practice- and arts-based research.

The development of research in creative, practice-based fields generates various questions and issues on the matter of what constitutes doctoral proficiency in these fields (or how this can be attained). Biggs and Büchler mention the emergence of a new incipient community of 'practitioner-researchers' (Biggs and Büchler 2011, 98). These practitioner-researchers are individuals who have experience and values as practitioners but who produce research in an academic context. Biggs and Büchler argue that there should be a distinct research model that is faithfully associated with the specific values of this new community of practitioner-researchers. One central question in this context is, then, how PhD students are to develop, master and manage their own creative capacity while being trained in the craft of research.

In parallel with the emergence of numerous different forms of doctoral programmes and degrees (with varying agendas and stakeholders with differing emphases and disparate historical and academic contexts, such as profession-based and artistic), a major discussion of the notion of 'doctorateness' and how it should be defined in the contemporary situation has developed (Denicolo and Park 2010; Philips, Stock, and Vincs 2009; Stock 2011). Several voices have coined the term 'doctorateness' while referring to the assessment of the production of doctoral research and the research competence of research students (e.g. Denicolo and Park 2010; Trafford and Leshem 2009). Important to notice in this respect is that 'doctorateness' requires a high-quality assessment practice that is transparent and arguably one that is relevant to the specificity of creative fields. In the oft-cited report *Practice-based Doctorates in the Creative and Performing Arts and Design*, about quality in doctoral theses in the creative and artistic spheres, issued by the UK Council for Graduate Education in 1997, 'doctorateness' is defined as follows: 'The essence of "doctorateness" is about an informed peer consensus on mastery of the subject; mastery of analytical breadth (where methods, techniques, contexts and data are concerned) and mastery of depth (the contribution itself, judged to be competent and original and of high quality)' (Frayling et al. 1997, 11). Artistic ability and research skills are assessed by examining boards and committees charged with evaluating the end products of doctoral studies, usually in the form of theses. These bodies investigate whether each thesis meets a sufficiently high standard for the candidate to be awarded the doctoral title. In other words, they judge

Editorial: the art of assessment xi

whether the end product shows that the candidate has attained a sufficient degree of 'doctorateness'.

In architecture and the arts the concept of doctorateness, however, has not yet attained a clearly articulated operational definition, linked to field-specific criteria and modes of assessment, that are academic-wide agreed upon. When developing their research environments in an academic context the creative fields have focused mainly on the production of doctoral theses. The discussion of doctoral research has been principally oriented to the modes of production and the output. The assessment of quality has been *practiced* by way of supervising, mentoring and evaluation of the dissertation but much less *discussed*. This has also been noticed by Biggs and Karlsson in the closing section of *The Routledge Companion to Research in the Arts* (2011), announcing that the next step in artistic research would be the problematic of evaluation and assessment. They assert that artistic research should understand its own value and the nature of its potential contribution to academia, so that existing evaluation systems can be adapted accordingly. What is required, in their opinion, is not to develop a special evaluation system for art but to ensure that the criteria for assessment are connected to the values and purposes of research in this field rather than rigidifying in obsolete forms or notions of where its value and significant contributions may lie (Biggs and Karlsson 2011, 405). They concluded that without serious stance in this regard, there is no possibility to establish serious research. The problem of assessment, however, is inextricably linked to the ongoing debate on the nature of the doctorate in creative fields. Every discussion on evaluation is necessarily anchored in a discussion on the nature of doctorates. The aim of this book therefore is to offer perspectives on *qualifying* doctoral research. Qualifying is a process in which identifying the characteristics (nature) and the quality (evaluation) are intertwined. At this stage of the maturity of research in creative fields, a better balance is needed between its production and the ongoing debate on its quality and how to assess this. The contributions in the book aim to give insight into pending qualification issues regarding research in architecture and the arts. With this we wish to feed the *discourse* on qualifying research in creative fields based on *qualifying practices* that have been developed in these fields of practitioners-researchers.

At the inception of the book we set up a special academic event as an alternative to the traditional blind peer review. Architecture and the arts being young academic fields, we consider the concepts of mutual learning in knowledge production as described in the knowledge-building discourse (Scardamalia and Bereiter 2010) to be very instrumental. This event was organized as an intense one day symposium during which the contributing authors presented the first draft of their chapter to the other authors and to expert panels of each university (Chalmers University of Technology, Telemark University College and the University of Agder) that had read the text beforehand and prepared questions and comments. That way

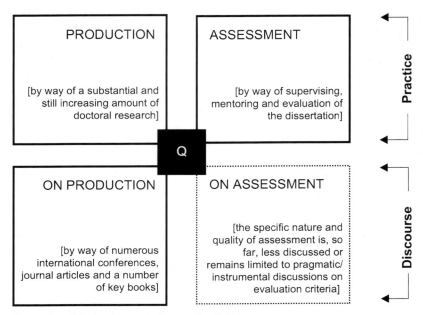

Q : *quality of doctorateness in the creative fields*

Fig. 0.1 Focus of the book
[Courtesy of H. Dunin-Woyseth, N. Janssens, F. Nilsson]

we established an extended scientific committee consisting of both authors and invited experts who engaged in a collective review and collective book production process. This helped articulate the relation among the different chapters and to sharpen the overall theme. Contributing authors and reviewers together with the editorial team discussed a number of recurrent and unresolved themes or issues that could be detected. One of these was the place of the doctorate in the educational system. Since the Bologna-Berlin Communiqué of 2003 it is supposedly the third cycle of education, which would arguably require a specific curriculum. The question then was raised whether the doctorate could be considered a kind of 'supermaster', a yet further specialisation or mastering – leading to the acquisition of even more knowledge and skills. Yet, it was said, doctorateness involves not merely a quantitative difference, it is about attaining a qualitative difference. This qualitative difference arguably is situated in the first and second levels (BA and MA), being mainly oriented to learning and exploiting the knowledge we already have, while the third level, doctoral research, is about producing new knowledge and acquiring and developing the techniques necessary to do so. In that sense the third level might not be well described as a kind of super MA. That the doctorate level implies a change of track from learning

Editorial: *the art of assessment*   xiii

and applying knowledge to developing knowledge is also illustrated by the example of some (British) university regulations that make it possible to do a PhD after completing the BA. However, in contradistinction to such a clear-cut change of track, we notice that most universities advocate a so-called research-based teaching in which everybody, from year one, starts to learn research skills. First, second and third levels (BA, MA and PhD) can then be considered a continuous educational curriculum in which a qualitative change in the sophistication and the amount of originality in handling and developing knowledge is expected by the time one gets to the PhD.

The third level, however, is very different from the first and second levels in terms of its financial base and its orientation to the professional world. While BA and MA are predominantly funded by state funding (with varying heights of tuition fees depending on the country) and lead to a diploma oriented to a professional career, the PhD is established on research funding and until fairly recently was almost exclusively oriented to an academic career. This however has started to change. In Sweden, for instance, about 20 percent of the graduated doctors stay or go back to academia. This means that 80 percent of the people with a doctoral degree leave academia. Especially in practice-based fields it is not yet clear what doctorateness adds to the educational trajectory of a practitioner, since the professional world has not clearly asked for this kind of specialisation in research. In architecture, however, there seems to be a growing demand for research expertise but also for research dissemination in the professional offices (see e.g. Hensel and Nilsson 2016). The current discourses on Mode 2 knowledge production and transdisciplinarity point out a changed relationship between research and society (Doucet and Janssens 2011; Dunin-Woyseth 2009; Gibbons et al. 1994; Thompson Klein et al. 2001), and this affects demands on the doctorate education, how it is formed, how it interacts through the process with society. The amount of so-called industrial doctorates is increasing also in practice-based fields. Large architectural firms contribute to the funding of a PhD student, working at the same time in the office. The company paying with external funding might then lead to a much richer interaction with society and also result in a type of dissemination in which people themselves go out into industry rather than their publications, which is a whole different idea, and take on the issue of dissemination of research results.

The relationship of academic and professional values and how they (dis)connect has been a topic of debate for a while now. But now the general trend of research, in all areas, not only in the creative fields, is to pull professional and academic values much more closely together. This is a consequence of the increasing use of research in professional, non-academic practices and transdisciplinary context in which present-day problems have to be investigated and solved. Given this evolving shift in the broad knowledge landscape, we might need to develop a different understanding of what is a scholar and what competence s/he needs to acquire. We might want to think of the xiv *Dunin-Woyseth, Janssens & Nilsson*

'adaptable' scholar, who can go into future problematising, having both research competence and the competence that is needed in practice, able to establish a direct contact between academy and practice. Such a profile also raises the question of the quality and nature of a (changing) learning environment. Doctorateness comes into being by what is achieved through a sort of shared community understanding around values and issues to address and methods to use while using certain languages and rewards attached to it. The question then becomes how to facilitate the highest-quality learning experiences and situations and which is the relation between individual and collective learning processes.

Another point raised during the peer-review event was the recurring discussion about the format of the thesis for doctoral work in the creative fields. The tension often debated is the relation between the written document and the artistic or design work. Some PhD programmes advocate that the artistic work itself can be the thesis; others insist on a written document accompanying the artistic work. The written part then is often considered a reflection on the creative work made and/or a contextualisation of the work in the broader field, but there is also another position which states that the act of writing is a key component for the creative project – in other words, writing does not have to be confined to the explanatory but can be equally part of the exploratory and the investigative. The re-deliberations on the position on writing and text already involves a considerable reconceptualisation of the format of a doctoral thesis. However, the stretch of the format continues when the pressure rises for adapting the standard to forms that are more suitable for specific artistic practices. Examples of such a stretch of the traditional PhD format are, for instance, a pair of acrobats applying for one PhD; a film collective of three people applying for one position and insisting that they're taken as three; music orchestras and so on. Since there are reasonable arguments for these 'out of the normal' requests, the pressure on the traditional (individual) format is rising and might soon lead to change. This means that we'll have to rethink the format of the PhD itself such that it supports the type of knowledge production that is at stake in creative fields. Although the idea of a shared, collective PhD or a zero-word PhD is apparently shocking. In the peer-review discussion of experts it was said that providing the community understands what that is, and it is considered to be a meaningful thing within a community, then we begin the process of actually consciously developing, validating and authorising it. In 1997 it was already reported in the UK Council for Graduate Education publication *Practice-based doctorates in the creative and performing arts and design* that for the music doctorates it is enough with 'accompanying commentary of 3.000–5.000 words' and in the particular case of a DPhil in composition at University of York, it said that 'Compositions may be submitted. May have accompanying notes, but not required' (Frayling et al. 1997).

The issues raised during the peer-review symposium of experts strengthened our conviction that production of doctoral work and assessment are

Editorial: the art of assessment xv

intertwined and closely dependent on each other. What became clear during the discussion was that although the main topic of the book is the issue of research assessment and evaluation, what was talked about the most was the nature of the doctorates. The problem of assessment remains inextricably linked to the ongoing debate on the nature of the doctorate in creative fields. We can only evaluate whether something has been successfully done or not in relation to some kind of agreed objective or purpose. What qualifies as doctorateness in creative fields has to relate to what ultimately are the objectives of practice-based research that is being developed and how these objectives are best met.

This book wants to contribute to this ongoing debate on issues of qualifying doctorateness and focuses this issue from different perspectives. The aim is to create a broader arena for discussion on doctorateness by establishing a framework for its application to creative fields. The book builds upon contributions that (1) offer general frameworks for further conceptualising doctorateness in the fields in question; (2) describe and discuss various experiences, cases and concerns in the production and assessment of doctoral research reporting from currently developing doctoral programmes; and (3) ask the question about how the ongoing, profound changes in academia are going to influence the concept of quality in both doctoral process and product.

The three groups of contributions are organised in three sections. Section 1 is about framing the concept of doctorateness. This is done by three contributions. The first one, written by Michael Biggs, addresses the societal context and specialist communities in which doctorates are evaluated. This chapter considers the possibility of an 'institutional theory of artistic research'. It proposes four distinct quadrants in which one might look for evidence for such a theory, which needs to have the capacity to accommodate the diverse positions on artistic research in the literature. The quadrants are named 'explicit', 'implicit', 'generic' and 'specific' and form a Boolean square with which one may also consider the contested term 'doctorateness' in any field.

The second chapter reflects upon the conceptual frameworks surrounding the concept of doctorateness and how it could be considered in the field of architecture, design and arts. The authors Halina Dunin-Woyseth and Fredrik Nilsson build upon their experiences from doctoral programmes in several countries, and in this chapter they use a study of the development of assessment practice at one institution during 10 years as the base for reflections on how the assessment frameworks have changed and can be elaborated further. The practice of assessment of doctorateness can be seen to have developed to include more of the field-specific character of the discipline and professional practice and has started to engage the emerging communities of 'practitioner-researcher' with their multiple competences and backgrounds. The chapter elaborates on the conceptual frameworks for assessment of research in the creative fields by using, for example, Elliot

xvi Dunin-Woyseth, Janssens & Nilsson

Eisner's model of connoisseurship and criticism and current discussions on different approaches and models for evaluation of transdisciplinary research.

In the third and last chapter of Section 1 Anne Solberg discusses the formal frameworks of regulations that surround the establishment of the third cycle of education in the creative fields, for instance, EU Bologna. The focus of this chapter is on the challenges facing doctorateness in architecture, design and the arts, with respect to the criteria of doctorateness in the Dublin Descriptors' third cycle, and the definition of research that is upheld in the descriptors. Questions regarding the obligatory nature and the scope of opportunities within formal frameworks of these international norms are discussed, and the consequent impact on national standards of doctorateness is exposed by a Norwegian case study.

In Section 2 expert witnesses provide insight into the various experiences, concerns and visions they have regarding doctorateness in their respective university departments (architecture, arts/design, music). The section opens with experiences from the Swiss context, and in the first chapter Oya Atalay Franck illustrates a situation in the country in which there is still a debate on the relevance of doctoral research in architecture. She dwells on what direction such doctoral studies should take in the future and suggests that one scenario could provide for two parallel kinds of studies, one to be called a 'Super Master', resulting in advanced expertise in designing complex buildings, and another one, based on theoretical underpinnings of the design, that is, its principles, concepts and methods, offering new insights into designing and building processes. The quality to be required from such work, that is, its doctorateness, should correspond with the general cross-disciplinary standards of advanced academic work as well as with the specific requirements of architectural design and of research into the art of building.

From the Swiss experience, the next chapter in Section 2 moves the perspective to the Anglo-Saxon context. Murray Fraser describes the development of doctoral studies at the Bartlett School of Architecture and at the University of Westminster. With their relatively long history of PhD studies in the UK in mind, the author concentrates on addressing criteria for the assessment of PhDs by design. He argues that it is essential to retain a sense of openness and experimentation in architectural design research. He finds it as crucial that 'doctorateness' be perceived through two criteria sets: first, what are the kinds of new knowledge being created as doctoral scholarship or 'doctorateness' and, second, what kinds of methodological approaches have been, or ought to be, used to do so?

In the third chapter Colin Fudge and Adriana Partal report from development of the doctoral studies at the RMIT University in Melbourne, Australia. They explain the origins and background to the RMIT model for design practice research and note that the model in operation today across three continents has developed considerably over the last thirty years with the foundational ideas remaining at the core of the model. They further discuss the model and the assessment component of the doctoral process

Editorial: the art of assessment xvii

with external and international jury members. Qualitative comments formulated by these jury members are included in the text, providing further insights on the assessment process and the value of the model. The authors conclude this chapter with their own reflections on the model and doctoral assessment, ideas on a wider research agenda on the development of design practice research, translation to other disciplines, applications in the wider policy and practice world and the notion and purpose of the contemporary university.

In the next chapter the perspective shifts from architecture to the field of music. Popular music performance is a new field for doctoral studies in Norway. A new doctoral programme in the field created by orally transferred musical traditions such as rock, pop, reggae, folk songs, jazz, world music and the like was established at the University of Agder in Kristiansand in 2008. Tor Dybo presents in his text this programme, where a particular emphasis is placed on knowledge areas characterised by intuitive and tacit knowledge among, for example, musicians, sound engineers and producers in recording studios and on stage. A serious challenge has been to develop theoretical and methodological approaches to this research field and, not least, to develop appropriate criteria for evaluating doctoral theses, addressing both academic and artistic-creative processes and their results. This duality and complementarity are reflected in the final products of these doctoral studies, as they consist of a practical, performative part and a traditional thesis.

Karen Burland, Michael Spencer and Luke Windsor from the University of Leeds then consider in their chapter practice-based research degrees (RDs) in music composition and performance in order to establish the characteristics of musical 'doctorateness'. Semi-structured interviews with supervisors and students at the University of Leeds were analysed thematically using interpretative phenomenological analysis and four key themes emerged: personal characteristics; defining practice, establish process; relationships with supervisors; and assessment, contexts and commonality. The data suggest that the shape and progress of the research is underpinned by three interrelating factors: practice–self-reflection–identity, in conjunction with positive working relationships with supervisors. Compared to their traditional counterparts, practice-based doctoral programmes in music are a relatively recent development in the UK. Their emergence is noted to the early 1980s, and they must satisfy both academic demands and those relating to professional practice. They must focus on both product and process and at the same time consider professional or personal identity – ensuring their voice is heard clearly. The authors therefore highlight the need for greater discussion and greater recognition of practice as research.

We end this section with a Belgian perspective provided by Liesbeth Huybrechts and Marijn van de Weijer, who explore the meaning of 'doctorateness' in PhD trajectories in art and design that engage with public issues, public spaces and/or act as resources that 'publics' can debate and contribute to in their own ways. They reflect on the challenges of defining doctorateness in art and design disciplines when doing research that constructs publics around the complex situations of contemporary society. In the chapter they present two Flemish PhD projects that deal with everyday issues, respectively employment and housing, and centre on constructing publics on spatial aspects of these broad societal concerns. This leads to a proposition of ways for nurturing a more nuanced debate on the richness and diversity of doctorateness in art and design that actively engage with societal issues and publics. They conclude by outlining specific requirements for PhD candidates in this field and point out that these can nurture a more nuanced debate on the richness and diversity of ways in which doctorateness in art and design can be understood and put into practice.

This second section of the book reports from experiences that illustrate the complex landscape of doctoral research in different countries and in various traditions. The context of the various countries and different creative and performing fields are of importance for demonstrating a growing awareness of significance of relevant assessment of doctoral scholarship as an indissoluble part of the process of producing new, relevant doctoral knowledge and insight of high quality.

Following this, Section 3 then offers more future-oriented perspectives on knowledge-building processes that can offer specific conceptualisations of doctorateness in the creative fields. Nel Janssens and Gerard de Zeeuw, in their chapter, argue that practice-based research cannot be positioned in the (still dominant) paradigm of observational research. Instead, they propose methods for 'non-observational research' as a suitable paradigm for the making disciplines. They discuss this type of research as a proper extension of observational research. Non-observational research takes individual values and preferences as its resources. In this light, they introduce the notions of 'instructions' as outcome and argue that in practice-based fields the development of instructions is about the improved recognition of structures and artifacts to extend the interactive performance of experiences. In addition, they address the base for evaluation and doctorateness this type of research generates.

Rolf Hughes, in his chapter 'When will it thunder?', argues that doctorateness should be treated as an open-textured concept (not unlike 'art' or 'artistic research'). It addresses the challenges for those developing learning resources for doctoral candidates in artistic research. How might we prepare our students for futures we are currently incapable of imagining? How is a practice changed by investigation into that practice? Research exposes the implicit assumptions that underpin habits, making the artist's own sensibility a legitimate area of inquiry. The relation between a standardised curriculum and resources tailored to the individual learning needs of each doctoral candidate accordingly becomes a central question.

In the last chapter of Section 3, Catharina Dyrssen discusses the artistic precision and judgment in relation to doctoral research. Judgement usually implies selection, an understanding embedded in Western traditions of

Editorial: *the art of assessment* xix

knowledge, law or taste, and this is reinforced by contemporary funding and career machineries. Dyrssen, however, explores judgement as precise, contextual and performative action with compositional logics and perspectives mainly from architecture and music. This stresses judgement as actions of spatial-compositional modelling that continuously enrich knowledge and avoid reductive indicators of standard evaluation. She further argues that artistic research and education, now maturing, rapidly diversify and merge into various practices in dynamic interactions between research fields, critically questioning romantic views on 'artistic processes' as well as traditional logics of cause and effect, academic procedures and criteria.

Our intention with this book is to offer different perspectives on the issue of how to develop relevant and fruitful research assessment practices and criteria in the practice-based and 'creative' fields of architecture and the arts. The three sections propose ways of framing this issue and its development conceptually, show the need for awareness of the specific context and tradition programmes develop in as well different phases and levels of their maturity and give proposals for various trajectories and potentials for the future. We hope that readers will get inspiration from the contributions in similar ways as we have got when working with this project and its contributors and that this book will trigger further discussions that will contribute to what a more operational definition of 'doctorateness' entails. Our hope is that this can serve as a means of strengthening dialogues between professional researchers and professional practitioners – who, more and more, will come to be the same people, being researchers and practitioners in the new community of 'practitioner-researchers'. These dialogues and discussions will need to be maintained and continued.

Bibliography

Biggs, Michael and Daniela Büchler. 2011. 'Communities, Values, Conventions and Actions'. In *The Routledge Companion to Research in the Arts*, edited by Michael Biggs and Henrik Karlsson, 82–98. London: Routledge.

Biggs, Michael and Henrik Karlsson. 2011. 'Evaluating Quality in Artistic Research'. In *The Routledge Companion to Research in the Arts*, edited by Michael Biggs and Henrik Karlsson, 405–424. London: Routledge.

Bologna Process. 2003. *Realising the European Higher Education Area: Bologna-Berlin Communique*. http://www.bologna-bergen2005.no/Docs/00-Main_doc/030919Berlin_Communique.PDF.

De Graeve, Peter. 2010. *No University without the Arts*. Brussels: Associated Faculty of Arts and Architecture.

Denicolo, Pam and Chris Park. 2010. *Doctorateness: An Elusive Concept?* Gloucester: The Quality Assurance Agency for Higher Education. http://www.qaa.ac.uk/Publications/InformationAndGuidance/Documents/doctorateness.pdf.

Doucet, Isabelle and Nel Janssens, eds. 2011. *Transdisciplinary Knowledge Production in Architecture and Urbanism: Towards Hybrid Modes of Inquiry*. Dordrecht, Heidelberg, London and New York: Springer Science+Business Media.

Dunin-Woyseth, Halina. 2009. 'On Designed Knowledge Artefacts'. In *Communication (by) Design*, edited by Johan Verbeke and Adam Jakimowicz, 277–293. Brussels: School of Architecture Sint-Lucas.

Frayling, Christopher, Valery Stead, Bruce Archer, Nicholas Cook, James Powel, Victor Sage, Stephen Scrivener, and Michael Tovey. 1997. *Practice-Based Doctorates in the Creative and Performing Arts and Design*. Lichfield: UK Council for Graduate Education.

Gibbons, Michael, Camille Limoges, Helga Nowotny, Simon Schwartzman, Peter Scott, and Martin Trow. 1994. *The New Production of Knowledge: The Dynamics of Science and Research in Contemporary Societies*. London: Sage Publications.

Hensel, Michael and Fredrik Nilsson. 2016. *The Changing Shape of Practice: Integrating Research and Design in Architecture*. London: Routledge.

Murphy, Peter. 2013. 'The Creativity Collapse: Why Creativity in the Arts and Sciences Is Declining and Why You Should Care'. Agnes Heller Lecture in Sociology, La Trobe University Faculty of Humanities and Social Sciences, November 6.

Philips, Maggi, Cheryl F. Stock, and Kim Vincs. 2009. 'Dancing Doctorates Down-Under? Defining and Assessing "Doctorateness" When Embodiment Enters the Thesis'. In *Dance Dialogues: Conversations Across Cultures, Artforms and Practices*, edited by Cheryl Stock. Canberra: Australian Dance Council & Queensland University of Technology. http://www.ausdance.org.au/resources/publications/dance-dialogues.html.

Scardamalia, Marlene and Carl Bereiter. 2010. 'A Brief History of Knowledge Building'. *Canadian Journal of Learning and Technology / La Revue Canadienne de L'apprentissage et de La Technologie* 36 (1): 1–16.

Stock, Cheryl F. 2011. 'Approaches to Acquiring "Doctorateness" in the Creative Industries: An Australian Perspective'. In *Pre-Conference Proceedings*, edited by Lorraine Justice and Ken Friedman. Hong Kong: Hong Kong Polytechnic University. http://www.sd.polyu.edu.hk/docedudesign2011/doc/papers/344.pdf.

Thompson Klein, Julie, Walter Grossenbacher-Mansuy, Rudolf Häberli, Alain Bill, Roland W. Scholz, and Myrtha Welti, eds. 2001. *Transdisciplinarity: Joint Problem Solving among Science, Technology, and Society*. Basel: Birkhäuser.

Trafford, Vernon and Shosh Leshem. 2009. 'Doctorateness as a Threshold Concept'. *Innovations in Education and Teaching International* 46 (3): 305–16.

Contributors

Fredrik Nilsson is Professor of Architectural Theory and Head of the Department of Architecture at Chalmers University of Technology, Sweden. Nilsson was head of R&D at White Architects 2007–2014. His research is directed to developments in contemporary architecture, especially the epistemology of architecture and interaction between theory, conceptual thinking and design work, aiming to reinforce exchange between research and architectural practice.

Nel Janssens is Associate Professor at the KU Leuven, Faculty of Architecture, campus Sint-Lucas Brussels, Belgium. She holds a MSc in architecture and spatial planning, and obtained a doctoral degree at the Department of Architecture, Chalmers University of Technology. Her research interest is directed to the link between critical theory and research by design. She is a founding member of the radical materiality research platform at KU Leuven Faculty of Architecture.

Halina Dunin-Woyseth is Professor Emerita at Oslo School of Architecture and Design (AHO). Since 1990 she has been the founding head of the doctoral programme at AHO, and she has contributed to developing several doctoral programmes in various creative fields internationally. Her main research interests are knowledge in design professions, epistemology of architecture and philosophy of science. She has a broad international teaching and research practice.

Oya Atalay Franck is an architect and architectural historian. Having taught architecture and construction, urbanism and architecture theory at RPI in Troy, NY, at Bilkent University in Ankara and at ETH Zürich, she is currently the head of architecture at ZHAW in Winterthur, Switzerland. Her research interests are architecture and politics, urbanism, research by design and architectural education.

Michael Biggs is Emeritus Professor of Aesthetics at the University of Hertfordshire and Adjunct Professor at the University of Canberra. Biggs is a leading figure in arts research. He is member of the board of the National

xxii *Contributors*

Research School in Architecture, Sweden, and the Interdisciplinary Expert Panel of the Belgian Research Council.

Karen Burland is Associate Professor of Music Psychology and Head of the School of Music at University of Leeds. Her research interests relate to musical identities, the career transitions of musicians and live music audiences and she supervises doctoral work primarily in these areas. She is currently a university student education fellow.

Tor Dybo is Professor of Musicology at the Department of Popular Music, University of Agder (UiA) in Kristiansand, Norway. Dybo is head of the doctoral programme in Popular Music Performance at UiA. His fields of research, teaching and supervising are ethnomusicology, jazz and popular music.

Catharina Dyrssen is Professor of Architecture and Design Methods at Chalmers University, Sweden. Her research cross-connects architecture, urbanism, design methodology, music and sound art, with twenty-five years of engagement in artistic research and doctoral education. In 2009–2015 she was a member and head of Swedish Research Council's Committee for Artistic Research.

Murray Fraser is Professor of Architecture and Global Culture at the Bartlett School of Architecture at UCL and Vice-Dean of Research. He has published extensively on design, history & theory, urbanism and cultural studies, including the award-winning book *Architecture and the 'Special Relationship'* (2008), and as editor for *Design Research in Architecture* (2013).

Colin Fudge is Emeritus Professor at RMIT University; Professor of Urban Futures and Design at Chalmers University; Senior Adviser to the EU Climate KIC; Global Adviser for the UN Global Compact Cities Programme and for UN Habitat and is Royal Professor of Environmental Science, Sweden. He has worked in universities in Europe and Australia and in government in the UK, Sweden, Australia and the European Commission.

Rolf Hughes is a prose poet, researcher and Professor of Artistic Research at Stockholm University of the Arts. He was previously professor, expert, and senior researcher at Konstfack, KU Leuven, the Swedish Research Council, and KTH School of Architecture and elected vice president of the Society for Artistic Research 2011–2015.

Liesbeth Huybrechts is a postdoctoral researcher in the area of participatory design and spatial transformation processes in the research group Arck, at the Faculty of Architecture and Arts, University of Hasselt. She is involved in the Living Lab the Other Market, a space for reflection and action on the future of (space for) work.

Contributors xxiii

Adriana Partal is a researcher on cultural policies, cultural sustainable development and cultural impact assessment and Project Officer, Urban Futures working for RMIT University Europe, Barcelona. Her career in the arts and media industries has specialised in research on cultural policies. She also worked for the EU in Germany, the Goethe University Frankfurt, and RMIT University in Melbourne.

Anne Solberg is Assistant Professor within Art and Design Education and a PhD candidate in Cultural Studies at University College of Southeast Norway. She is an artist within ceramic art and a jurist and has a professional background as head of institute and dean of faculty. Her research interest is in the international development of doctorates in the creative fields.

Michael Spencer is Associate Professor of Music and Head of Composition at University of Leeds. Between 1998 and 2004 he worked privately with James Dillon, on whose work he has published three articles. His music has been performed nationally, internationally and on BBC Radio 3 and is available on CD.

Marijn van de Weijer is a postdoctoral researcher at the Faculty of Architecture and Arts, Hasselt University, interested in spatial transitions in (post) industrial landscapes. He holds an MSc in architecture from Eindhoven University of Technology, a MA in human settlements from KU Leuven, and a PhD in engineering and architecture from KU Leuven and Hasselt University.

Luke Windsor is Associate Professor of Music Psychology and Faculty Pro-Dean for Student Education at University of Leeds. He has been researching and teaching psychological, aesthetic, analytical and semiotic aspects of music since the mid-1990s. He has supervised doctoral work on a range of topics including improvisation.

Gerard de Zeeuw is Emeritus Professor of Mathematical Modelling of Complex Social Systems at University of Amsterdam, the Netherlands. He is Visiting Professor of Systems Management at University of Lincoln and Senior Professor of Architectural Design Research at KU Leuven and holds various honorary memberships.

Section 1

Framing 'doctorateness'

Doctorateness: where should we look for evidence?

Michael Biggs

Emerging epistemic communities and cultures of evidence: on the practice of assessment of research in the creative fields

Halina Dunin-Woyseth & Fredrik Nilsson

Setting the scene: the development of formal frameworks for doctorates in Europe

Anne Solberg

1 Doctorateness
Where should we look for evidence?

Michael Biggs

Discussion and debate about the nature and role of the doctorate, and therefore how it should be evaluated, can be found in all disciplines. However, there are certain disciplines in which the debate seems particularly wide ranging, and therefore the topic of evaluation has less consensus. In the creative arts, including music, architecture, creative writing, fine arts and design, and the like, the debate about doctoral research often includes fundamental issues about art and knowledge (Eisner 2008) and consequently what the creative arts can contribute to academic research (Knowles and Cole 2008). In education, the debate is often focussed on the transferable concept of level of achievement or competencies called 'doctorateness' (Trafford and Lesham 2009). I intend to approach the issue of the contribution to the arts of doctoral research by looking at a recent dispute in the educational debate about doctorateness. In this dispute, Wellington and Poole adopted different analyses of doctorateness, resulting in opposing conclusions.

Wellington offers five main arenas in which the concept of the doctorate can be discussed: the purposes of doctoral study, the impact of doctorates, written regulations for the award of the doctorate, the examination process and the voices of those involved in it (Wellington 2013, 1491). He assumes that what is being evaluated is the written thesis rather than the competencies of the candidate, and despite analysing various constituent categories in each arena he concludes 'we should give up a search for some sort of "inner essence" of doctorateness' (Wellington 2013, 1501). Wellington believes that 'doctorateness' is an 'essentially contested concept' and that it suffers from the same kind of indeterminacy as Wittgenstein's concept of a game (Wittgenstein 1953, §66). His main positive conclusion is that being 'publishable' is 'the single most necessary (though not on its own sufficient) quality that makes up a doctorate' (Wellington 2013, 1502). Poole (2014), on the other hand, rejects this response to the polysemous nature of many of the terms used in the debate about doctorateness. He argues that by unpacking some of the plurality or ambiguity we may yet refine the concepts and reveal the causal variants between the disputants. For example, he finds many opposed assumptions made by Wellington and others, including whether it is the thesis or the candidate that is being evaluated, whether it is the process or

4   Michael Biggs

the outcome, whether the examiner is acting as gatekeeper or community builder and where on the 'cline of originality' we require a successful thesis to lie (Poole 2014, 7).

The disagreement between Wellington and Poole reveals two different approaches to where one should look for evidence. Wellington's interpretation is based on case studies of doctoral supervision, whereas Poole's is based on a structural analysis of the doctorate as a process. Both agree that the outcome should be significant to the community but disagree whether this consists in making an individual 'contribution' (Wellington) or in meeting community-endorsed criteria for being 'publishable' that is assured through the process of peer review (Poole). These differences can be explained by looking more closely at the evidence that is being used and in particular by looking at the broader social context in which doctorates are evaluated.

Social authorisation

Our expectations of the nature of doctoral study do not arise out of the blue – advanced study of any kind is rooted in the requirements and expectations of individual disciplines and framed within overall notions of training, accreditation and qualification in institutional settings such as universities, training colleges, industry and so forth. The doctorate is differentiated from other levels of education by its requirement that the candidate contributes to the knowledge or understanding we already have in the subject. This places two obvious requirements on the doctoral candidate. The first is that they gain a thorough understanding of the subject (sometimes known as the literature review) so that they know what is the current state of knowledge and where an original contribution might be made (sometimes known as the gap analysis). The second is that the candidate has techniques (sometimes known as research methods) that will allow him or her to make a valid contribution that is accepted by the community and other stakeholders (Park 2007, 7f.). The second requirement is normally satisfied by what is known as discipline-specific research training that connects generic knowledge-production techniques to the specialist interests of particular academic or professional communities.

What we understand by 'research training' looks very different from one discipline to another. For example, in the hard sciences, research training is often training in specific techniques that constitute the industry standard for competent professional practice, such as 'the leaching test'. In the humanities, there tends to be less standardisation about what are current professional competences, and so research training tends to involve exposure to different interpretational frameworks such as post-structuralism, critical theory and so forth. In the creative arts the situation is even more diverse than it is in the humanities. Here one finds that research training takes a wide variety of forms but still has the same role in a doctoral programme, that is, to make the candidate aware of the ways in which different intellectual and critical approaches to an issue change the responses that would be appropriate and the kind of artistic outcomes that would result. Thus as one moves from the hard sciences through humanities and social sciences into creative arts, one sees that the nature of research training changes from training in specific technical competencies into training in a particular intellectual or artistic stance. I believe that both professional competencies and critical rigour are necessary in all disciplines, and so perhaps it would be better to say that in the hard sciences the emphasis is on technical competencies with less emphasis on but still a presence of intellectual and critical awareness and that in creative arts the emphasis is the reverse. As a thought experiment one can imagine that a doctoral candidate in science who failed to exhibit technical competencies would probably fail, but equally a doctoral candidate in creative arts who only exhibited technical competencies would also probably fail.

This balance of intellectual and technical competencies relates to the values of the individual disciplines. I have claimed elsewhere that research training enables the candidate to make a valid contribution to knowledge and understanding in their discipline (Biggs and Büchler 2007). Part of the validity of this contribution consists in demonstrating that the candidate understands how knowledge is currently produced in the field. It is a professional competence that in the humanities one reaches for an intellectual position rather than a piece of laboratory equipment in order to gather or interpret data. By engaging in a legitimised professional activity the candidate demonstrates membership of the community. The candidate also demonstrates that he or she is able to understand the current state of knowledge in the field and to undertake a gap analysis precisely because the intellectual and professional framing of the discipline is an integral part of identifying the content of the discipline. We therefore have a virtuous circle containing the knowledge and understanding of the discipline, the training that is necessary for a doctoral candidate, gap analysis and contribution of the candidate that ultimately feeds back into the shared knowledge and understanding of the discipline. This fairly traditional structural description of research practice is equally applicable to the creative arts and sciences given a certain flexibility about the reference of each of the terms beyond their traditional uses, for example, 'literature review'.

The virtuous circle of knowledge is endorsed and authorised by the professional community, and the broader intellectual context in which it is situated gives us a clue as to how we might deal with paradigm shifts or novel worldviews (Guba and Lincoln 2005). The difference between a paradigm shift and what is simply incompetent professional activity lies in the ability of the community to perceive an advantage in the new way of thinking. This may take time, and there is always a certain amount of intellectual inertia or resistance. However, a permanent failure to persuade is perhaps the indicator of incompetence rather than revolution. Artistic practices are

6   Michael Biggs

sometimes called transgressive, but the difference between what is transgressive and what is madness also lies in the ability of the community to find value in what is presented. Indeed, what is madness is also a notion of society and collective agreement rather than having objective criteria. Park (2005, 196) claims that the doctorate, rather than being an objective construction, is a social construction, echoing a broader contemporary trend in philosophy of science (cf. Bloor 1991 [1976]) towards social rather than epistemic foundationalism.

This thought experiment with notions of professional competence and community legitimisation reveals the way in which our notions of what is normal, transgressive or madness are grounded in consent, particularly amongst persons who are societally authorised to 'tell us what to think'. For example, in the art world, expert representatives of the community such as curators find value in some practices that are regarded as madness by the general public – the 'institutional theory of art' defines 'what is art' by what curators say is art. The content and boundaries of disciplines and intellectual practices are not fixed, and we can expect that doctoral candidates who are working at the highest levels of intellectual training and creative artists who normally work at the maximum reaches of innovation might find themselves working on sites of tension. These tensions will also be exacerbated because of the societal situation in which the establishment, for example, the university, is authorised to endorse a candidate as someone who understands the limits of the discipline and becomes qualified to extend those limits. This implies a new 'institutional theory of artistic research' that defines 'what is artistic research' by what academics say is artistic research, with its concomitant tensions between academia, the art world and society as a whole.

Professional and academic values: what to look for

The assessment process has three principal stakeholders: the assessor, the person or work being assessed and the context in which the assessment is used – for example within an institution or within a social group who recognise the validity of that judgement. This social context may authorise the assessor to make judgements on behalf of the community, for example, we authorise certain assessors to make judgements about the competence of medical practitioners on our behalf, and we accept the consequence that some people are therefore allowed to practice medicine while others are not. Whether at a micro or macro level this process of assessment is normally undertaken by one group on behalf of and with the consent of another. At the moment, doctoral evaluation in the arts often lacks representation from the professional art world, reflecting the perception that artistic doctorates are relevant in academia but not necessarily in the gallery. As a result the dominant concept of doctorateness in creative arts constitutes an 'institutional theory of artistic research'. I was once in discussion with a Swedish curator

Doctorateness: where should we look? 7

who said to me that she would only be interested in doctoral research in the arts when it produced good art, which revealed an erroneous assumption on her part that the institutional theories of art and artistic research are the same.

The difference between these two theories lies in the difference between professional and academic values in the arts and whether the professional objectives of curators and gallery owners are the same as the academic objectives of doctoral programmes or advanced training in the arts. There is no intrinsic reason these objectives should be the same, although there may be political reasons academic objectives should be brought more in line with professional objectives, for example in order to demonstrate that taxpayer/ stakeholder investment is meeting real-world needs. The academic structure of research in any discipline does not necessarily result in commercial benefit, although it may so result. The commercial exploitation of knowledge in the form of R&D is often a separate process to the generation of theoretical or academic knowledge (by which I do not intend to imply any hierarchy of values). So it is that a process that satisfies the academic requirements for a doctorate or of doctoral training in the arts does not necessarily result in good gallery art. Similarly, good art does not necessarily warrant the award of a doctorate. The institutional theories of art and artistic research are not the same principally because those who are authorised by society to make value judgements are not the same, that is, curators on one hand and academics on the other.

Analysis of sources of data: where to look

Depending on the country in which the doctoral examination takes place, the evidence for awarding a doctorate may be intrinsic or extrinsic. Evidence that I describe as intrinsic would include the written thesis and any portfolio of artwork or previous publications that may constitute the formal submission. In Australia this is normally all that the examiner has as evidence, whereas in Europe the examiner is also presented with the candidate at a *viva voce* examination. Evidence that I describe as extrinsic would include all those extra-textual references that are not included in the submission, and the academic and societal context to which the study refers and against which it must be evaluated. In addition to differentiating intrinsic and extrinsic evidence we can differentiate between the generic and the discipline-specific aspects of the work. At a generic level we have the requirement that the doctoral candidate has been trained in some way as a researcher. At a discipline-specific level we have a requirement that the candidate or the study makes a contribution to the discipline. These four sources of data form a Boolean square within which we may consider the contested term 'doctorateness' (see Table 1.1).

The extrinsic-generic quadrant comprises the social context in which we have a class of persons with doctoral qualifications who normally pursue

8 Michael Biggs

Table 1.1 The contested field of "doctorateness"

	generic	*specific*
extrinsic	social context	academic context
intrinsic	competences	contribution

careers as researchers. The examiner comes from this class, and whether she is acting as a gatekeeper or a community builder, society authorises her to make judgements on its behalf. These judgements may have consequences that permit the candidate to work as a professional in sensitive areas such as medicine or managing the national economy. It is therefore a position of trust. As a society we have developed a construct in which going to university and completing a doctorate in some way equips the candidate to have the competencies that we demand in order to undertake certain roles. Whether this is actually a training or merely a rite of passage is a meta-level question that lies outside the diagram. What can be noted is that the pathway to the professions is determined by society, and one could easily find societies in which formal academic education was not a prerequisite to undertake these societal roles. Indeed, our own society has changed over time as to whether academic qualifications are necessary to practice as a mechanic, a psychologist, an artist and the like, and we are currently in a period of increasing academicisation.

The extrinsic-specific quadrant comprises the academic context in which one finds a subset of society as a whole who operate in academia and/or in the same discipline as the candidate, depending on whether one wants to take a macro or micro view of the quadrant. Here one finds the discipline-specific values and rhetoric that characterize 'artists', 'designers', 'musicians' and so on. Each discipline tries to mark itself out as a tribe through a process of differentiation and distinction that creates its own culture (Biggs and Büchler 2012). At least one but perhaps not all of the examiners will come from this subset, reflecting the requirement in many disciplines that the successful candidate will be part of a wider community, not merely a member of his or her own discipline, and that the examination team should therefore include both generalists and specialists.

The intrinsic-generic quadrant comprises the idea that to be a researcher one must learn certain skills and competencies. These are the competencies that will enable the candidate to earn a living as a professional researcher. Research training may include problem analysis, learning various research methods and approaches whether or not they are actually used in the candidate's research project, writing and presentation skills and so on. Appeals to the importance of transferable skills in the criteria for doctorateness refer to this quadrant, for example Poole.

Doctorateness: where should we look? 9

The intrinsic-specific quadrant comprises the contribution that the research makes to the specific discipline of the candidate. This normally requires that the candidate understands the scope of the existing knowledge and understanding in the field through a literature review or its equivalent and the identification of a claim for a particular addition to that field. The claim constitutes the intellectual property of the candidate. The fact that such a contribution could only be identified by an indigenous professional or peer, and therefore the hermetic tendency of such judgments, results in a resistance to generalisation and criteria and an emphasis on individual cases, for example Wellington.

Considering Wellington and Poole as particular instances of the broader debate about doctorateness, one can further examine relationships within the Boolean square. The issue of whether the examiner is acting as a gate-keeper or community builder lies in the extrinsic-generic quadrant. Here one can also place national quality standards and policy documents (e.g. QAA 2011) that are designed by society and its representatives to ensure that those who are authorised to make certain decisions do so within a frame-work that is socially acceptable, that is, that the experts do not lose sight of their social responsibility. Societal failure to control the experts leads to the kind of rupture of confidence in the example of the madness of the art curator in the eyes of the general public.

Whether the candidate has sufficient competencies to undertake the role of professional lies in the intrinsic-generic quadrant. The candidate has to be trained for his or her role as a researcher, and some aspects of this are not discipline-specific, for example techniques for identifying whether research is original. Furthermore, there is an expectation that this training is train-ing as a researcher in addition to any training there may be in a specific discipline, such as an artist. Discipline-specific training includes knowledge of current practices and practitioners and falls within the intrinsic-specific quadrant.

Finally, in the extrinsic-specific quadrant one can locate the academic debate about knowledge production as it applies in specific disciplines, including the debate mentioned previously about how the arts can contrib-ute knowledge (Eisner 2008) and in so doing whether the arts bring with them any particular and unique requirements such as combined connois-seurship and criticism (Dunin-Woyseth and Nilsson 2012).

The two extrinsic quadrants are linked by the variety of types of doctorate mentioned by Wellington (2013, 1490). In recent times – for the concept of a doctorate is fairly recent – we have created a societal role for those with the title 'Dr'. Since the award is only made by universities and is their highest award, the title has generally implied academic as well as or perhaps instead of professional competencies. With the advent of professional doctorates the title is also being conferred on those with advanced professional competen-cies, such as one might find in commercial R&D and applied areas. Thus the societal expectation and perhaps status of 'Dr' is being modified by actions

10   *Michael Biggs*

in the extrinsic-specific context. According to one's causal explanation, these might be motivated by an increased requirement for vocationalisation or as a consequence of political reorganisation in the extrinsic-generic quadrant (Deer 2002).

The two intrinsic quadrants contain the debate about whether it is the thesis or the candidate that is being evaluated. Even in countries where the candidate is not required to be present at the evaluation, there are implications that the training and personal skills of the candidate will be evidenced in the thesis. The two extrinsic quadrants contain the debate about whether the successful candidate is entering a community of researchers (RCUK 2008) or entering a specific profession (Abbott 1988).

The two generic quadrants contain Wellington and Poole's disagreement about whether there are any common criteria to doctorateness. Although the advocates of doctorateness identified by Wellington (e.g. Park 2007; Trafford and Lesham 2009) locate their argument in the extrinsic-generic quadrant, Wellington's objections arise from the disagreement between individual disciplines that is located in the extrinsic-specific quadrant. This explains why Wellington is forced to conclude that the problem suffers from indeterminacy, that is, that evidence from one quadrant cannot be used to resolve issues in another. Poole, on the other hand, can be located together with his evidence in the extrinsic-generic quadrant and therefore finds no problem in continuing the quest for a structural rather than a case-based account of doctorateness.

The two specific quadrants contain the debate about whether arts practice can contribute traditional academic knowledge or whether its entry into academia fundamentally reframes our notions of knowledge and expertise. I think this can be compared to the development of qualitative methods in 1970s and the impact this had not only on sociology by providing more relevant methods but also the way in which quantitative methodologists had to re-describe what they were doing in terms of discipline-specific values and assumptions instead of truth-claims (Guba 1990, 25f.).

Somewhere in the extrinsic quadrants we need to locate the examiner's training. Winter *et al.* (2000) note that whilst effective evaluation depends greatly on experience, passing on that expertise directly as training is not common. The generic aspect of creating career paths in research, in this case as a doctoral examiner, are problematised by a low desire for inexperienced examiners, coupled with a structure that relies on a master–apprentice model. Whether this examiner training is found or perceived as necessary in the intrinsic or extrinsic quadrants depends on whether one regards examination or peer review as something that belongs to the academic community as a whole, thereby reinforcing a notion of transferable academic values (doctorateness), or whether one regards it as something discipline specific, thereby accounting for why it is sometimes deemed unnecessary to have additional representation from the professional world on examination teams.

Conclusion

I have previously claimed that the evaluation of what is relevant as research in creative arts and what kind of activities produce significant outcomes for the creative arts community is something that has to be undertaken within the value and belief structure of the community itself. Hence my controversial and often misunderstood assertion that artistic research rarely produces outcomes of significance to the artistic community (Biggs and Büchler 2011, 89). The lack of significance is not a comment on the quality of the research but a consequence of the activities and methods being borrowed from other disciplines rather than arising naturally from within the arts themselves. In other words, one cannot import evaluation systems from other disciplines, because these will have been developed in relation to different aims and objectives. However, I have also resisted the 'isolationist position' in which creative arts practitioners might therefore infer that they are free to claim whatever they wish as valid research (Biggs and Büchler 2008). The Boolean square clarifies how both positions can be maintained by revealing that there are four quadrants that provide both criteria and evidence and not just one. How the world looks depends on the quadrant from which one is viewing it.

In the extrinsic-generic quadrant there are certain general qualities that research must meet in order to be recognised as research. These qualities have been appealed to in order to refute isolationism (Borgdorff 2011, 54) and satisfy cross-disciplinary demands for transferable 'doctorateness'. In addition, and not as an alternative, in the extrinsic-specific quadrant one finds the discipline-specific values of the creative arts community. These values have been used to define a novel paradigm particular to creative arts research and distinct from traditional models of research that Elkins calls 'the Nordic Model' (Elkins 2013, 11). A compromise is sometimes formed between these two quadrants (Borgdorff 2011), but I believe they can be synthesised not just by adding certain requirements to artistic practice but by re-describing our understanding of research in all areas (Coessens *et al.* 2009). When qualitative research legitimised the subjective researcher with his or her opinions into the activity of research, it revealed the essentially human and constructed nature of all research, even the apparently objective (Bloor 1991 [1976], 5). In the same way, the legitimation of the visual, the tacit, the embodied and the non-linguistic in creative arts research reveals the multiple ways in which we engage with our world and find out about it.

Thus my conclusion is that certain common principles may be found in each quadrant, but their manifestation in the discourse of each discipline is very different. This does not only apply, as one might expect, in the specific quadrants but also in the generic quadrants. For example, when we speak of 'methodology' in the sciences we probably refer to current accepted practices that lead to valid outcomes, but when we speak of methodology in the humanities we probably refer to the selection of an interpretative framework within which judgments are made. What exactly we mean when

12 *Michael Biggs*

we use the term 'methodology' in relation to creative arts is, as yet, unclear. However, we should expect that the meaning will incorporate the 'artistic values' of the Nordic Model in addition to a reframed notion of the critical competences necessary to 'be aware of the knowledge landscapes in which professional researchers have to find their way . . . and to be able to position themselves and expand knowledge in their own fields' (Dunin-Woyseth and Nilsson 2013, 147). At the same time we can expect that the extrinsic-generic quadrant is modified by what is happening in the neighbouring extrinsic-specific quadrant, in ways comparable to how the extrinsic-generic scientific descriptions are being impacted by Bloor's extrinsic-specific Strong Programme in Sociology of Knowledge.

As a result of adopting a socio-cultural approach this paper does not conclude that there are specific criteria for doctorateness but instead that a meaningful evaluation can only be made with reference to the values and worldviews of specialist communities. We should therefore expect that 'meaningful and significant' outcomes (Hirsch 1984) will look very different from one discipline to another yet will share certain common features qualifying the candidate as being of doctoral standing. Previous studies have differed about what these criteria should be, owing to different perspectives. This chapter does not argue that we should resolve this plurality by creating a hybrid of rules and criteria from academia as a whole, but instead it argues for a fundamental reassessment of what impacts on our concepts of doctorateness and research and how these might be expressed in ways that are inclusive of the creative arts. The chapter proposed four quadrants in which one might look for evidence and thereby attempts to contribute to an institutional theory of artistic research.

As new disciplines are incorporated into academia, so the language we use to describe the fundamentals of research is altered – to be more accommodating of social rather than scientific concepts, for example. In due course, artistic research will seem less strange not because it will become more familiar but because we will have to re-describe research in other disciplines as a consequence of the way in which we describe artistic research. Each rhetorical shift reveals the cultural assumptions of academic disciplines. In addition, the external conditions in which research is conducted are themselves changing. Changes in the extrinsic social climate affect what is needed and expected intrinsically in doctoral submissions. Thus any institutional theory of artistic research will be a product of these rhetorical and social factors.

Bibliography

Abbott, Andrew. 1988. *The System of Professions: An Essay on the Division of Expert Labor*. Chicago: University of Chicago Press.

Biggs, Michael A. R., and Daniela Büchler. 2007. "Rigour and Practice-Based Research." *Design Issues* 23 (3): 62–69.

Doctorateness: where should we look? 13

———. 2008. "Architectural Practice and Academic Research." *Nordic Journal of Architectural Research* 20 (1): 83–94.

———. 2011. "Communities, Values, Conventions and Actions." In *The Routledge Companion to Research in the Arts*, edited by Michael Biggs and Henrik Karlsson, 82–98. London: Routledge.

———. 2012. "Research into Practice and A/r/tography: A Study of Kinship." *Visual Arts Research* 38 (2): 28–38.

Bloor, David. 1991 [1976]. *Knowledge and Social Imagery*. Chicago: University of Chicago Press.

Borgdorff, Henk. 2011. "The Production of Knowledge in Artistic Research." In *The Routledge Companion to Research in the Arts*, edited by Michael Biggs and Henrik Karlsson, 44–63. London: Routledge.

Coessens, Kathleen, Darla Crispin, and Anne Douglas. 2009. *The Artistic Turn: A Manifesto*. Leuven: Leuven University Press.

Deer, Cécile. 2002. *Higher Education in England and France since the 1980s*. Oxford: Symposium Books.

Dunin-Woyseth, Halina, and Fredrik Nilsson. 2012. "Doctorateness in Design Disciplines: Negotiating Connoisseurship and Criticism in Practice-Related Fields." *FORMakademisk* 5 (2): 1–11.

———. 2013. "Emerging 'Doctorateness' in Creative Fields of Architecture, Art and Design: Some Experience from a Nordic – Belgian Context." In *Artistic Research Then and Now: 2004–13*, edited by Torbjörn Lind, 133–147. Stockholm: Vetenskapsrådet.

Eisner, Elliot W. 2008. "Art and Knowledge." In *Handbook of the Arts in Qualitative Research*, edited by J. G. Knowles and A. L. Cole, 3–12. London: Sage Publications.

Elkins, James. 2013. "Six Cultures of the PhD." In *SHARE Handbook for Artistic Research Education*, edited by Mick Wilson and Schelte van Ruiten, 10–15. Amsterdam: ELIA.

Guba, Egon, ed. 1990. *The Paradigm Dialog*. London: Sage Publications.

Guba, Egon, and Yvonna Lincoln. 2005. "Paradigmatic Controversies, Contradictions and Emerging Confluences." In *Sage Handbook of Qualitative Research*, edited by Norman Denzin and Yvonna Lincoln, 191–215. London: Sage Publications.

Hirsch, Eric D. 1984. "Meaning and Significance Reinterpreted." *Critical Inquiry* 11 (2): 202–225.

Knowles, J. Gary, and Ardra L. Cole. 2008. "Arts-Informed Research." In *Handbook of the Arts in Qualitative Research*, edited by J. Gary Knowles and Ardra L. Cole, 55–70. London: Sage Publications.

Park, Chris. 2005. "New Variant PhD: The changing nature of the doctorate in the UK." *Journal of Higher Education Policy and Management* 27(2): 189–207.

Park, Cris. 2007. *Redefining the Doctorate*. http://eprints.lancs.ac.uk/435/1/Redefining TheDoctorate.pdf, accessed on 21 March 2014.

Poole, Brian. 2014. "The Rather Elusive Concept of 'Doctorateness': A Reaction to Wellington." *Studies in Higher Education* 39 (1): 1–16.

QAA. 2011. *UK Quality Code for Higher Education: Chapter A1: The National Level*. London. http://www.qaa.ac.uk/Publications/InformationandGuidance/Documents/Quality-code-Chapter-A1.pdf, accessed on 30 March 2014.

RCUK. 2008. *The Concordat to Support the Career Development of Researchers*. http://www.researchconcordat.ac.uk, accessed on 1 April 2014.

14 *Michael Biggs*

Trafford, Vernon, and Shosh Lesham. 2009. "Doctorateness as a Threshold Concept." *Innovations in Education and Teaching International* 46 (3): 305–316.

Wellington, Jerry. 2013. "Searching for 'Doctorateness'." *Studies in Higher Education* 38 (10): 1490–1503.

Winter, Richard, Morwenna Griffiths, and Kath Green. 2000. "The 'Academic' Qualities of Practice: What Are the Criteria for a Practice-Based PhD?" *Studies in Higher Education* 25 (1): 25–37.

Wittgenstein, Ludwig. 1953. *Philosophical Investigations*. Oxford: Basil Blackwell.

2 Emerging epistemic communities and cultures of evidence

On the practice of assessment of research in the creative fields

Halina Dunin-Woyseth & Fredrik Nilsson

Recent decades have witnessed the emergence of both new modes of research and new theoretical models for knowledge production in practices and contexts of application. This has led to the development and proliferation of arts- and design-based research. In parallel, the evaluation of research and assessment criteria has become a focus of debate internationally, particularly during the last decade. Issues of quality have increasingly been debated in PhD and senior research circles, as have notions of the 'impact' of research and 'doctorateness' in PhDs in both traditional academic disciplines and in the creative fields of architecture, design and the arts.

In this context it has become increasingly important to discuss how to evaluate and assess quality in the rapidly growing transdisciplinary, practice-based or artistic approaches in research. We have ourselves engaged in these discussions in various contexts in order to contribute to the development of relevant frameworks for the assessment of research in these fields (Dunin-Woyseth and Nilsson 2012a, 2012b, 2012c, 2013a, 2013b). This chapter draws on some of our studies of how the concept of 'doctorateness' could be considered in the field of architecture, design and the arts and discusses the development of assessment as an attempt to develop the conceptual framework further. So before looking more in detail at some cases of assessment, we summarise aspects of our previous writings based on our experience of research training and research assessment in several European environments, sometimes in joint studies together with doctoral students from various backgrounds and contexts.

Becoming a doctor . . .

The current debates on 'doctorateness' are to a large extent about how to define the concept in the contemporary situation, not least in relation to the increasing number of different types of doctoral programmes, including professional and artistic doctorates and awards with different stakeholders and agendas (Denicolo and Park 2010; Philips, Stock, and Vincs 2009; Stock 2011). It has been argued that when doctoral candidates understand the nature of 'doctorateness' they are usually able to provide the quality of thesis

16   *Dunin-Woyseth & Nilsson*

that examiners expect and that 'doctorateness' can be seen as a 'threshold concept' hitherto underemphasised by examiners, supervisors and candidates (Trafford and Leshem 2009, 315).

The concept and meaning of having a doctoral degree has also changed through history. Today, it is not only about specific deep knowledge but also about having certain abilities, skills and capacities in relation to research as well as acquiring a position in a certain community. The doctoral degree proclaims that the recipient 'is worthy of being listened to as an equal by the appropriate university faculty', and to be a doctor means 'to be an authority, in full command of the subject right up to the boundaries of current knowledge, and able to extend them' (Phillips and Pugh 2005, 20–21). It is about becoming a professional researcher in one's field, and as with all contemporary professionals, one needs to have the ability to 'push the limits' of what is known or of mainstream practice, especially when confronted with new conditions and circumstances (Dunin-Woyseth and Nilsson 2012b). Thus one current challenge is to reform doctoral assessment to meet contemporary situations whilst maintaining continuity and congruence with the past (Denicolo and Park 2010, 2–3).

In the context of the new emerging modes of research, Julie Klein has argued that while interdisciplinarity and transdisciplinarity have become widespread mantras for research, 'evaluation, however, remains one of the least-understood aspects' (Klein 2008, 116). Inter- and transdisciplinary research performance and evaluation are generative processes of using and integrating multiple kinds of expertise. New flexible environments and collaborative collectives are needed, capable of communicating across borders and with novel means. 'Appropriate epistemic communities must also be constructed and new cultures of evidence produced', Klein argues (Klein 2008, 117).

Today there are several different approaches to and interpretations of transdisciplinary research. Christian Pohl and colleagues have delineated three different approaches: 'mastering multiple disciplines', 'emphasising integration and synergy', and 'critiquing disciplinarity'. The approach of 'mastering multiple disciplines' is what most funding organisations and research institutes promote, and in this view, disciplinary knowledge production is enriched by cross-fertilisation from different disciplines. An evaluation within this approach would be based on the respective disciplinary standards, and a good project would have to fulfil standards of several disciplines in parallel. The approach of 'emphasising integration and synergy' is promoted mainly by interdisciplinary organisations and practitioners for whom inter- and transdisciplinary research are alternative, integrative models of knowledge production that integrate knowledge from different disciplines. An evaluation here has to combine existing disciplinary standards with new standards of quality of synthesis and integration. Finally, in the approach of 'critiquing disciplinarity', the evaluation of research cannot be based on existing standards but requires their transformation into new kinds of standards. Here research goes beyond traditional disciplines to establish knowledge production systems with permeable boundaries (Pohl et al. 2011, 3). The variability of criteria and indicators mirrors the on-going and open debate on the nature of inter- and transdisciplinary research, and the question of how inter- and transdisciplinary research is defined goes hand in hand with the question of how it can be evaluated.

When discussing what evaluation criteria and frameworks to use, one can find a good starting point in the criteria delineated in 'Framework for Qualifications' in the so-called 'Dublin Descriptors' (EHEA 2005; see also Dunin-Woyseth and Nilsson 2012b). These general criteria can be seen as valid for and must be met by all kinds of research. The question is therefore whether these criteria can be applied in the creative fields. Several scholars say they could. Most general and established descriptions of academic research leave room for wide variation of research programmes and strategies, irrespective of whether researchers come from technology or natural sciences, social sciences or humanities – or the arts (Borgdorff 2011, 54). So many argue that it is not necessary to develop a special evaluation system for, for example, artistic research. But artistic – as well as design and practice-based – research should understand its own value and its potential contribution to academia, so that one can ensure that the criteria for assessment are connected to the values and purposes of research in the field (Biggs and Karlsson 2011, 405).

. . . in new kinds of communities

New types of research communities emerge from new collaborations across borders and the cross-fertilisation of various practices, academic disciplines and contexts of application. For instance, Daniela Büchler and Michael Biggs have argued that there is a third community emerging from the previous distinction between professional practice and academic research: a new community of 'practitioner-researchers' (Biggs and Büchler 2011, 98). These practitioner-researchers are individuals who have experience and values as practitioners but who also produce research in an academic context. Büchler and Biggs argue that there should be a distinct research model that is faithfully associated with the specific values of this new community.

In relation to the concept of 'doctorateness' and the evaluation of research in design disciplines, we have elsewhere discussed the potential usefulness of the 'connoisseurship model' using the concepts 'connoisseurship' and 'criticism' based on the work by the Stanford University professor of art and education Elliot W. Eisner (see e.g. Dunin-Woyseth and Nilsson 2012b, 2013b). Connoisseurship is here the art of appreciation, and criticism is the art of disclosure. Connoisseurship can be defined as a competence that makes possible the appreciation of complexity; it is the ability to make fine-grained discriminations among complex qualities. To be a connoisseur in a field is to be informed about the qualities of the particular material or topic

18 *Dunin-Woyseth & Nilsson*

of the field; it is about a certain *awareness* of the field's characteristics, and such awareness provides the basis for judgement (Eisner 1975, 2–3; 1976, 140). Criticism is about disclosing characteristics and qualities. But what the critic aims for, in Eisner's view, is not only to describe the character and qualities of the object or event, he or she also strives to articulate or render communicable those ineffable qualities outside of the sometimes ephemeral or silent space of connoisseurs. Through criticism, the connoisseur reveals the complexities of the particular field and its objects and re-educates the perception of it by others (Vars 2002, 70). Judgement and the evaluation of qualities are present in both connoisseurship and criticism, but the critic needs to have the abilities and skills to make the qualities and arguments for judgement explicit and communicable.

Following this, we argue that in relation to the assessment of practice-based research, the competence of the connoisseur – the ability to perceive and appreciate nuances in a particular field of practice – has to be combined with the competence of the critic – the ability to disclose and communicate characteristics and qualities to a broader audience. A connoisseur is someone immersed or embedded in practice, where the experience and perception of the qualities and competences of that particular practice is crucial. A critic builds upon those experiential and perceptual components and competences but also needs to step outside and assume a somewhat critical distance and be able to articulate and communicate with others who do not possess the connoisseurship or are not in the field.

We have also observed the emergence of more 'permeable practices' within the new hybrid modes of research, combining and using the potentials in both design and research, as well as trained capacities in various making and discursive practices (Dunin-Woyseth and Nilsson 2013a). The 'practitioner-researchers' described by Biggs and Büchler can be seen as part of these developments, forming new 'epistemic communities' that need to be taken into account and which can form bases for developing and implementing other frameworks and criteria.

These practices do not only include the exchange between academic research and professional practice, but also includes a 'permeable' practice triad of design, education and research, which opens the door to an innovative future for designers (Dunin-Woyseth and Nilsson 2014a, 2014b). This new group of professionals combines all the three aspects – of professional practitioners, of educators and of field-specific researchers – in one compound skill set. This group of 'new practitioners' will not replace academics, researchers and professional practitioners, but they can together contribute to a more robust, self-confident and dialogue-oriented field of practice and inquiry in architecture and design (Dunin-Woyseth and Nilsson 2014a).

The development of new epistemic communities of permeable practices must also include the practice of assessing research. The new modes of research demand specific criticism and assessment better tuned to this 'permeability' between modes of practice. These 'permeable practices' work

Emerging epistemic communities 19

over the borders between research and professional practice, making some previous distinctions obsolete and putting scientific inquiries and creative work in new relations. Therefore, we have argued that the adequate assessment of research in practice-based fields should build on a double judgement of both practitioners and scholars through negotiation between connoisseurship and criticism (Dunin-Woyseth and Nilsson 2012b).

Developing the assessment of 'doctorateness' – a brief study

In the earlier section we have discussed the need for and emergence of new kinds of environments and collectives, as well as for appropriate epistemic communities and new cultures of evidence, in order to engage in inter- and transdisciplinary research, as maintained by Julie Klein. We agree with Pohl and his colleagues that new research approaches should be developed in order to tackle this kind of research, but it also influences what criteria the assessments should be based on. With Biggs and Karlsson we ask whether the general criteria defined by the Dublin Descriptors can be applied to creative fields or, more generally, to new modes of research. What kind of competencies would be adequate to practice assessment in the new circumstances?

We decided to examine these frameworks for assessment through a brief case study of the assessment of four doctoral theses. We compared the development of criteria in relation to the specific doctoral projects by looking at the professional background of the candidates, at the content of the doctoral theses in question, at the format of the doctoral output, at the background of the adjudication committees and at the way they worked in the assessment processes including the public defence. Three of the four authors of the presented and discussed doctoral theses agreed that we used the written assessment documents of their thesis. In relation to one of the theses we had to rely on the assessment as it was expressed during the public defence of that thesis. We examined how these assessment documents as well as the oral response and comments of the external examiners illuminated the evaluation processes in each instance, whether the examples have some commonalities and interdependences and whether and how they can be discussed in the light of the assessment discourse and its development as discussed in the first section.

All four PhD projects were completed at the Oslo School of Architecture and Design (AHO). They were assessed in the period between 2004 and 2015. The system of assessing doctoral theses at this academic institution builds upon the common Norwegian formal doctoral framework and the institution's own doctoral regulations. The formal criteria for assessment include that it should be undertaken by three independent experts, all of whom hold PhDs and at least two of whom are international. The supervisors are not allowed to participate in the assessment process. The adjudication committee is obliged to deliver a jointly written evaluation document. When the decision is unanimously positive, the doctoral candidate

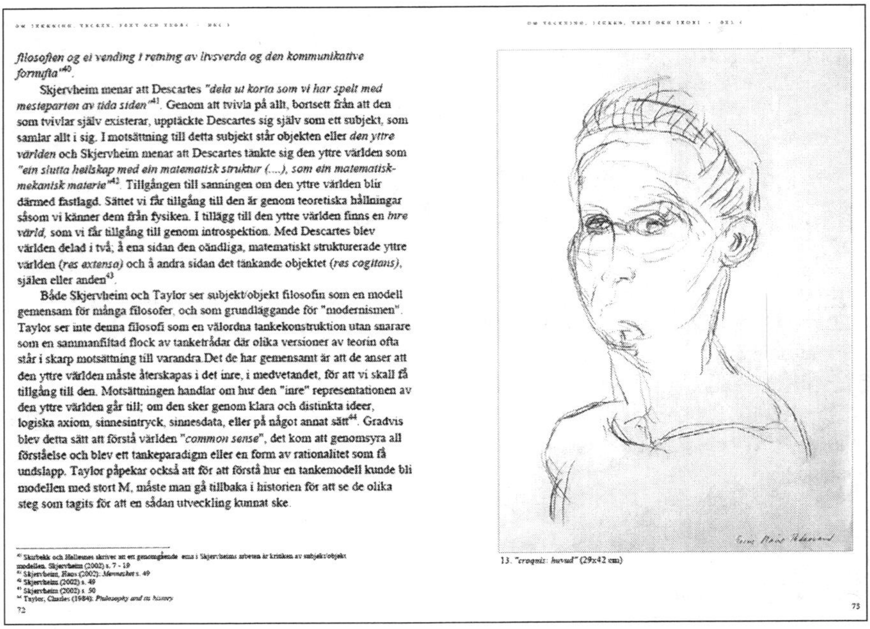

filosofien og ei vending i retning av livsverda og den kommunikative fornufta"[40].

Skjervheim menar att Descartes "*dela ut korta som vi har spelt med mesteparten av tida siden*"[41]. Genom att tvivla på allt, bortsett från att den som tvivlar själv existerar, upptäckte Descartes sig själv som ett subjekt, som samlar allt i sig. I motsättning till detta subjekt står objekten eller *den yttre världen* och Skjervheim menar att Descartes tänkte sig den yttre världen som "*ein slutta heilskap med ein matematisk struktur (....), som ein matematisk-mekanisk materie*"[42]. Tillgången till sanningen om den yttre världen blir därmed fastlagd. Sättet vi får tillgång till den är genom teoretiska hållningar såsom vi känner dem från fysiken. I tillägg till den yttre världen finns en *inre värld*, som vi får tillgång till genom introspektion. Med Descartes blev världen delad i två; å ena sidan den oändliga, matematiskt strukturerade yttre världen *(res extensa)* och å andra sidan det tänkande objektet *(res cogitans)*, själen eller anden[43].

Både Skjervheim och Taylor ser subjekt/objekt filosofin som en modell gemensam för många filosofer, och som grundläggande för "modernismen". Taylor ser inte denna filosofi som en välordna tankekonstruktion utan snarare som en sammanfiltad flock av tanketrådar där olika versioner av teorin ofta står i skarp motsättning till varandra.Det de har gemensamt är att de anser att den yttre världen måste återskapas i det inre, i medvetandet, för att vi skall få tillgång till den. Motsättningen handlar om hur den "inre" representationen av den yttre världen går till; om den sker genom klara och distinkta ideer, logiska axiom, sinnesintryck, sinnesdata, eller på något annat sätt[44]. Gradvis blev detta sätt att förstå världen "*common sense*", det kom att genomsyra all förståelse och blev ett tankeparadigm eller en form av rationalitet som få undslapp. Taylor påpekar också att för att förstå hur en tankemodell kunde bli modellen med stort M, måste man gå tillbaka i historien för att se de olika steg som tagits för att en sådan utveckling kunnat ske.

[40] Skirbekk och Hellesnes skriver att ett genomgående tema i Skjervheims arbeten är kritiken av subjekt/objekt modellen. Skjervheim (2002) s. 7 - 19
[41] Skjervheim, Hans (2002): *Mennesket* s. 49
[42] Skjervheim (2002) s. 49
[43] Skjervheim (2002) s. 50
[44] Taylor, Charles (1984): *Philosophy and its history*

72

13. "*croquis: huvud*" (29x42 cm)

73

Fig. 2.1 Book spread from dissertation 'On drawing, sign, text and theory' 2004 [Courtesy of Eirin Marie Solheim Pedersen]

is allowed to defend the doctoral thesis at a public defence. The process of establishing adjudication committees is thorough, and several instances at the institution assure the impartiality of the committee members. It is the aim of these offices to select three experts who are jointly competent to cover the area of research of the thesis at hand.

The four theses span 10 years of development at the institution. These doctoral theses have different backgrounds, approaches and contents, but are to large extent characteristic examples of the discussions, research intentions and development of their respective periods. We have chosen two examples at the beginning of the period, from 2004 and 2005 respectively, and two examples at the end of the period, from 2014 and 2015 respectively. In what follows we briefly present the doctoral theses and their assessments.

2004 – 'On drawing, sign, text, and theory'

Eirin Marie Solheim Pedersen, an artist and MA in art education, is the author of the doctoral thesis 'On drawing, sign, text and theory: drawing the nude in a contextual, discursive and paradigmatic perspective' ('Om teckning,

Emerging epistemic communities 21

tecken, text och teori: aktteckning i ett kontextuellt, diskursivt och paradigmatiskt perspektiv'; Pedersen 2004).

The objective of the thesis was to theoretically problematise and practically elaborate some basic questions concerning artistic work in life drawing, as it has been taught at various art academies based on the doctoral student's own artistic experience. Furthermore, the thesis historically examined the processes in which the role of practice itself was recognised as central and which have constituted the artist as a creative performer.

The thesis is a monograph, based on empirical and theoretical foundations that also includes a practical artistic part ('research-based art'). In addition to the thesis volume of 334 pages the doctoral student submitted a CD with five portfolios including 21 representations of drawings that were mainly executed on paper. Most of the drawings included in the thesis are expressions of her visual reflection, executed as fieldwork during her residence as a doctoral student at the State Art Academy in Oslo. Prior to and during the public defence she organised an exhibition of her own works, created for and used in the doctoral project.

The appointed adjudication committee consisted of three experts: a professor in art history; a famous Swedish artist and art critic holding a PhD; and one author, playwright and professor. The committee found the thesis satisfactory for granting the candidate the right to publicly defend it. The committee did not include the exhibition in the assessment material, as the doctoral regulations at that time did not permit such an epistemological stance, that is, the inclusion of artefacts into the thesis 'argumentation'.

In their assessment document the committee recognises the aim of the thesis to be relevant, but their formulations reveal a certain distance concerning the artworks and an uncertainty regarding the status of the artistic material. Among the weaknesses they put forward, the theoretical structure of the thesis is seen as unclear, and its character is regarded as a report from the doctoral student's own theoretical studies rather than being the systematic reasoning expected from a doctoral thesis. According to the committee, the objective of the doctoral project – to illustrate mutually productive impacts of the artistic and theoretical parts of the thesis – had not been made in a convincing way, and therefore the connection between theory and art practice was weak. Much was left to the reader's associative abilities rather than following a consistent line of argument. The committee wanted a more general reflection on the part of the artist/researcher, especially in the context of the feminist theoretical framework, which is strongly articulated in the thesis.

The committee acknowledged some strengths of the thesis, but the formulations reveal strong reservations concerning the fulfilment of the formal requirements, and they state that the 'minimum demands' concerning theoretical research competence are fulfilled. They see the thesis as an interesting attempt to try a method in which theoretical and practical reflections can illuminate and strengthen each other, and they recognise the thesis as a contribution to what they state is, in many ways, an unclear field.

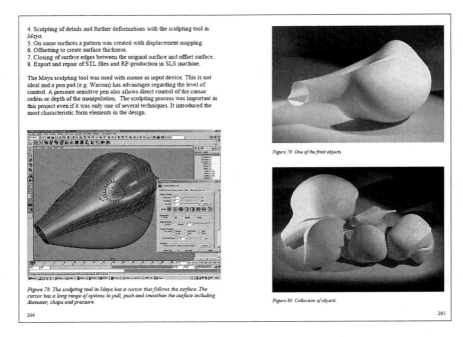

Fig. 2.2 Book spread from dissertation 'Developing digital techniques' 2005
[Courtesy of Birger Sevaldson]

The assessment committee for Pedersen consisted of experts with broad experience and backgrounds in the field: one being an academic; one being a practitioner and academic; and one a highly recognised practitioner and critic as well as an academic. But the assessment document shows that the committee mostly assessed the thesis from a traditional academic perspective. They gave no feedback on the artistic or creative parts, and their perspective in this context shows an identification with the academy despite their own broad backgrounds, expertise and experience also as practitioners. The art practice is to a large extent neglected, and the doctoral student's perspective from within practice is not acknowledged or seen as convincing.

2005 – 'Developing digital techniques'

Birger Sevaldson, a designer with practice ranging from architecture and interior architecture to furniture, product design, boat design and installations, is the author of the doctoral thesis 'Developing digital techniques – investigations on creative design computing' (Sevaldson 2005).

The point of departure for the doctoral project was that computer technology within design and architecture is most often designed and used

Emerging epistemic communities 23

in order to rationalise the work of the designer. Furthermore, the software for digital visualisation available at that time typically 'imported' techniques, representations and types from a conventional and method-focused approach to design, which did not take advantage of the generative potential of this technology. In order to use this generative capacity, the candidate proposed and demonstrated a set of creative practices based on emergence. This led him to establish a long series of design experiments, to design processes open to negotiation and collaboration both between different people and between the designer and the form generated. Sevaldson extensively used the form of 'first-person practitioner research' throughout the thesis, which made his a study 'from within' the process of designing. Nevertheless the dissertation offered a review of the most important literature in the field, and the author positioned his own research in this knowledge landscape. Sevaldson employed his own experimental practice as the method of inquiry.

The thesis is a monograph consisting of 357 pages. Additionally an appendix in the form of a CD was delivered, but as it reached the committee late they chose not to include it in their assessment. Prior to, during and some time after the public defence, an exhibition was arranged by Sevaldson for a broader audience at AHO. The committee did not take a view regarding this exhibition because that form of research material was not permitted by the doctoral regulations in force at that time.

The adjudication committee consisted of a professor of architecture with internationally renowned expertise in computer design who was a highly appreciated educator but with no MA or PhD degree; an engineer and renowned researcher with a PhD in design; and a designer, design educator and leading design education researcher. AHO broke the regulations by appointing to the committee a person without a PhD, with the argument that this person had strongly contributed to developing the field in question.

The assessment document expresses the committee's thorough and broad knowledge of this field. They position the doctoral thesis within contemporary benchmark practice and discourse. They acknowledge the PhD student's orientation within the field and his substantial contribution to it. Of special interest to them is the methodology of the doctoral project, which builds upon the field-specific way of thinking and acting as a creative and reflective designer. They see the experimental work to be well disciplined and the practice to be structured in line with the needs of the research. The committee also point out the candidate's remarkable awareness of the context and the work in a range of increasingly related fields of academic inquiry. The thesis is regarded as well written and clearly structured, but the clarity of the conceptual framework could have been more developed. All in all, the committee concluded their assessment stating the thesis to be 'one of the more substantial bodies of work in the field of computer design'.

The adjudication committee for Sevaldson consisted of one highly acclaimed practitioner and teacher; one academic with an engineering background and one practising designer, design educator and academic. The committee as a whole is well anchored in both academia and design practice, and the assessment document shows that they position and view the doctoral work from both these complementary perspectives. They acknowledge the practice competences, and they also regard them as integrated and structured in a convincing way in relation to academic and scholarly criteria.

2014 – 'The photographic absolute'

Eight years later, in 2013, Pavlina Lucas submitted her doctoral thesis 'The photographic absolute: an architectural beginning' (Lucas 2013), to subsequently be defended in March 2014. She had a BSc in photojournalism and an MA in architecture, and she had practised photography, architecture, installation, performance and creative writing.

The doctoral student applied to the school's research committee to be allowed to submit her doctoral work in a non-traditional format, which she regarded as more adequate to the character of her project. Her thesis consists of six independent parts. The part 'User's manual' provides an introduction to the project, outlining its aims and methods and summarising the content of each section. The part 'In my beginning is my end' contains a discussion

Fig. 2.3 The unusual format of the dissertation 'The photographic absolute: an architectural beginning' by Pavlina Lucas.
Photo by Fredrik Nilsson.

on how analytic thought over the last two centuries has come to dominate the design of architecture on behalf of creative processes. She argues for a renewal and strengthening of the intuitive, creative aspect of architecture and that this renewal could be done through observations captured through the photographic lens. The part 'Practicing-research; towards a mathesis singularis' offers a wide-ranging and insightful overview of the development of *practice-led research, research-by-design* and *artistic research* and how they relate to established research paradigms in art, architecture and design. The part 'Logbook' contains her photographs taken over 10 years, and these are put in dialogue with poetic and reflective texts. The part 'Photography in practice' reports on an elective course taught by the candidate at the Oslo School of Architecture and Design in the years 2010 and 2011. The part '. . . In my end is my beginning' addresses the contribution of the thesis and sums up the project as well as including acknowledgements, literature and three appendices.

In 2007 AHO intended to expand the existing PhD programme in the direction of 'research by design', and the doctoral regulations were regarded as flexible enough to permit this without the need for change. An internationally announced call for applications for doctoral projects in this new direction found a broad response, and this call was also submitted to the adjudication committee as part of the basis for their assessment.

The adjudication committee consisted of a creative writer and head of a cross-professional doctoral school in the arts; a mathematician, previous head of a school of architecture and currently head of a practice-based doctoral programme; and a practising sculptor and researcher. All of them held PhDs. In the assessment document they make an introductory comment that 'much is at stake' for the parties involved, including the candidate, the institution, the authority of Norwegian third-level education, as well as the credibility of the committee members themselves. They also state their appreciation for being allowed the opportunity of having an extra committee meeting before submitting their assessment. This, along with other formulations, might reflect that there had been tense discussions before the final assessment was agreed.

Among the core qualities of the thesis the committee states that it is a 'valuable and genuine contribution to the development of design-led architectural research, breaking with conventions', and that it is original and courageous. The methods applied were found adequate to the research task and the format suitable for understanding the intentions. While the artistic core of the work is the most important and the artistic drivers are strong, it could have been presented in a more forceful and cogent manner. A better combination of image and text could have greatly strengthened the correspondence between the artistic work and the essays. The presentation of the evolution of research by design was acknowledged as a well-written overview, and in this part the committee recognized Lucas's capacity for sustained academic argument and analysis. The weaknesses concern the further possibilities of improvement to the structure of the work, of the pedagogic emphasis and of the author's scholarly craft in the parts which aspire to academic writing.

In the conclusion, the committee recognises it to be publicly defended but also offers several recommendations for improving the work. They wish the core of the work, the photographic and ceramic production, to be foregrounded, and they recommend the host institution to finance an exhibition as a supplement to the printed part of the submission for the final examination. The doctoral candidate responded in writing to the assessment, as the doctoral regulations allow. She designed an exhibition and executed a performance, both of which were presented and very positively evaluated during the public defence.

The adjudication committee for Lucas consisted of one writer, academic and teacher; one mathematician and academic; and one practising sculptor and academic. These people were all very involved in and acquainted with the international developments of practice-, arts- and design-based research, but all of them can be seen as having an outside perspective in relation to architecture and design as a practice. They acknowledge the artistic qualities and drivers and see the evaluation of the thesis as a crucial point in the institutional development. The assessment process was also done in a slightly new procedural and more dialogical way, since it also took into account the call for the position, an extra meeting was arranged during the process, and they were in dialogue with the candidate, who gave responses to the assessment before the final defence. The committee was also instrumental in making the exhibition part of the final defence and therefore of including artefacts as part of the final assessment.

2015 – 'The gap between design and vision'

Julia Dorothea Schlegel holds a degree as an engineer (Diplom-Ingenieur). She has experience in several countries of working with architecture as well as in visualisation. She was the first 'industrial doctoral student' at AHO, working part time in the renowned architectural office Snøhetta while doing her doctoral work 'The gap between design and vision. Investigating the impact of high-end visualisation on architectural practice' (Schlegel 2015).

The starting point for the doctoral project was the evolving character of architectural practice, mainly due to the changing technologies and media used for its production and dissemination, as well as the resulting challenges in organisational and creative processes in architecture. The PhD thesis discusses the role of high-end visualisation in architectural competitions, with an emphasis on the involvement of visualisation specialists and the linked cooperation process between them and the designing architects.

The thesis is a monograph of 259 pages in a traditional format. It is structured in seven chapters, where the first starts with introducing the objectives, research questions, and the positioning of the research. The study continues with Methodology, Literature Review, Interviews, Case Studies, Triangulating the results, Summary and Conclusion.

As announced in the presentation of the adjudication committee by the Master of Ceremony at the public doctoral defence, the committee for this doctoral dissertation consisted of three architects: an internationally renowned theoretician, researcher and educator; a practitioner with a special competence in digital design who was also a professor; and an architectural scholar with a long experience in doctoral research, research education and the international discourse on these issues. All three of them held PhDs.

During the public defence, the external examiners pointed out that they found the thesis to be well structured, and they describe it as exemplary regarding the standards of scholarly craft. As to the originality of the doctoral project, the subject of the research is new, and there is rather sparse literature on the issue. Therefore the research had to take an exploratory approach, resulting in significant but not original findings in themselves, and the thesis is most original where it generates further questions. By triangulating the results of the three methods used – literature review, empirical studies (the interviews) and case studies – the candidate was able to present a convincing overview of the situation and to point out a number of gaps. During the public defence the examiners emphasised that all three kinds of investigation were executed in an exemplary way, testifying to the doctoral student's mastery of scholarly craft. The committee also stated that the thesis is done according to the rules; in which everything is correct and is easy to follow, but few risks are taken, that could have led to more unexpected conclusions and results.

The adjudication committee for Schlegel consisted of one academic and educator; one practitioner, academic and educator; and one academic and an educator especially at doctoral level. All of them were highly regarded researchers with a close connection to and involvement in architectural practice. In the public discussion they acknowledged the very strong academic craft in the thesis. But even though the doctoral candidate is well embedded in practice, both from experience and during the research project, the research uses traditional methodologies from humanities and social sciences. During the defence the external examiners pointed out that few risks were taken, which leads to no surprising or ground-breaking results, and in parallel to the acknowledgement of the very strong academic competence of the candidate, including the choice of methodology, one can sense a wish for an approach that was bolder and made more use of the specific position of being within practice.

Concluding remarks

The four doctoral projects have a background in artistic or practical aesthetic fields of arts and art education (Pedersen), various kinds of design (Sevaldson), architecture and photography (Lucas) and architecture and architectural visualisations (Schlegel). All of them have chosen issues that they encountered and developed in their artistic and professional careers as the objects of their study. It is quite clear that without their practice-based background they would not have been able to identify and formulate these research questions or topics.

One can see different characteristic traits between the committees' assessments in 2004 and 2005 compared to those in 2014 and 2015. The committee for Pedersen consisted of one expert from academia and two experts based in both practice and academia. Despite their joint background, at the time they seem to have had difficulties in dealing with the practice component of the research, and they mainly assessed the work in the light of traditional academic craft. The committee for Sevaldson consisted of one expert from academia, one expert mainly based in practice and one based in both. They clearly acknowledge the practice component as important and central but regard it mainly as well structured according to established academic criteria. Both the committees from the period 2004–2005 assess the practice-based research from the perspective of traditional academic standards and rely on established formats of research assessment and criteria.

Around 10 years later the committee for Lucas included one academic and two experts based in both academia and practice, but all of them are from fields other than the doctoral student's. Nevertheless, this committee was active in developing the assessment process and encouraged the practice and art components to be integrated and central to the assessment. The committee for Schlegel consisted of two experts from academia and one expert based in both practice and academia. They recognised and acknowledged the high standard of the doctoral student's scholarly craft from a traditional perspective, but they also indicated that they wanted to have more risks taken and more of the approaches from practice to be included in the research. In the committees of the period 2014–2015 there seem to be, based on either the assessment documents or in what was discussed during the public defences, greater confidence around what are the characteristics and knowledge base of the field, and they take more active roles in the assessment process as part of developing field-specific criteria and formats.

The first of the projects (2004) was evaluated based on traditional interpretation of the generic national doctoral regulations and on the institution's own doctoral criteria, which did not allow the inclusion of the more field-specific, creative part of the project into the assessment. The 'doctorateness' of this project was academically traditional and was assessed by a team of what could be described as one 'critic' and two 'connoisseur/critics'.

The second doctoral project (2005) was assessed by a committee of which, against the doctoral regulations at that time, one member was not a PhD. The research authority of the school invited a practitioner-expert to the committee, as he represented the highest level of competence in the emergent

Emerging epistemic communities 29

field of digital architectural practice and education. This assessment process was executed by a team consisting of one 'connoisseur', one 'critic' and one 'connoisseur/critic'. This case shows a growing scholarly self-confidence on the part both of the institution and of the committee. Their competences covered the field of studies and synergically formed the joint assessment competence. Yet they chose to disregard the creative part of the doctoral work and its output, the exhibition, while assessing this doctoral project. The 'doctorateness' of this project was inviting a new field of inquiry, recognising the contribution of the doctoral work to this field, even if evaluation of its creative part was not included.

A few years later (in 2008) the AHO as an institution decided to develop their research competence with regard to a more field-specific research, research by art/research by design, and invited research proposals of this kind. The institution seems to have developed a new epistemic community with a stronger scholarly self-confidence, ready to supervise and promote a new kind of practice-based doctoral research. A few years later (2013), the AHO appointed an adjudication committee for the evaluation of such doctoral work consisting of three highly competent scholars with a triadic competence of practice, teaching and research. Their practices are 'permeable'. The school allowed them to develop a new, innovative assessment process, dialogical with regard both to the institution itself and to the doctoral candidate. As a result, the doctoral work was further developed in its creative aspect and was more adequately communicated by an exhibition and a performance. The 'doctorateness' of the project could be described as well attuned to the field of studies and was assessed by one 'critic' and two 'connoisseur/critics'.

The fourth PhD project (2015) was an illustration of how a practice-derived research problem can be discussed in an appropriate mode while using traditional research approaches combined with the creative insight of the doctoral student. This project was assessed according to the traditional practice of academic evaluation and in tune with Borgdorff's point of view that it is not necessary to develop a special evaluation system for, for example, artistic research. Here the 'doctorateness' could be regarded as examining the adequacy of traditional scholarship in creative fields, and was assessed by a team of two 'critics' and one 'connoisseur/critic'.

The two most recent assessment processes illustrate the international development of a new research community, in which the institution AHO has been open to a new mode of assessment. While doing so, they followed the generic criteria of the Dublin Descriptors and extended their mode of assessment from the traditional academic one to a new, more field-specific but also integrated one. The research community at the institution seems to have become increasingly aware of the value and potential of creative fields as fields of inquiry.

Examined through the 'lenses' of the theoretical frameworks introduced earlier, the study of the four assessment processes has contributed to an

30 Dunin-Woyseth & Nilsson

extended understanding of how 'doctorateness' has changed over time. It has been generically formulated in response to the European guidance of the Dublin Descriptors and national and even institutional doctoral regulations. The 'doctorateness' has been defined by each of the adjudication committees with regard to these regulations but, first and foremost, with regard to their joint competences and epistemic stances as both 'connoisseur/critics' and 'researcher-practitioners'.

The four assessments also show traits of the approaches described by Pohl, not only regarding the contribution and integration of different disciplines but also through integration and combination of different practices within one discipline. So to paraphrase Pohl's framework of approaches, one can say that the examples show how the doctoral projects and 'doctorateness' have been assessed from approaches and criteria of 'mastering multiple practices' (Pedersen, Schlegel) and 'emphasising integration and synergy between practices' (Sevaldson, Lucas). One of the assessments is also 'critiquing disciplinarity' by stressing the need to introduce new quality criteria and cultures of evidence from practice (Lucas).

The study has shown the evolution and changeability of 'doctorateness' over time in the context of one institution. It demonstrates that 'doctorateness' needs to be continuously defined and re-defined while also being discussed within open and flexible frameworks that are valid for all kinds of research. It further suggests that these assessments have to be practised within the emerging new epistemic communities and supported by new cultures of evidence.

Bibliography

Biggs, Michael, and Daniela Büchler. 2011. 'Communities, Values, Conventions and Actions'. In *The Routledge Companion to Research in the Arts*, edited by Michael Biggs and Henrik Karlsson. London: Routledge.

Biggs, Michael, and Henrik Karlsson. 2011. 'Evaluating Quality in Artistic Research'. In *The Routledge Companion to Research in the Arts*, edited by Michael Biggs and Henrik Karlsson. London: Routledge.

Borgdorff, Henk. 2011. 'The Production of Knowledge in Artistic Research'. In *The Routledge Companion to Research in the Arts*, edited by Michael Biggs and Henrik Karlsson. London: Routledge.

Denicolo, Pam, and Chris Park. 2010. *Doctorateness: An Elusive Concept?* Gloucester: The Quality Assurance Agency for Higher Education. http://www.qaa.ac.uk/Publications/InformationAndGuidance/Documents/doctorateness.pdf.

Dunin-Woyseth, Halina, and Fredrik Nilsson. 2012a. 'Creating Stronger Awareness of Traditional Academic and "by Design" Scholarship: Investigating "Doctorateness" in Belgium, Sweden and Norway'. In *Reflections +16*, edited by Gudrun De Maeyer. Brussel-Ghent: Sint-Lucas Architectuur.

———. 2012b. 'Doctorateness in Design Disciplines: Negotiating Connoisseurship and Criticism in Practice-Related Fields'. *FORMakademisk* 5 (2).

Emerging epistemic communities 31

————. 2012c. 'Negotiating "Doctorateness" in Practice-Related Design Disciplines: Some Notes from a Scandinavian Perspective of Research Education'. In *3rd International Conference on Professional Doctorates: Conference Proceedings*. Florence.

————. 2013a. 'Developing Making Scholarship: From Making Disciplines to Field-Specific Research in Creative Practices'. In *Knowing (by) Designing*, edited by Johan Verbeke and Burak Pak. Brussels: LUCA.

————. 2013b. 'Emerging "Doctorateness" in Creative Fields of Architecture, Art and Design: Some Experiences from a Nordic-Belgian Context'. In *Artistic Research Then and Now: 2004–13*, edited by Torbjörn Lind. Stockholm: Swedish Research Council.

————. 2014a. 'Design Education, Practice, and Research: On Building a Field of Inquiry'. *Studies in Material Thinking* 11.

————. 2014b. 'Research as a Driving Force for Change: On Triadic Practice in Architecture'. In *Reflections +17* edited by Johan Verbeke. Gent: KU Leuven Faculty of Architecture.

EHEA. 2005. 'A Framework for Qualifications in the European Higher Education Area'. http://www.ehea.info/Uploads/Documents/QF-EHEA-May2005.pdf.

Eisner, Elliot. 1975. *The Perceptive Eye: Toward the Reformation of Educational Evaluation*. Stanford: Stanford University.

————. 1976. 'Educational Connoisseurship and Criticism: Their Form and Function in Educational Evaluation'. *Journal of Aesthetic Education* 10 (3/4): 135–50.

Klein, Julie. 2008. 'Evaluation of Interdisciplinary and Transdisciplinary Research'. *American Journal of Preventive Medicine* 35 (2): 116–23.

Lucas, Pavlina. 2013. *The Photographic Absolute: An Architectural Beginning*. Oslo: Oslo School of Architecture and Design.

Pedersen, Eirin. 2004. *Om Teckning, Tecken, Text och Teori: Aktteckning i ett Kontextuellt, Diskursivt och Paradigmatiskt Perspektiv*. Oslo: Oslo School of Architecture and Design.

Philips, Maggi, Cheryl F. Stock, and Kim Vincs. 2009. 'Dancing Doctorates Down-Under? Defining and Assessing "Doctorateness" When Embodiment Enters the Thesis'. In *Dance Dialogues: Conversations Across Cultures, Artforms and Practices: Refereed Proceedings of the World Dance Alliance Global Summit, Brisbane, Australia, 13–18 July 2008*, edited by Cheryl Stock. Canberra: Australian Dance Council & Queensland University of Technology.

Phillips, Estelle M., and Derek S. Pugh. 2005. *How to Get a PhD*. Berkshire: Open University Press.

Pohl, Christian, Pasqualina Perrig-Chiello, Beat Butz, Gertrud Hirsch Hadorn, Dominique Joye, Roderick Lawrence, Michael Nentwich, et al. 2011. 'Questions to Evaluate Inter- and Transdisciplinary Research Proposals'. Working paper, td-net for Transdisciplinary Research. Berne. http://www.transdisciplinarity.ch/documents/td-Evaluation2011_workingpaper.pdf.

Schlegel, Julia. 2015. *The Gap between Design and Vision: Investigating the Impact of High-End Visualization on Architectural Practice*. Oslo: Oslo School of Architecture and Design.

Sevaldson, Birger. 2005. *Developing Digital Design Techniques: Investigations on Creative Design Computing*. Oslo: AHO.

Stock, Cheryl F. 2011. 'Approaches to Acquiring "Doctorateness" in the Creative Industries: An Australian Perspective'. In *Pre-Conference Proceedings*, edited by Lorraine Justice and Ken Friedman. Hong Kong: Hong Kong Polytechnic University.

Trafford, Vernon, and Shosh Leshem. 2009. 'Doctorateness as a Threshold Concept'. *Innovations in Education and Teaching International* 46 (3): 305–16.

Vars, Gordon F. 2002. 'Educational Connoisseurship, Criticism, and the Assessment of Integrative Studies'. *Issues of Integrative Studies* 20: 65–76.

3 Setting the scene
The development of formal frameworks for doctorates in Europe

Anne Solberg

The issue of this chapter is the European formal frameworks of qualifications that delineate the scope of doctoral works in architecture and the arts. At present there are policies for integrating these disciplines into universities, even though they have not had the same research traditions as the classical university disciplines. In this situation, the challenge is for them to be accepted by the academic community whilst at the same time maintaining their relevance to the practice field. This chapter claims that there is a reciprocal interaction between the formal frameworks and academic endeavours of these disciplines.

One consequence of architecture and the arts entering academia is raised by Biggs and Karlsson, who asks whether it is significant that art-based research generates artefacts such as musical compositions, performances, paintings, and so forth. In their view this is a striking difference of output compared to that of research in other subjects. Most universities have had to modify their doctoral regulations in order to accommodate this difference in the kinds of submission doctoral candidates can make. The expectation has traditionally been for an extensive written report (a thesis) that contains a critical analysis and makes an explicit claim regarding the original contribution that the study makes to the field. The newly incorporated art faculties have often demanded that they be allowed to, additionally or alternatively, submit non-textual material in the form of artefacts and artistic productions (Biggs and Karlsson 2011, 2).

European university politics is a driving force for the process of integrating architecture and the arts in academia. First, there are extensive restructuring processes in higher education throughout Europe. Small institutions are merged into larger ones, and schools of art and architecture are incorporated into universities. Second, there is a shift from direct governmental steering to the so-called New Public Management, which includes result-based financing, increasing competition for research funding, and, as a result of this, rigorous regimes of benchmarking and reporting to the authorities. Third, there is a thorough process of international harmonisation in higher education, through the Bologna Process in particular. The Dublin Descriptors, an

34 Anne Solberg

overarching European framework of qualifications, is a major achievement of the Bologna Process.

Disciplines, faculties, and institutional autonomy

The integration of new disciplines is a characteristic of university dynamics: a constant grouping and regrouping of disciplines and specialisms and the creation of new disciplines. At present there is also a notable transgression of discipline borders, as reflected in the concept of Mode 2 knowledge production (Gibbons et al. 1994). There seem to be two parallel movements: an increasing number of disciplines entering the academic community and an expanding amount of research projects transgressing the borders of disciplines.

> The ebb and flow within the various fields and sub fields that go to make up a discipline, fragments large units and brings about the merger of smaller ones. And since this pattern of movement is determined by the way the particular field of research evolves in the light of the findings made in it, it is a dynamic not easily controlled by administration, be it institutional or national. Indeed, the acceleration of knowledge which lies at the heart of the university enterprise, is one of the major uncontrollable factors of that undertaking.
> (De Groof, Neave, and Švec 1998, 73)

In general, the acceptance of new disciplines is within the power of faculties, owing to their role of assessing the academic quality of the newcomers. The faculty is the crossing point where the authority deriving from the expertise and the personal influence of the scholars meets the formal authority of the institution, deriving from the law and the government. The role of faculties can be traced back to the medieval origin of universities. From the start, universities were exercising a monopoly, given by the pope or by the emperor, of training for the professions of law, medicine, and theology. These were the original faculties, in addition to a faculty of basic disciplines, the *artes liberales*. Universities were private associations, recognised by the state for pursuing a public purpose (Tarschys 1998), organised in what may be characterised an academic guild model: free standing, self-regulating, self-financing, and eventually property owning. The guild model accounted for a collegial model of governance (De Groof, Neave, and Švec 1998).

Developing policies and standards of doctoral competences

In the last decades the scope of doctorates has been extended to include professional and practice-based doctorates. In the mid-1990s the emergence of these kinds of doctorates in the UK had raised confusion as to what should be the structure and assessment standards for them. For this reason, the UK Council for Graduate Education (UKCGE) ordered a report on practice-based doctorates within the creative and performing arts. The task was given to a working group chaired by Christopher Frayling, then rector of the Royal College of Art. Although disputed, their report (Frayling et al. 1997) may serve as an introduction to the challenges for doctoral degrees in architecture and the arts. The report deals with the question of field-specific standards for the creative and performing arts.

The report is based on a survey of doctoral programmes in the UK. In this survey, some of the doctorates with practice elements in them could be regarded as traditional 'doctorates by research' rather than practice-based. On the other hand, practice-based doctorates might contribute to knowledge production by means of practice itself, in which the doctoral characteristics of 'originality, mastery and contribution to the field are held to be demonstrated through the original, creative work'. These submissions must show 'doctoral level powers of analysis and mastery of existing contextual knowledge, in a form which is accessible to and auditable by knowledgeable peers' (Frayling et al. 1997, 18). The working group described a continuum from research to creative practice. They argued that there is no need to differentiate a PhD in practice-based subjects from a PhD in other subjects, because it is the research orientation that is paramount (Frayling et al. 1997, 20). The intention of the candidate could be decisive: the researcher/academic role would be suited to those who aim at the analysis or evaluation of the creative product, as well as excellence in its expression, as an integral part of the thesis. A Doctor of Art would be appropriate when the purpose of the candidate is to achieve a formal recognition of the highest achievement within his subject area (Frayling et al. 1997, 37).

The working group asked for nationally agreed standards for the award of doctorates 'sufficiently rigorous to secure demonstration of the qualities necessary, but sufficiently inclusive to allow all subjects to find expression within them' (Frayling et al. 1997, 20). They recommended that:

> Where 'equivalence' is concerned, it appears both possible and desirable to formulate criteria for a submission for a PhD award in which the production of original pieces of work is an integral part of the process as well as the product, and to employ the same judgemental stance as if they were a more conventional research-based submission.
>
> (Frayling et al. 1997, 23)

In parallel, a number of initiatives, nationally and internationally, were taken for developing common standards of higher education. The Bologna Declaration was launched by the turn of the millennium, at a time of looking forward into a new millennium and back at almost 900 years of European university history. It was an initiative by ministers in charge of education, aiming at the harmonisation of the structure of European higher education. The declaration emphasised the European cultural dimension and aimed 'to establish a more complete and far-reaching Europe, building upon and

36   *Anne Solberg*

strengthening its intellectual, cultural, social and scientific and technological dimensions' (Bologna 1999). Major action lines were the development of a common European framework for teaching and learning in two consecutive cycles, a system of European Credits, and a mutual, cross-national recognition of degrees and examinations. For this purpose, a European Higher Education Area (EHEA) was to be established within 2010. At present there are 47 member states of the EHEA.

Ten years earlier, rectors of European universities had proclaimed another document: the *Magna Charta Universitatum* (Magna_Charta 1988), at present signed by 788 universities in Europe and beyond. Fundamental principles of the Magna Charta are that a university is the trustee of the European humanist tradition. It must be morally and intellectually independent of all political authority and economic power. Research and teaching must be inseparable, and there must be freedom in research and training. The document recognises the need for restructuring higher education and includes a number of objectives of international harmonisation.

The Magna Charta and the Bologna Declaration are basic policy documents for higher education reforms in Europe. Their formal status is different: the Magna Charta addresses national governments, while the Bologna Declaration is an intergovernmental enterprise. Additionally, while Magna Charta takes a global outlook, the Bologna Declaration has a European focus. The cultural dimension is emphasised in both. However, while the Magna Charta promotes academic freedom and institutional independence, the Bologna Declaration stresses European attractiveness and competitiveness. On the other hand, the Bologna Declaration explicitly endorses the principles of the Magna Charta:

> European higher education institutions, for their part, have accepted the challenge and taken up a major role in constructing the European area of higher education, also in the wake of the fundamental principles laid down in the *Magna Carta Universitatum* of 1988. This is of the highest importance, given that the universities' independence and autonomy ensure that higher education and research systems continuously adapt to changing needs, society's demands and advances in scientific knowledge.
>
> (Bologna 1999, n.p.)

Of note is the modification embodied in this statement: the principles of the Magna Charta are endorsed as long as the universities' autonomy does not preclude their willingness to change. Over the course of time a certain shift of agenda can be observed in the Bologna Process. Progressively a focus on knowledge as an economic factor has gained importance. This is not explicit in the Bologna Declaration. Neave and Maassen describe a development from initially leaning on the ideals of the *Magna Charta Universitatum* towards an influence from the EU Lisbon strategy. The economic perspective was

Setting the scene 37

explicit for the first time in the Bologna Berlin Communiqué of 2003 (Neave and Maassen 2007). In addition, there are other international agreements that may interfere with the Bologna Process. The World Trade Organisation (WTO) has stated that education is a trade of services (WTO 1998). Thus government funding and legislative priority to the classic universities may be questioned by regulations of free trade and competition laws.

As is seen, a need for agreed standards of doctoral qualifications was recognised in academic milieux. Major initiatives for the international harmonisation of higher education represent, on the one hand, the university rectors in the *Magna Charta Universitatum* and, on the other hand, the ministers in the Bologna Declaration. In my view, these represent a double driving force for developing formal frameworks, one academic and one governmental.

The Dublin Descriptors

Ministers adopted the Dublin Descriptors at the Bologna Bergen Conference 2005. They describe learning outcomes in three cycles: bachelor, master and doctorate level. The descriptors include five components: knowledge and understanding, applying knowledge and understanding, making judgements, communication, and lifelong learning skills (Bologna_Follow-Up_Group 2005, 9). The descriptors constitute a progression of qualifications, with formulations that are recognisable from one cycle to the next. For the doctorate level, the third cycle, the descriptors demand that the students

- have demonstrated a systematic understanding of a field of study and mastery of the skills and methods of research associated with that field;
- have demonstrated the ability to conceive, design, implement, and adapt a substantial process of research with scholarly integrity;
- have made a contribution through original research that extends the frontier of knowledge by developing a substantial body of work, some of which merits national or international refereed publication;
- are capable of critical analysis, evaluation, and synthesis of new and complex ideas;
- can communicate with their peers, the larger scholarly community, and society in general about their areas of expertise; and
- can be expected to be able to promote, within academic and professional contexts, technological, social, or cultural advancement in a knowledge-based society.

The term 'research' is used in the first three descriptors. There is a definition of this term in a footnote to the descriptors, called 'Glossary':

The word 'research' is used to cover a wide variety of activities, with the context often related to a field of study; the term is used here to

38 *Anne Solberg*

represent a careful study or investigation based on a systematic understanding and critical awareness of knowledge. The word is used in an inclusive way to accommodate the range of activities that support original and innovative work in the whole range of academic, professional and technological fields, including the humanities, and traditional, performing, and other creative arts. It is not used in any limited or restricted sense, or relating solely to a 'scientific method'.

(Bologna_Follow-Up_Group 2005, 66–67)

Reception of the Dublin Descriptors

The Dublin Descriptors have been widely disputed. Formal comments are scarce at the international level, since there was no hearing procedure before the adoption of the descriptors. However, there have been hearings in national legislative processes, at which institutions of higher education have been consultative bodies. Comments from the Norwegian legislative process may serve as an example: In the Norwegian Qualification Framework, *artistic development work* is included. The formulation is 'research and academic and artistic development work'. Nonetheless, at the hearing, the Oslo School of Architecture and Design (AHO) and the Bergen Academy of Art and Design (KHIB) commented that the descriptors were inappropriate for education in the arts. There was also critique from the Norwegian Academy of Music. KHIB referred to the Frayling concept of research *in*, *on*, or *through* the arts (Frayling et al. 1997). They argued that the descriptors were based on knowledge *of* the arts, while research *through* the arts is the fundamental approach for art and design practice. KHIB requested learning outcomes through personal, independent work and the transforming of knowledge into art or design results. Hence, in spite of the addition of 'artistic development work', the descriptions of learning outcomes were regarded as deficient. The Ministry of Education had foreseen this opposition and suggested that adjustments might be necessary to meet the special character of art education (NQHE 2007, 27). Artistic development work is also included in the Norwegian Law of Universities and University Colleges (LOV-2005–04–01–15 §§ 1–1 and 1–3) as a parallel to research and academic development work. A three-year programme, the Norwegian Artistic Development Fellowship Programme, now renamed the Artistic Research Fellowship Programme, was established in 2003. The criteria of this programme demand works of art at a high international level. This is a postgraduate programme but not a doctorate. At present the board of the programme is working for the candidates to be awarded a PhD degree.

In Sweden, the term *artistic development work* was introduced into university law in 1977 as an equivalent to research. Since then there has been a discussion as to how to understand artistic development work and artistic research. The questions have been on the extent of scholarship and how and

Setting the scene 39

by what measures artistic development work should be related to knowledge building. In a ministerial report on research and innovation (prop. 2000/01:3) artistic development work was characterised as activities at the intersection between artistic work and research. During recent years, there has been a change of terms from 'artistic development work' to 'artistic research'. In 2010 a new category of doctorate, Doctor of Art, was established in Sweden as a parallel to the PhD. In the proposition for this legal reform, the government declared that at a later stage, it may be necessary to reconsider the term 'artistic development work' in the Swedish Law of University Colleges (Högskolelagen 1992, 1434) in order to change it for better terms for artistic research, development, and knowledge building (Prop. 134 2008/09, 21). At present §2 of the law states that education is founded on scientific (*vetenskaplig*) or artistic basis, and includes the categories of *research*, *artistic research*, and *development work*, which are slightly different from the formulations of the Norwegian law. In the proposition it is argued that research education has been the domain of sciences but that artistic education at research level has emerged, partly through interaction with scientific education in other fields. Scope should be given for the artistic research to contribute to knowledge building on the premises of the artistic field itself. This way there will be no need to re-interpret conventional scientific norms and practices in a way that dilutes the concept of science (Prop. 134 2008/09, 14). While research education in art is leading to a conventional PhD, the further development of artistic research education may be hampered because the descriptions of exams at research level that were given in 2007 were elaborated for scientific work and not for research education in the artistic field (Prop. 134 2008/09, 16).

> In order to meet the demands of the descriptors of exams, artistic education must emanate from conventional scientific terminology and the structure of research education, while at the same time the established scientific concepts, norms and practices must be extended to be used for this education. Adapting conventional scientific norms and practice to the needs of the artistic fields can, as the Government sees it, cause a risk of eroding the concept of research. The Government also considers that in the adaptation of artistic research to traditional scientific norms there is a potential risk that artistic education may lose its particular content and character.
>
> (Prop. 134 2008/09, 16; my translation)

Hence, the Norwegian and Swedish examples illustrate different solutions to research education in the creative fields in Bologna member states, even in two neighbouring countries where reforms of higher education have traditionally paralleled one another.

At the international level, a field-specific framework within music, elaborated by the Polifonia network, may also serve as an example. Since its

40 Anne Solberg

launch in 2004, the ERASMUS Network for Music, Polifonia, has proactively addressed European higher education policy issues from the perspective of higher music education. The Polifonia framework follows the Dublin Descriptors word for word, with a few additions (in italics): Initially music is referred to as 'a field of *musical* study'. Further on in the document the more general term 'artistic' is used: '*artistic and* scholarly community', '*artistic and* scholarly integrity', '*artistic* understanding'. The Dublin Descriptors formulation 'national or international refereed publication' is changed to 'national or international *recognition or dissemination through appropriate channels*'. The Dublin Descriptors' definition of research is included as an appendix to the framework (Tomasi and Vanmaele 2007, 11).

Of note is that in the present debate, there are also authors who welcome the Dublin Descriptors as appropriate to the making disciplines. Henk Borgdorff finds that artistic research coincides with the Bologna Process, which he regards as part of the practice turn in philosophy, and he refers to broad definitions of research as employed in the Dublin Descriptors. In this respect, he defines four positions regarding artistic research: the *academic* perspective, related to the UK and the English-speaking world, valuing traditional academic criteria; the *sui generis* perspective, related to the Nordic countries by some preferring artistic values for assessing research in the arts; and the *critical* perspective, that may be related to the protest against the Bologna Process by German-speaking countries; and the critical force of research in the arts, as opposed to the neoliberal tendency to subsume deviance under one single umbrella (Borgdorff 2013, 148).

Thus, there is a paradox: the Dublin Descriptors, regarded as a problem for the creative fields, and for research education in the field of art in particular, are also used as I understand it as a legitimation of artistic research, particularly through the definition of research.

Doctoral candidates within art and architecture tend to meet conventional standards of doctorateness. One example is the criterion of mastering the methods of research, since these disciplines do not yet have commonly agreed research methods. For this reason, candidates in these fields of study tend to give much attention to discussions and legitimation of their working methods. A couple of statements from doctoral candidates illustrate this situation:

> This thesis is part of the emerging field of artistic research, in which the studies are not framed and focused on specific research questions and do not aim at results that can be applied independent of the context. This type of research is based on ideas for development of a new kind of art and on the practice of art and practical projects. It is a matter of presenting unknown possibilities . . . This thesis can be regarded as a refinement of the kind of knowledge production and knowledge distribution that normally guides design practice.
>
> (von Busch 2008, 27–28)

Setting the scene 41

The integration of intuitive production and analytical thinking that is at the core of practicing-research prompts the reconsideration of academic research *en masse* as this mode of knowledge production enters the academic environment. Notwithstanding the state of uncomfortable tension in which the wedlock of practicing-research and academic research now stands, and regardless of all the questions that still remain on the table, it is generally agreed that the process of their reciprocal adaption is inevitable and bound to bring about a radical evolution of the established concept of research.

(Lucas 2013, 16)

The reception and discussions of the Dublin Descriptors may derive from conflicts of interest as well as different understandings of the formulations as such. In the next section is an interpretation of the descriptors, including the degree of obligation and their substantive content. Information sources for this interpretation are preparatory documents, comments from the working process, and the context of their adoption. There has been a comprehensive working process preparing the descriptors. Documents from seminars are filed in digital archives, while, in general, documents from work meetings and the like are not publicly available. However, some presentations of summaries and such from work meetings are available at the Bologna Process websites.

The question of obligation and commitment

The Bologna Process is an intergovernmental enterprise with the Bologna Declaration as the basic guiding document. There has been no national ratification procedure. Thus, when the 29 ministers signed the declaration in 1999, it was not legally binding for their respective states. Commenting on this, the European university rectors argued that 'the Bologna Declaration is not just a political statement, but a binding commitment to an action programme' (CRE 2000). However, a 'binding commitment' for the ministers does not constitute legal binding for the member states. This is also the case for the adoption of the Dublin Descriptors. There is only one legally binding treaty integrated in the Bologna Process: the Lisbon Recognition Convention (CETS No.: 165) on the mutual recognition of qualifications in higher education. This is a Council of Europe convention. By the adoption of the Dublin Descriptors, the ministers committed themselves to elaborating national frameworks for qualifications compatible with the overarching framework for qualifications in the EHEA by 2010 (EHEA 2005, 2). This was later postponed to 2012. This follows the same structure as the Bologna Declaration that was signed by the ministers, explicitly committing themselves to implement the decisions.

The Bologna Process reflects a characteristic feature of international harmonisation: there is no superior authority. For the same reason, international law is grounded on state sovereignty. However, at present there is a tension

42   *Anne Solberg*

between traditional international law and 'new or nascent law, often soft and hazy, inspired with new community values' (Cassese 2005, V). According to Jan De Groof, president of the European Association of Education Law and Policy and UNESCO Chargé de Mission for the Rights to Education, the Bologna Process may be regarded as an example of *soft law* (De Groof 2009, 87). Karseth and Solbrekke say,

> in our view, the Bologna Process and the policy of 'standardisation' of higher education and the expectations of the 'new architecture' as expressed in European Higher Education policy documents are regulations that are typically soft processes ('soft laws'). Its approach to regulation is through a political convergence which includes implicit discursive mechanisms such as language used, knowledge making and meaning making in general.
>
> (Karseth and Solbrekke 2010, 565)

However, since the Bologna Process does not include the ambition of legal regulation, the concept of 'soft law' can be questioned. De Groof suggests it to be of *para-law* rank, with a *quasi-binding* effect. In his view, the technique of this process questions the traditional top-down and supranational EU method and explores to what extent new forms of European governance, intergovernmental, and non-governmental, can be promoted (De Groof 2009, 88).

As a complement to the Dublin Descriptors, the EU developed the European Qualifications Framework of Lifelong Learning (EQF), adopted by Parliament in 2008. The EQF covers the whole span of education, structured in eight levels, with higher education as the top three. EQF introduces the categories *knowledge, skills*, and *(general) competence*. By their adoption of the Dublin Descriptors in 2005, the Bologna ministers underscored the importance of securing complementarity between the Dublin Descriptors and the forthcoming EQF. Like the Dublin Descriptors, the EQF does not impose legal obligations on the member states. However, the structure of three levels of higher education is mandatory to the EU and EEA states. Various combinations of the Dublin Descriptors and the descriptors of the EQF are seen in national qualification frameworks.

The non-binding status of the reforms that are necessary for achieving international harmonisation does not mean that the effects of the reforms are soft and non-binding. One example is the mutual recognition of degrees. This facilitates the implementation of the EU directive on the recognition of professional qualifications (European_Parliament 2005, 2013), ensuring free movement of professionals. Architecture is included in this directive, and the specification of qualifications in this directive is interfering with the curriculum of architect education. The principle of free movement of professionals is also interfering with national legislation for the authorisation of architects.

Setting the scene 43

The substantive content of the descriptors

Ministers at the Bologna Berlin Conference of 2003 initiated the development of an overarching set of descriptors for higher education. They gave a mandate including a system of transfer credits, descriptions of learning outcomes, and a three-cycle structure through the addition of the doctoral level. This was not defined as a separate cycle in the Bologna Declaration. A working group was appointed in 2004. The report of this group contains a thorough discussion of the structures of higher education but no profound discussion of the academic content of the descriptions, such as 'methods of research', 'extending the frontier of knowledge', and others. One reason for this may be that the working group did not actually formulate the descriptors. Instead they endorsed the Dublin Descriptors, which had already been developed by another working group; the Joint Quality Initiative (JQI). This was an informal group of higher education specialists from a number of Bologna Member States, gathered by a personal initiative. The JQI group had elaborated a draft of descriptors as early as 2002. The JQI group also focussed on the structural level. Tone Flood Strøm, a member of the JQI group, states that they regarded the further development of the academic content based on the descriptors to be an issue for the academic expertise.[1]

Three different types of doctorates are mentioned in the report: predominantly research based doctorates, professional doctorates, and the so-called higher doctorates. The Dublin Descriptors were to cover both the PhD and the professional doctorates. For the formulation of the descriptors, the JQI group used four previous frameworks as models, from Denmark, Scotland, Ireland, and England (including Wales and Northern Ireland).[2]

The Danish framework was for the PhD degree. Criteria were that the candidates should be able to:

> communicate large amounts of knowledge both orally and in writing. Formulate and structure long-duration, continuous research projects on an independent basis. Conduct research on an international level and in international context. Evaluate the appropriateness of methods for research projects on an independent basis. Demonstrate specialist understanding of cutting-edge scientific theories and methods in the international research world. Display responsibility in relation to own research (research ethics). Plan and maintain academic and professional responsibility for complex tasks based on scientific theories and/or experimental methods. Make decisions supported by complex documentation.

The English 'summary of descriptors'[3] at level 8 seems to be directed to the PhD. It demands significant and original contribution to a specialised field of inquiry, methodological issues, and critical dialogue with peers (QAA

44 *Anne Solberg*

2001, 7). The report also describes the professional doctorate, or practitioner's doctorate, to be achieved through a study programme based on a validated curriculum, for this reason sometimes called a taught doctorate (QAA 2001, 12).

The Scottish framework included both PhD and professional doctorates, which would frequently involve both work-based and HEI-based research and study. There were five categories, one of which was called 'practice: applied knowledge and understanding'. In this category, outcomes of learning were to include the ability to:

> Use a significant range of the principal skills, techniques, practices and materials associated with the subject or discipline. . . . Apply a range of standard and specialised research/equivalent instruments and techniques of enquiry. Design and execute research investigative or development projects to deal with new problems and issues. Demonstrate originality and creativity in the development and application of new knowledge, understanding and practice.
>
> (QAA 2001, 37)

There is no practice category in the Dublin Descriptors. Thus, even if intended to cover both PhD and practice-based doctorates, the specific criteria for practice from the Scottish framework are not included. However, the definition of the Dublin Descriptors reflects this broad scope of doctorates: 'the word is used in an inclusive way to accommodate the range of activities that support *original and innovative work* in the whole range of academic, *professional* and technological fields, including the humanities, and traditional, performing, and other creative arts. *It is not used in any limited or restricted sense, or relating solely to a "scientific" method*' (my italics). However, this is not embodied in the descriptors but in a footnote.

None of the model frameworks had a glossary added. A memo from a JQI working meeting in London, February 2004, refers to a discussion on this issue, concluding that a glossary was needed (JQI 2004). In a draft of the descriptors in April 2004 a glossary had been added.

In addition to preparatory documents, the context of the adoption of the descriptors is of relevance. As an effort in international harmonisation, the Dublin Descriptors had to be adopted by ministers representing states with a variety of cultural and political backgrounds. In a working group at a Bologna Seminar (Workshop 1, Copenhagen II, January 2005), it was concluded that 'the descriptors represent the best current consensus on the generic outcomes of Higher Education. Experience has shown that they can be applied in greater detail within national systems, but that it is not possible to reach multinational consensus for more detailed generic descriptors'. This working group also discussed whether *profile* should have been added to the descriptors. The inclusion of *profile* had been encouraged by the ministers at the Berlin Conference (2003) for field-specific qualifications. The conclusion

Setting the scene 45

was 'while the view was expressed that cycle should be an optional element in the European framework, it emerged that there was no agreement on what the profile description should look like, so it cannot be proposed at this time' (Leegwater and Magire 2005). Hence, the lack of a practice component in the descriptors may rely on these considerations. Flood Strøm states that when formulating the Dublin Descriptors and the definitions in the glossary, the group kept in mind the need to obtain consensus at the ministerial meeting. She also states that the formulation of the definition of research was elaborated within the JQI working group.[4]

The need for consensus is a characteristic feature of international agreements, since there is no overarching authority. In order to obtain this, wide and inclusive formulations are frequently required. For the adoption of the Dublin Descriptors, consensus was needed between European ministers representing cultural and political diversity, as well as a broad spectrum of disciplines and fields of study. The generic formulations must be understood in this context, as must the felt need for a definition ensuring the wide and inclusive concept of research.

The Bologna Bergen Communiqué (Bologna Process 2005) states that the ministers adopted the overarching framework for qualifications in the EHEA. In the proposition, the footnote with the definition of research was included. However, at the EHEA website, the descriptors are presented without the footnote. Hence, the glossary with the wide and inclusive definition of research, which was included in the preparatory report, seems to have been suppressed in the process of adoption and publication. In my view the conflicting understandings of the Dublin Descriptors may depend on whether importance is attached to the definition of research.

Concluding remarks

The structural reforms are a major achievement of the Bologna Process. However, structural reforms also affect the academic sphere. One example is the three-cycle structure, crucial for transparency and mobility. This building block structure makes the third cycle the top education for professional as well as research careers, which may change the profile of doctoral education, hence even the concept of research. As I see it, this is part of the present debate on doctorates in architecture and the arts.

On the other hand, since the assessment of doctoral qualifications is an issue for academic expertise, the academic community, by approving doctoral submissions, is filling the descriptors with academic content. Thus, the academic community and the doctoral candidates are defining the borders of doctorateness over the course of time, particularly in the case of the new disciplines that are now entering academia. Hence, the present debate about doctoral qualifications in creative fields needs to continue.

As an overarching framework, the Dublin Descriptors are a common reference for differing national standards. It is my view that because of the

46 *Anne Solberg*

national differences, this overarching framework serves as a point of reference that affects the understanding of learning outcomes at the national level. De Groof describes 'the inevitable enforceability of the international norm', arguing that the constant penetration of international conventions and declarations into domestic legal systems is inevitable (De Groof 2009, 85). In this perspective the principles of the Bologna Declaration, and its endorsement of the *Magna Charta Universitatum* in particular, should be uplifted, focusing the basic ideals of the European higher education and the Bologna reforms.

Notes

1 This comment was given in a dialogue with Flood Strøm in May 2014.
2 The framework of Northern Ireland was not available for this book chapter.
3 Referring to the NICATS of Northern Ireland, the CQFW of Wales, NUCCAT of Northern England, and SEEC of Southern England.
4 Comments given in a dialogue with Flood Strøm in May 2014.

Bibliography

Biggs, Michael, and Henrik Karlsson. 2011. 'Foundations'. In *The Routledge Companion to Research in the Arts*, edited by Michael Biggs and Henrik Karlsson, 1–2. London: Routledge.

Bologna_Follow-Up_Group. 2005. *Framework for Qualifications of the European Higher Education Area*. Copenhagen: Ministry of Science, Technology and Innovation.

Bologna Process. 2005. *The European Higher Education Area – Achieving the Goals Communiqué of the Conference of European Ministers Responsible for Higher Education*. Bergen: EHEA.

Borgdorff, Henk. 2013. 'A Brief Survey of Current Debates on the Concepts and Practices of Research in the Arts'. In *SHARE Handbook for Artistic Research Education*, edited by Mick Wilson and Schelte van Ruiten, 146-152. Amsterdam: ELIA European League of Institutes of the Arts.

Cassese, Antonio. 2005. *International Law*. Oxford: Oxford University Press.

CRE. 2000. *The Bologna Declaration on the European Space for Higher Education: An Explanation*. http://www.msgsu.edu.tr/Assets/UserFiles/unverst_xyonetim_xulik/ulik_genel/bologna.pdf

De Groof, Jan. 2009. 'European Higher Education in Search a New Legal Order'. In *The European Higher Education Area: Perspectives on a Moving Target*, edited by Barbara M. Kehm, Jeroen Huisman, and Bjørn Stensaker, 79–106. Rotterdam, Boston, Taipei: Sense Publishers.

De Groof, Jan, Guy Neave, and Juraj Švec. 1998. *Democracy and Governance in Higher Education*. The Hague: Kluwer Law International.

EHEA. 2005. 'The European Higher Education Area – Achieving the Goals'. Communiqué of the Conference of European Ministers Responsible for Higher Education, Bergen, 19–20 May 2005. http://www.eurashe.eu/library/modernising-phe/Bologna_2005_Bergen-Communique.pdf

European_Parliament. 2005. *Directive 2005/36/EC*. The recognition of professional qualifications. http://eur-lex.europa.eu/legal-content/en/TXT/?uri=CELEX%3A32005L0036

European_Parliament. 2013. *Direktiv 2013/55/EU*. Amending of 2005/36/EC. http://eur-lex.europa.eu/legal-content/EN/ALL/?uri=celex%3A32013L0055

Frayling, Christopher, Valery Stead, Bruce Archer, Nicholas Cook, James Powel, Victor Sage, Stephen Scrivener, and Michael Tovey. 1997. *Practice-Based Doctorates in the Creative and Performing Arts and Design*. Lichfield: UK Council for Graduate Education.

Gibbons, Michael, Camille Limoges, Helga Nowotny, Simon Schwartzman, Peter Scott and Martin Trow. 1994. *The New Production of Knowledge: The Dynamics of Science and Research in Contemporary Societies*. London: Sage Publications.

Högskolelagen. 1992 [1434]. Svensk författningssamling. https://www.riksdagen. se/sv/dokument-lagar/dokument/svensk-forfattningssamling/hogskolelag-19921434_sfs-1992-1434

JQI. 2004. 'Towards an Overarching Framework'. London 6 February 2004. http:// archive.ehea.info/getDocument?id=2126

Karseth, Berit, and Tone Dyrdal Solbrekke. 2010. 'Qualifications Frameworks: The Avenue towards the Convergence of European Higher Education?'. *European Journal of Education* 45 (4): 563–576.

Leegwater, Marlies, and Bryan Magire. 2005. 'Report from Workshop 1: Cycles, Levels and Credits as Elements in the EHEA Framework'. Paper presented at Bologna Seminar, Copenhagen 13–14 January. http://www.ehea.info/Uploads/ Seminars/050113–14_Report_Workshop1.pdf

Lucas, Pavlina. 2013. *The Photographic Absolute: An Architectural Beginning* (PhD diss). Oslo: Oslo School of Architecture and Design.

Magna_Charta. 1988. *The Magna Carta Universitatum*. http://www.magna-charta. org/magna-charta-universitatum

Ministerial Conference Bologna. 1999. *The Bologna Declaration of 19 June 1999. Joint declaration of the European Ministers of Education convened in Bologna on 19 June 1999*. 1999. http://www.ehea.info/cid100210/ministerial-conference-bologna-1999.html

Neave, Guy, and Peter Maassen. 2007. 'The Bologna Process: An Intergovernmental Policy Perspective'. In *University Dynamics and European Integration*, edited by Peter Maassen and Johan P. Olsen, 135–154. Dordrecht: Springer.

NQHE. 2007. *Forslag til nasjonalt rammeverk for kvalifiasjoner i høyere utdanning. Rapport fra en arbeidsgruppe*. https://www.regjeringen.no/globalassets/upload/ KD/Hoeringsdok/2007/200703620/Rapport_Forslag_til_nasjonalt_rammeverk_ for_kvalifikasjoner_i_hoeyere_utdanning.pdf.pdf

Prop.134. 2008/09. *Forskarutbildning med profilering och kvalitet. Prop. 2008/ 09:134*. Stockholm. http://www.regeringen.se/rattsdokument/proposition/2009/ 03/prop.-200809134/

QAA. 2001. 'An Introduction to the Scottish Credit and Qualifications Framework'. The Quality Assurance Agency for Higher Education. Publication code: AE1243. http://web.inf.ed.ac.uk/sites/default/files/atoms/files/scqf-guide.pdf

Tarschys, Daniel. 1998. 'Foreword'. In *Democracy and Governance in Higher Education*, edited by Jan De Groof, Guy Neave, and Juraj Švec, xiii–xiv. The Hague: Kluwer Law International.

48 *Anne Solberg*

Tomasi, Ester, and Joost Vanmaele. 2007. *Doctoral Studies in the Field of Music – Current Status and Latest Developments.* http://www.aec-music.eu/userfiles/File/aec-report-doctoral-studies-in-the-field-of-music-current-status-and-latest-developments-en.pdf

von Busch, Otto. 2008. *Fashion-Able: Hachtivism and Engaged Fashion Design.* PhD dissertation. Gothenburg: University of Gothenburg.

WTO. 1998. 'Education Services: Background Note by the Secretariat'. Report. https://docs.wto.org/dol2fe/Pages/FE_Search/FE_S_S009-DP.aspx?language=E&CatalogueIdList=41567&CurrentCatalogueIdIndex=0&FullTextHash=

Section 2

Various experiences, cases and concerns

Criteria for 'doctorateness' in the creative fields: a focus on architecture
Oya Atalay Franck

Preserving openness in design research in architecture
Murray Fraser

Design practice research in architecture and design at RMIT University: discovery, reflection and assessment
Colin Fudge & Adriana Partal

Doctoral scholarship in popular music performance
Tor Dybo

Exploring, enhancing and evaluating musical 'doctorateness': perspectives on performance and composition
Karen Burland, Michael Spencer, Luke Windsor

Constructing publics as a key to doctoral research: a discussion of two PhD projects engaging in societal issues with artistic and design-based methods
Liesbeth Huybrechts & Marijn van de Weijer

4 Criteria for 'doctorateness' in the creative fields

A focus on architecture

Oya Atalay Franck

The following thoughts on doctorateness in the creative fields take architecture as discursive setting, although the ideas brought forward may also apply to the other disciplines in the creative fields that deal with the design of concrete objects, such as industrial and landscape design (but probably less for other disciplines such as arts and media). The thoughts proposed are also strongly informed by the specific conditions of architecture in Switzerland – the understanding of architecture and professional practice, the role of the architect in the building process, and the characteristics of architectural education – which in many ways differ considerably from those abroad.

Doctorate programs at Swiss schools of architecture

For quite a few years now, schools of architecture at universities in various countries have started to offer doctoral degrees in architectural design while continuing to offer a 'classical' PhD as well.[1] Not so in Switzerland: of the three Swiss universities with architectural education in their curricula – the Eidgenössische Technische Hochschule Zürich (ETHZ), the Ecole Polytechnique Fédérale Lausanne (EPFL) and the Università della Svizzera Italiana Mendrisio (USI) – only the school in Lausanne currently offers an explicitly design-based doctorate degree.[2]

Due to its federal political system and its consensus-based approach to problem solving, many things developed elsewhere take a while to settle in Swiss society. This is also true in academia. The tertiary-level educational landscape was shaken quite forcefully by the Bologna Process. The adoption of the Anglo-Saxon model led to a re-thinking of professionalism and a restructuring of academic requirements.[3] With two different professional degrees – a Bachelor and a Master – the discussions at the universities and in the professional organisations about the relative merits of these degrees – and the qualifications they represent – are still going on.

Prior to the Bologna reform, there were basically two tracks leading to a professional degree in architecture in Switzerland. There was the academic track requiring A-Level or equivalent qualifications and leading to

52 Oya Atalay Franck

a university-based school of architecture (almost exclusively at the federal polytechnic schools in Zurich and Lausanne) and there was the non-academic track consisting of a four-year apprenticeship in the dual education system and a four-year education at a tertiary-level technical school.[4]

The degrees awarded were in both cases "diplomas in architecture". The titles of university and technical-school graduates differed only in the suffix, which indicated the type of school attended – 'ETH' and 'EPFL' for the university graduates or 'HTL'[5] for technical-school graduates. Here it must be taken into account that the professional title of the architect was and still is not protected in Switzerland; in fact, anybody can call themselves an architect and practice as such. The school suffix is therefore of importance in distinguishing architects with a qualification from those without. Behind the three-character suffix, however, a completely different understanding of professional qualification was subsumed, and a clear hierarchy existed. The university-trained architect was particularly skilled in designing, with strong theoretical knowledge and capable of handling complex tasks. The practitioner-architect on the other hand was equipped with a good understanding of the down-to-earth, practice-oriented aspects of constructing and building.

In the process of adapting the Bologna reform in Switzerland, the higher technical learning institutes were turned into universities of applied sciences, giving them a more elevated status in the educational system. Access to these schools is still granted primarily based on a vocational education in the Dual Education system. However, with the structures at both universities and at universities of applied science being basically identical, and with a high degree of permeability between the two systems, there is considerable anxiety amongst the universities in Switzerland that the various stakeholders might no longer recognise the 'superiority' of their education. There is one field, however, in which universities still hold a monopoly in Switzerland: doctoral education. Until now the consensus of education specialists and politicians alike has been that universities of applied science cannot provide the necessary environment for doctoral studies because their focus is primarily on teaching, and research has only played a relatively minor role. But this is about to change too, as can be seen for example at the Zurich University of the Arts.[6]

The changing role of the architect

Swiss architecture is internationally renowned for its adherence to the principles of modernity, for its understatement, for the way in which design and construction are fused into one, for the thoughtful use of materials, and for the high quality of execution at every scale. A general idea of the importance of craft – in design, in construction, in execution – permeates the best projects. In fact, in the traditional dichotomy of the architect as artist and as 'Baumeister' (master builder), the overwhelming majority of the architects at the forefront of the profession will identify themselves with the latter. Andrea Deplazes, architect and professor at ETH Zurich, speaks for many of his colleagues when he postulates that designing and constructing are inseparable:

> For me, designing and constructing is the same thing. I like the idea that form is the result of construction; and material, well, that's something finite. Nevertheless, confining myself to this formula would be a mechanistic reduction because the shape of the form, deliberate or not, bears – beyond its material or constructional component – information, an intent.[7]

(Deplazes 2005, 19)

According to this understanding of the architectural profession, design educators at universities, too, are mostly chosen for being successful practitioners not successful academics or researchers. It is quite obvious that in such a professional setting there is no real urge for a design degree demonstrating academic excellence, such as a doctorate. In fact, a doctorate in architecture is not a requirement – nor a boost – for either a professional or an academic career *as a designer*. Quite the contrary: an architect-designer with a doctoral degree is regarded at best as an oddity. At worst, a doctoral degree may be interpreted as a sign of either a lack of interest in the core activity of an architect – to design and construct – or a lack of talent! It shouldn't come as a surprise, then, that professors at the Department of Architecture at ETH Zurich complain about 'too many doctorate students' for which there is no need in the job market.

This may explain why in Swiss professional circles the support for a doctorate degree 'in architectural design' – a 'Doctor of Architecture' – has not really arisen. Indeed, before tackling the main questions regarding the *criteria for doctorateness* in the field of architectural design, these should perhaps be the first questions answered: what is a doctorate in architectural design, and what is it good for?

What is a doctorate – and what is a doctorate in architectural design?

A doctorate is an academic 'post-professional' degree – that is, it is awarded for the successful completion of an education that goes beyond the requirements for a full professional degree (usually a Master degree). It distinguishes its bearer (the 'Doctor') as having reached a level of expertise beyond basic (Bachelor) or even advanced (Master) professional and academic requirements.

Doctoral studies consist in most cases of coursework and of a research project of some kind carried out independently by the student. These doctoral studies usually result in a 'document' commonly referred to as a

54 Oya Atalay Franck

'doctoral thesis' or a 'dissertation'. The requirements for being admitted to a doctoral programme and for graduating as a doctor vary from place to place. There is, however, a 'common understanding' regarding the qualifications of the doctoral candidate (see e.g. AK DQR 2011; Denicolo and Park 2010; QAA 2011):

- the possession of advanced knowledge and understanding of the subject matter and the research field as a whole and of the methods associated with this field;
- the capability of critical analysis, evaluation, and synthesis of new and complex ideas;
- the ability to carry out research in a methodical and systematic way, thus contributing to the progress of knowledge in the field; and
- the capability of communicating the ideas and research findings to the scientific community and others.

A key component of doctoral studies is advanced independent research. There is a considerable 'bias' when we use the term 'research', because there is a widespread understanding that 'research' is a scientific endeavour. However, not all disciplines taught at universities consider themselves as part of science, especially not the so-called creative disciplines. Nonetheless there is research being conducted in the creative disciplines, too. In fact, most architects and artists would also consider the process of designing a research endeavour.

In many areas of science, the concepts of doctoral studies are not far from those of studies at Master level. In both cases, the requirements comprise coursework as well as a research project. The distinction between the two types of academic education is therefore not categorical but relative to the methodological, conceptual, and intellectual depth of coursework and research. A doctoral thesis is in many cases like a Master thesis but at a clearly higher level of expertise and innovation regarding ideas and knowledge.

This is not the case in architecture – at least not in Switzerland. Today's doctorates in architecture at Swiss universities are for the most part studies belonging not to the core activities of architecture – design and construction – but to 'side branches' such as the history of art and architecture, urbanism, materials sciences, sociology, theory and philosophy, or information technology.

This absence, in architecture, of a doctoral education and degree 'in line' with the curricular sequence leading from Bachelor to Master would be striking if it were not for the fact that there is so far no clear need for such a degree. Indeed, what would be the benefits of a doctoral program as a continuation of the Bachelor–Master sequence? What would a 'doctor of architecture' be other than a highly educated 'theoretical' architect who lacks professional experience and knowledge? Who might employ an architect who has acquired 'advanced design skills' but quite possibly does not have the portfolio of practical work to prove it?

Criteria for 'doctorateness' 55

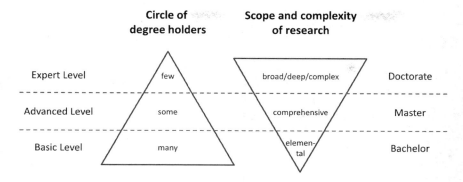

Fig. 4.1 Circle of degree holders by level and scope and complexity of research involved
Copyright by the author

In order to gain acceptance in the professional market and to secure employability for its graduates, any kind of doctorate program 'of architecture' or 'in architectural design' would have to make a meaningful addition to the spectrum of architectural education and to its range of degrees and qualifications. The hierarchy of these degrees can be visualised as shown in Figure 4.1.

As the illustration shows, a doctorate in architectural design of this type would further broaden and deepen the educational spectrum provided by the Bachelor and Master programs, factual as well as processual. Based on this trivial but fundamental concept of levels of expertise, there are two types of doctorate studies that I can think of which have the potential for a relevant contribution to the portfolio of doctorate degrees of universities – even in reluctant Switzerland:

- doctorate programs in architectural design forming 'super masters' – extremely qualified, highly experienced and creative designers equipped with an extensive critical/theoretical framework who can tackle the most complex building endeavours in systematic, structured ways;[8]

or

- doctorate programs in architectural design shaping 'intellectual specialists' – architectural theoreticians/critics who can lead an intellectual discourse on topics important for architecture today and who may find jobs as teachers in academia, as journalists, as experts in public administrations, or as 'critics in residence' in large design firms.[9]

What should be the criteria for a doctorate in architectural design?

Having concluded that there is both an argument for a doctorate in architectural design and professional potential for holders of such a degree (though probably a limited potential), it is time to tackle the question at the core regarding the criteria for 'doctorateness in architecture' and adequate modes for their assessment.

In science, the notion of 'doctorateness' is closely tied to the research work conducted in the course of studies and to its qualitative requirements. It is obvious that doctorateness in the creative fields, too, must have a strong association to the particular kind of research done in these fields, which may – or may not – be similar to the research done in other fields. Therefore when reflecting on 'doctorateness in architectural design' one must first reflect on the kind of research associated with the core business of architecture, that is designing and constructing. One way to approach this might be by looking at the ways in which doctoral work in the natural or the social sciences or engineering builds on the work at Master level. The difference between Master and doctorate programs observed in these disciplines (the 'vector', so to say) might then be added to the requirements for a Master degree in architectural design, resulting in the requirements for a doctoral degree in architectural design. Doctorateness in architectural design would thus be formulated as an 'extrapolation' of the requirements for a Master degree. This implies, however, that a doctorate in architectural design is 'structurally similar' to a Master degree.

A more open and – in my eyes – altogether more interesting approach would be to look at the way research is done in architectural practice and deduce the requirements for doctoral-level research from these observations. In fact, many architects claim to perform research when designing a building. However, there is a fundamental difference if the research is executed in an ad-hoc and unstructured manner or in a systematic, thorough, and 'scientific' manner.

Also relevant for the discussion is the distinction between research 'on design' – that is research done about designing or for the purpose of designing – and research 'by design' – that is research done by means of designing. In research 'on design', the focus may be on all kinds of aspects related to a specific design problem. It may for example be programmatic or morphological, typological, or historiographic. This kind of research is 'auxiliary' to the primary task of designing (Fig. 4.2). Research *by* design, however, has as its objective not the design of a building but an issue investigated by means of designing – and somehow related to it (Fig. 4.3). This distinction is relevant because, in my opinion, a designed object cannot be considered the 'main outcome' of research. Research must always lead to knowledge – it is knowledge that is the principal outcome of academic research. A design may be the carrier – or, as Nigel Cross puts it,

Criteria for 'doctorateness' 57

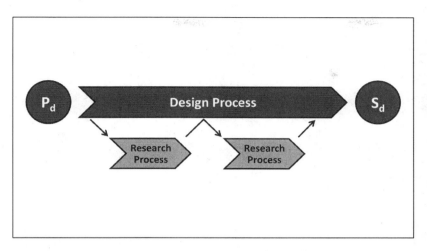

Design-Triggered Research Process

Fig. 4.2 Design process supported by 'auxiliary research': P_d denotes a design problem, S_d a design solution; with knowledge transfer from the auxiliary to the primary process

Copyright by the author

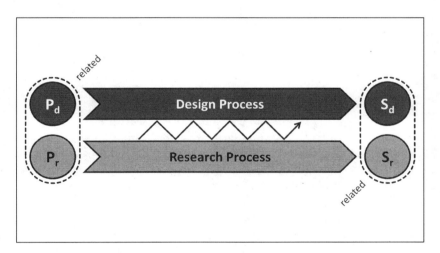

Research-by-Design Process

Fig. 4.3 Research-by-design process: P_d = Design Problem, S_d = Design Solution; P_r = Research Problem, S_r = Research Solution; with knowledge transfer from one process to the other

Copyright by the author

58 Oya Atalay Franck

the 'source' of knowledge (Cross 2007, 47). A design is either the object to be studied – in research 'on design' – or the means by which knowledge is gained – in research 'by design'. Research produces all kinds of knowledge, but in order for this knowledge to be acceptable at doctoral level in academia it must have specific attributes: it must be distinct and clear (i.e. resistant to different interpretations), communicable (i.e. describable in words or illustrations), and repeatable (i.e. others repeating this research must come to the same findings). Buildings as results of architectural design processes are by themselves none of the three: they are highly susceptible to personal interpretation; their qualities are notoriously hard to communicate in words; and the result would differ even if the same designer were to approach the same problem a second time, never mind other designers.

Research 'on design' and 'by design' – two illustrative examples

I will discuss two examples to illustrate how both research 'on design' and 'by design' can be directly linked to architectural designing. Neither of these is the outcome of doctoral work, but both show which direction such doctoral work could take. One is a recent publication by the Federation of Swiss Architects BSA[10] on research regarding a specific building type ('hunks' or 'clusters' – dense urban developments for mixed use); the other is the design by Staufer & Hasler Architects for the Federal Administrative Court in St. Gallen. The selection of these illustrative examples is discretionary; however, each of the two represents a particularly interesting – and important – aspect of the involvement of research in the design process.

Buildings as 'hunks' – a typological research

On the occasion of its 100-year anniversary in 2008, the Federation of Swiss Architects, for the first time in its history, issued a stipend for the promotion of design-related research activities by young architects living in Switzerland. Since then it has sponsored two more research projects with such a stipend, and a call for proposals for a fourth has been published. The grants are meant to support research on questions of urban, architectural, and constructive designing; purely historiographic topics or research in materials or technology are not requested. The criteria for selection are originality and critical relevance of the topic for designing.[11]

Of course it is not unusual for larger architectural firms to publish findings from work related to planning and design in magazines and reports. A publication stemming from a research stipend – a stipend expressly devoted to architectural designing with a particular focus on

Criteria for 'doctorateness' 59

current developments – granted by an organisation outside the academic realm was, however, new to Switzerland at that time. In their research on 'hunks', published in 2014, the authors investigated a building type which, according to them, is not entirely new (Euler and Reimer 2014), pointing to various historical predecessors especially from the early 20th century such as the Chile-House in Hamburg by Fritz Höger, the Ca'brutta in Milan by Giovanni Muzio and the Casa Economica ICP S. Ippolito II in Rome by Innocenzo Sabatini. However, in their opinion, the 'hunk' type of building has gained considerable significance in inner-city settings in Switzerland and elsewhere over the past 30 to 50 years: large, compact urban blocks of mixed use that, because of their size, are hardly ever built by single investor/owners, but rather by consortia. The developed territories typically belong to the inner periphery of the cities, areas freed from former industrial or infrastructural use. They are characterised by mixed, sometimes even highly fragmented ownership, a comparatively large size, an often amorphous or 'accidental' shape, usually with excellent connections to public transportation and potential for high-density, high-profit development investments.

The functional program of the 'hunk' is invariably hybrid, typically encompassing shopping facilities, offices, and housing. The attractiveness to investors of these projects depends particularly on the ability of winning an important, high-profile, key tenant or anchor store that in turn attracts other stores, services, and residential users. The buildings are typically of medium rise, in Switzerland usually not more than 25 meters high (buildings higher than that are considered 'high-rise' and require increased safety levels regarding earthquake and fire resistance, making them less economical). 'Hunk' buildings usually occupy the entire lot, their facades following the building lines; they are clearly distinguishable as single objects even though they are not free-standing solitary volumes.

As mentioned before, such research into design typology is not unusual. In fact, such an analysis and categorisation of buildings for the purposes of establishing a typological taxonomy is quite common. The authors of the study point out three main goals of their research. The first is to differentiate buildings according to their functional and morphological nature, thereby 'enhancing the typological library' of architecture in general – which is, after all, the quintessential idea of research: to further humankind's knowledge of the world. Second, the research serves as a 'primer' or as a 'manual' for architects, giving specific knowledge of the principles and rules that govern 'hunk' buildings – from the early phases of investment-project development to their realisation. Through processual and economic, morphological, and typological analysis, the authors developed criteria and assessment tools which are meant to guide the design process in a manner beneficial to 'good architecture'. The third goal is that the research benefits from the first two aims and, in order to overcome the

60 Oya Atalay Franck

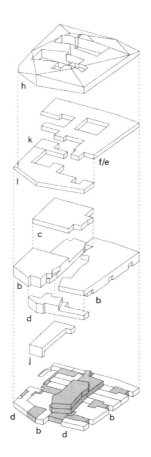

Fig. 4.4 BDE Architects, Archhöfe, axonometric drawing. Winterthur 2013
Copyright by Euler and Reimer

increasing fragmentation of responsibility, re-establishes a holistic view on the design of such buildings by uniting programmatic aspects with architectural, structural, and urban.

This is also why research such as this is of interest for the Federation of Swiss Architects: because it investigates – and helps understand – phenomena of current professional practice. Such understanding, or such 'knowledge', is of particular use when the traditional role of the architect (with the Federation being its safeguard) is threatened by economic and social developments. The fact that the Federation sponsors such research also shows a growing awareness for its benefit to professional practice.

Criteria for 'doctorateness' 61

Fig. 4.5 BDE Architects, Archhöfe, Winterthur, 2013
Copyright by Euler and Reimer. Photography by Christian Weyell

The Swiss Federal Administrative Court – a complex building task

In a referendum in 2000, the Swiss electorate voted for a reform of the federal judiciary, whose main goal was to improve on legal protection and to relieve the Federal Supreme Court of its workload through the establishment of two additional, specialised federal courts, one being the Federal Penal Court and the other the Federal Administrative Court. The Federal Administrative Court deals with appeals against decisions of federal authorities, examines cantonal decisions, and issues judgments in individual litigation proceedings; its seat was to be in St. Gallen in eastern Switzerland.

For the design of the building, a competition was held.[12] The winning entry was by the architectural firm of Staufer & Hasler from Frauenfeld.[13] The building was inaugurated in 2012. Its spatial program is quite straightforward: some shared spaces – lobby, a few courtrooms, cafeteria, library, archives, and such – and a large number of individual and group offices for

Fig. 4.6 Staufer & Hasler Architects, Swiss Federal Administrative Court, St. Gallen, 2012

Copyright by Staufer & Hasler. Photography by Roland Bernath.

the judges, their clerks, and the general secretariat. The court building has three distinct parts: a low pedestal-like volume, an elongated extension to this 'pedestal' defining a terrace, and a cubic tower. The tower houses the offices of the five divisions of the Federal Administrative Court, the so-called pools, each being assigned two floors. The pedestal beneath the office cube provides room for the general secretariat, and the extension contains the courtrooms and other shared facilities.

Between 1997 and 2001, while working at the Zurich School of Applied Sciences, Astrid Staufer and others had developed the concept of 'Synchrones Entwerfen' or 'Synchronous Design' (Staufer and Hasler 2009, 18). This concept abolishes the traditional model of designing in 'stages' – starting on the largest scale, with the highest degree of abstraction, and working continuously towards a more and more precise and detailed design, from site analysis to massing studies to constructive solutions – in favour of simultaneous thinking at all relevant scales and parallel exploration of different aspects and levels. While teaching at the ETHs in Zurich and Lausanne, the architects added to this method the dimension of 'textual work' in which certain aspects of the design were addressed not only from an architectural but also from a linguistic point of view and referred to the process as 'simultaneous projection'.[14]

Through the application of this method, designing the Federal Administrative Court building in St. Gallen led to (potentially shareable) knowledge gained both 'on design' and 'by design'. Knowledge gained 'on design' may include:

- typological knowledge regarding the design of courthouses in general and especially in Switzerland with its particular judiciary system
- knowledge regarding the urban specificities of the site – its location at the edges of neighbourhoods of various density and at the transition from the flat bottom of the valley to the hillside
- knowledge regarding the construction – the ways in which the load-bearing outer columns are connected to the floor slabs or the articulation of the four corners
- knowledge regarding architectural elements and their production, such as the patterned terrazzo floors and the tinted stucco walls.

Knowledge gained 'by design', on the other hand, may include:

- methodological knowledge regarding the further development of the 'Synchronous Design'/'Simultaneous Projection' design method (Staufer and Hasler 2009, 14–22)
- conceptual knowledge regarding the adequate representation of justice and the expression of the dignity of the judiciary – and of other public functions – in architecture (Staufer and Hasler 2015).

The architects see the latter as the key aspect of the task of designing this specific building: that this building should reflect the 'dignity of the court'.

64　*Oya Atalay Franck*

As Astrid Staufer puts it, 'That is the far-reaching social, philosophical and cultural question. If you ever begin to reflect [on this], it offers endless raw material with which you can busy yourself as an architect' (Staufer and Hasler 2015).

Conclusion: 'doctorateness' in architectural design – its prerequisites and its assessment

As mentioned, neither of the two examples cited here can be considered 'doctoral work'. First, neither has been submitted, in conformity with rules and regulations, as a doctorate proposal in a program at a university. But this is 'only' the formal aspect. More important is that neither example shows all the characteristics and requirements of doctoral research to the required extent. Nonetheless, both can be seen as having the potential for full-fledged doctoral work, containing the necessary elements 'in nucleo': a number of topics worthy of a doctoral examination with considerable relevance to the academic and professional debate; a critical stance; and a systematic and coherent analytical and synthetic method.

The examples also show that knowledge gained 'on design' is more easily identifiable than knowledge gained 'by design' – just as 'researching for the purpose of design' is much more common than 'designing for the purpose of research'. But there is a limit to what can be learned factually both about and through a design. This has to do with the inherent subjectivity of both the design process and the product: the former in its creation by the designer, the latter in its perception and use by the public. Every building is as individual as its designer. Some important aspects of a design will always be inaccessible to explicit knowing, limited to other ways of perception and interpretation because they belong to the world of emotions and feelings, of the senses, not readily accessible to logic and reasoning.

When we look at the two illustrative examples: what might constitute the core of a doctorate in architectural design in these projects? Reading the publication on 'hunks', it is obvious that it contains all the typical ingredients for a doctoral proposal and could well serve as an application exposé. It is by no means a finished thesis, though, because both the analysis and the critical reflection on the findings do not reach the breadth and depth expected of a doctoral work – after all, it was not meant to.

A design project such as the Federal Administrative Court, on the other hand, is never an individual effort but the work of many. To my knowledge, there are no 'team degrees' yet awarded in architectural programs. That means that all doctoral work must be attributable to a single person. It is also not possible to award a doctorate degree purely 'ex post', when the building is finished, based on the material produced in connection to the design process. Otherwise, formal and processual criteria for doctoral research – such as the admission to studies and approval of a study plan

Criteria for 'doctorateness' 65

or the assignment of advisor and co-advisor and the fulfilment of other requirements such as coursework and the proof of independent, original research – could not be met. Such a degree 'ex post' for work done beforehand could only be 'honoris causa' as an architectural award.

A project such as the new Federal Administrative Court represents a complex, multi-layered body of work, which is evident in its ideas and concepts, in its tectonics of space and construction, in its contribution to the genealogy of this particular building type and program, in its materialisation and in the way the design process evolved. 'Doctorateness' as a concept is tightly linked to the object with which it is to be proven: the doctoral thesis or dissertation (Dunin-Woyseth and Nilsson 2012, 8). The criteria for doctorateness in architectural design depend on the nature of the 'doctorate thesis'. But whatever the thesis primarily consists of – a report on empirical research, a philosophical reflection, a concrete architectural design project – a key aspect of 'doctorateness' is always that the doctoral candidate demonstrates that he or she belongs to a professional élite and has excelled through doctoral work in specific, describable ways.

Of course, the 'pièce de résistance', when discussing for what kind of doctoral work and on what 'grounds of doctorateness' a doctoral degree in architectural design could be awarded, is whether the doctoral work has produced 'new and shareable knowledge' and whether it is 'innovative' – these are the 'key components' of doctoral work in all disciplines.

To pick up on the two professional tracks for a doctor in architectural design described earlier: if we think of a doctoral program in architectural design as a 'super master', having at its centre a complex design project, then it is mainly the quality of the design work – and of the auxiliary research supporting and feeding the design – which has to be judged by the doctoral jury. The jury's assessment will also be based on the ways in which the requirements of the program are fulfilled and whether the design succeeds in making a bold, new, artistic statement. If, on the other hand, a doctorate in architectural design were based on the intellectual-critical treatment of an 'ideological' aspect relevant to architectural design – with the design project merely as a vehicle for shaping the ideas and concepts brought forward in the doctorate thesis – the jurors must not look primarily at the design itself but at how these ideas are exposed through texts or images or other means of communication, at the intellectual depth and rigour of the argument and how it is rooted in the context of the history of ideas leading up to today, and whether the thoughts proposed constitute a form of 'new and shareable knowledge'. Here the results could and should be measured quite like those of a doctorate in philosophy.[15]

What are, then, the overarching 'brackets' holding together as truly doctoral work such cases as might be worked up from the two illustrative examples? As Nigel Cross points out, there are fundamental criteria which count for any and all research work, whether designerly or not: all research

66 Oya Atalay Franck

work has to be purposive, inquisitive, informed, methodical, and communicable (Cross 2007, 48). These criteria – in my opinion – are indeed valid for all doctoral work in architecture, too, whether 'classical' PhDs or 'new' doctorates in architectural design.

What should not be forgotten is that any kind of academic degree – whether bachelor, master, or doctorate – is the result of a contract fulfilled. The graduates having committed to their side of the deal by paying tuition fees, attending courses, and producing 'by their own hands' a product (the thesis), the school then conforms to its side of the contract by bestowing the degree upon the candidates. Furthermore, such a degree is not only an affirmation of a specific quality of its holder but also of the school assigning it. For the relationship is reciprocal: by awarding the degree, the school transfers some of its prestige and renown onto the degree holders – through their research work, the degree holders give proof of the quality of the education of the school they attended. The consequent adherence to clear and convincing criteria governing 'doctorateness' is in this sense a key element in securing the quality of the educational system.

Notes

1 There may be some confusion arising from the distinction between PhD and doctoral degrees in architectural design, because in English the term 'PhD' does not denote doctorates in philosophy only but all types of doctorates from such diverse fields as engineering and the formal and the natural sciences. In German, however, these doctorates are all specifically designed; examples include Dr. theol. (Doctor of Theology), Dr. iur. (Doctor of Law), Dr. sc. (Doctor of Science) and Dr. oec. (Doctor of Economics). In this context, a Doctor of Architecture or in Architectural Design does not seem entirely far-fetched.
2 The 'ComplexDesign' doctoral program is offered by the Laboratory of Architecture and Urban Mobility, which is a division of the Institute of Architecture and the City at the EPFL School of Architecture, Civil and Environmental Engineering ('ComplexDesign – Thinking at a Large Scale', EPFL, March 2011).
3 The Qualifications Framework of the Swiss Higher Education Area (nqf.ch-HS, version from 20 September 2011) describes and defines the levels and qualifications in higher education in Switzerland on the basis of generic descriptors, admission criteria, ECTS credits, and academic degrees.
4 Well-known architects who pursued this second, non-academic track include Theo Hotz, Peter Zumthor, and Gion A. Caminada.
5 Höhere Technische Lehranstalt HTL (Higher Technical Learning Institute).
6 The Zurich University of the Arts (Zürcher Hochschule der Künste, ZHdK) has recently opened joint doctorate programs with the Universities of Oldenburg, Germany, and Linz, Austria, a.o. Until now, however, for formal and other reasons, doctorate diplomas from the joint program are only awarded by the foreign universities, not by ZHdK itself.
7 There is a distinct problem when translating these ideas of architectural designing from German to English, for the meaning of the English verb 'to design' does not correspond fully to the German 'entwerfen' (as in 'Entwerfen und Konstruieren' used by Deplazes in the German original). The word 'design' has the same root as the German 'zeichnen' and French 'dessiner' – to draw. The meaning of the German Word 'entwerfen', however, is not tied to the act of drawing at all;

Criteria for 'doctorateness' 67

it is rather 'to give a form/a shape to something'. The duality of *'Entwerfen und Konstruieren'* is therefore that of giving something simultaneously a *shape* and a *structure*.

8 Such a 'super master' might be, for example, particularly skilled in dealing with so-called wicked problems – problems which are manyfold, difficult to define and highly complex to solve (Rittel and Webber 1973, 155–169).

9 In such a program, current design problems would serve as 'case studies' for the development of ideas and concepts. Such a specialisation should therefore not be confused with a doctorate in art history, dealing with historical phenomena purely.

10 The Bund Schweizer Architekten BSA (Federation of Swiss Architects) is an association of renowned architects devoted to the conscientious and critical appraisal of the designed environment and the promotion of valuable architecture, urban design, and city and regional planning.

11 For the other research topics sponsored by BSA, see http://www.architekten-bsa.ch/de/medien

12 http://www.hochbau.sg.ch/home/wettbewerbe/ueberbauung_chruezacker.html

13 http://www.staufer-hasler.ch

14 The purpose of this methodological approach, which uses inspiring texts, condensed visual statements, directive sketches, and models as catalysts in the design process, is to open up new mental spaces for projection (Staufer 2009, 19–20).

15 Of course there are a lot of 'designerly ways of knowing' – to use Nigel Cross's expression – in such design-based doctoral theses (Cross 2007). However, only a small part of such knowing will be shareable in a way acceptable to the scientific community. Indeed, 'to know' is not equal to 'knowledge': this is the crux of the matter when one tries to apply scientific concepts to the outcome of creative processes.

Bibliography

AK DQR – Arbeitskreis Deutscher Qualifikationsrahmen. 2011. *Der Deutsche Qualifikationsrahmen für lebenslanges Lernen.* http://www.dqr.de/media/content/Der_Deutsche_Qualifikationsrahmen_fue_lebenslanges_Lernen.pdf

Canton of St. Gallen (Ed.) 2012. *Staufer & Hasler Architekten: Bundesverwaltungsgericht – Bauen für die Justiz.* Zurich: Niggli.

Cross, Nigel. 2007. *Designerly Ways of Knowing.* Basel: Birkhäuser.

CRUS/KFH/COHEP. *Qualificationrahmen für den schweizerischen Hochschulbereich – nqf.ch-HS, Version from 20 September 2011.* http://www.swissuniversities.ch/fileadmin/swissuniversities/Dokumente/DE/UH/NQR/nqf-ch-HS-d.pdf

Denicolo, Pam, and Chris Park. 2010. *Doctorateness – An Elusive Concept?* Gloucester: The Quality Assurance Agency for Higher Education. http://www.qaa.ac.uk/Publications/InformationAndGuidance/Documents/doctorateness.pdf

Deplazes, Andrea. 2005. *Constructing Architecture: Materials Processes Structures: A Handbook.* Basel: Birkhäuser.

Dunin-Woyseth, Halina, and Fredrik Nilsson. 2012. 'Doctorateness in Design Disciplines: Negotiating Connoisseurship and Criticism in Practice-Related Fields'. *FORMakademisk* 5 (2): 1–11.

Euler, Lisa, and Tanja Reimer. 2014. *Klumpen Auseinandersetzung mit einem Gebäudetyp.* Zürich: gta.

QAA – The Quality Assurance Agency for Higher Education. 2011. 'The UK Quality Code for Higher Education'. http://www.qaa.ac.uk/assuring-standards-and-quality/the-quality-code

68 Oya Atalay Franck

Rittel, Horst W. J., and Melvin M. Webber. 1973. 'Dilemmas in a General Theory of Planning'. *Policy Sciences* 4: 155–169.

Staufer, Astrid, and Thomas Hasler. 2009 Band 2. *Methoden/Methods*. Zurich: Niggli.

Staufer, Astrid, and Thomas Hasler. 2015. www.youtube.com/watch?v=ebWo BlKOTpg

5 Preserving openness in design research in architecture

Murray Fraser

While there is an understandable desire to stipulate criteria for the assessment of PhDs by design, this chapter argues that it is even more essential to retain a sense of openness and experimentation in architectural design research. Indeed, it is the dual ability to produce new knowledge while at the same time engaging in self-doubt that is regarded as constituting the essence of any kind of doctoral scholarship, or 'doctorateness'. Both aspects can obviously be tested in creative disciplines just as they can in more traditional academic disciplines. Hence the most crucial questions for any assessment criteria to address are: first, what are the kinds of new knowledge/insight being created through the demonstration of 'doctorateness' within a creative PhD; and second, what kinds of methodological approaches have been or ought to be used to achieve this aim. These issues will be analysed with reference to two specific examples of PhDs by design from the Bartlett School of Architecture and the University of Westminster in the UK, and in doing so I will be arguing explicitly against narrow-minded writers who appear to want to close down the possibilities of design research in architecture. The background for the case being made in this chapter was set out at greater length in the book that I edited on *Design Research in Architecture*, which in turn is but part of a wider book series of the same title that is now being published by Routledge (Fraser 2013).

What is design research in architecture?

As a working definition, architectural design research can be described as the processes and outcomes of inquiries and investigations in which architects use the creation of projects, or broader contributions towards design thinking, as the central constituent in a process which also involves the more generalised research activities of thinking, writing, testing, verifying, debating, disseminating, performing, validating, and so forth. Architects have been deploying a combination of these modes of expression for a rather long time in their work. Likewise, design research is able to blend into other more established research methodologies in the arts, humanities, and science, with no intrinsic antagonism. It is vital that the design element and these other modes

Fig. 5.1 Front cover of *Design Research in Architecture: An Overview*
[Courtesy of Routledge]

of research activity and research methodology operate together in an interactive and symbiotic manner, with each feeding into the others throughout the whole process from start to finish. In turn this raises an important point about temporality, in that design research should never be something that just happens at the beginning of a project, as a sort of R&D stage, before the architect 'lapses' into more normative and routine productive modes. Indeed, architectural design research, if undertaken properly, is open to the full panoply of means and techniques for designing and making that are available to architects – including sketches, drawings, physical models, digital modelling, precedent analysis, prototyping, digital manufacture, interactive design, materials testing, construction specification, site supervision, building process, user occupation, user modification, and the like. Architectural design research does not of course need to use all of these possibilities in every instance, but they indicate the sorts of techniques that ought to be brought into the frame.

Design research in architecture cannot however be conceived as synonymous with the immensely broad subject of architecture, or indeed of architectural practice; rather, it is a significant seam that runs through design work with a particular focus on the creation of new insight and knowledge. Here there is a useful parallel with practice-led research in the fine arts, as Jane Rendell has pointed out (Rendell 2013). She notes that compartmentalising the four main disciplinary approaches within architecture (building science, social science, humanities, and art/design) works directly against what we realise is the multi-disciplinary nature of architecture as a whole. Instead, Rendell believes that design research offers a means to bring these disciplinary strands together and also – importantly – for them then to be able to critique their own methodological assumptions. In this regard, architecture can learn a lot from the development of PhDs by practice in other artistic fields. Yet while accepting that the influence of practice-led research in the fine arts is important, there are of course other approaches within architectural design research which stem from very different impulses: there are many types of research in design research, just as one can see there are many types of research in science or social science or history or fine art.

This then leads on to the issue of the methodology of design research. Other forms of research in architecture openly proclaim their methodological approach, for example science (repeatability) or history (transparency), while in social science, for instance, an articulation is made between theory testing (deductive) and theory building (inductive) approaches. Yet in each case, research methodology is not just a narrow matter of being rigorous and consistent and diligent. The importance of speculation and imagination to the scientist or the social scientist or the historian, is well testified. Hence the only difference with design research in architecture is a matter of degree, since in the latter – while borrowing where appropriate from the other, more established research methodologies – the creative aspect becomes the dominant part of the investigation, and to achieve that it has to introduce its own ideas of testing and evaluating, even in rather lateral or unexpected ways. Hence there is no methodological schism. Each of the other kinds of architectural research also rely on creative leaps and lateral thinking in their methodological process, if not nearly as much. In other words, the issue of the methodology of design research as a contested site – in that it clearly opens up a new paradigm of research – is one of its real strengths.

To give an example, I continue to be fascinated by what as far as I know is the first reference to design research in architecture, by the Finnish émigré architect Eliel Saarinen in a book on *The City* written in wartime America (Saarinen 1943). In the final section of his book, Saarinen postulated a scenario in which the research element of the work involved the architect or urban designer in imagining what a city might be like in 50 years' time and then extrapolating their thoughts backwards in 10-year jumps in order to inform the more practical design projects required to construct the city. It thus involved what he termed a 'two-fold movement' that expressed well the

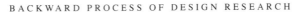

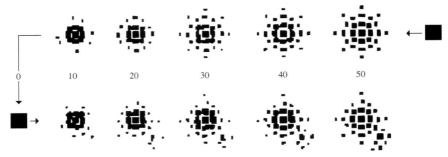

FIG. 50. DIAGRAM ON ORGANIC URBAN DESIGN

Assumptions: Fifty percent of the concentrated city is decayed. It takes fifty years to rehabilitate this—The number of years being a more symbol —during which period of time the city's site will be doubled. This process of rehabilitation and growth is divided into five ten-year periods, as the above diagram indicates.

Fig. 5.2 Diagram of design research
[Courtesy of Eliel Saarinen, *The City* (1943)]

desire of the architect to be able to imagine in different temporal zones – from present to future and from future back to present – in their designs. Saarinen's brilliant and conceptual schema helps remind us of the complex and varied methods required to conceive innovative and relevant architecture.

This degree of openness – both in the acceptance of design research as a valid activity and in what it involves as a practice – is of course highly relevant. We know that architects, through their design work and professional practice, carry out forms of research that produce their own particular kind of new insight and knowledge. In other words, they are engaged upon a research process that is noticeably different from yet equal in value to the kinds of insight and knowledge from natural scientists, social scientists, historians, geographers, humanities scholars, and the like. It is essential to hold this catholic and tolerant view of design research, for if there has been a weakness in previous thinking on design research in architecture, it was that they were far too defensive and limited in their conception. In turn, this caused such writers to attempt to justify design research in terms of what it was not – mostly in relation to misconstrued or exaggerated notions of objectivity in the natural sciences – rather than trying to say what it actually was.

Two examples of 'doctorateness' in architectural design research

Turning now more specifically – and positively – to the issue of PhDs by design and how they now sit within the international academic scene of

Preserving openness in design research 73

architectural schools, there are two major models that have emerged to date, both of which started to emerge in the mid-1990s. The first model is that being followed by an extremely large cohort of PhD students at the Bartlett School of Architecture in London. In a programme devised by Jonathan Hill, these kinds of doctoral studies primarily involve design research investigations that are carried out as speculative and theoretical attempts to advance the discourse of architecture as a broad intellectual subject. In this regard, it is notable that the Bartlett's PhD by Architectural Design programme is not exclusively intended for architects but also includes artists, musicians, and those from many other disciplines. As a result, the diverse range of research subjects being tackled serves to demonstrate the breadth of architecture as a discipline. It has always been Jonathan Hill's intention that the PhD by Architectural Design programme should reflect the spectrum of approaches undertaken in the Bartlett School of Architecture as a whole, so that any Masters student who wishes to is easily able to find relevant doctoral supervisors. Much of this climate of investigation in the Bartlett focuses on the nature of drawing and other forms of representation in architecture or in the active participation of other kinds of agency, such as the building user, in the creation of works of architecture. The conscious aim is to create a highly theoretical and challenging intellectual environment for doctoral students. Hill's own PhD by design, which in 2000 was the first to be awarded anywhere in the world, contained two of his projects that were then published in his book on *Actions of Architecture: Architects and Creative Users* (Hill 2003). The second and slightly later model derives from the Graduate Research Conference system that is run by RMIT University (previously the Royal Melbourne Institute of Technology), largely under the aegis of its founder, Leon van Schaik, and other colleagues such as Richard Blythe (van Schaik and Johnson 2011). The RMIT approach places its emphasis much more on enabling architectural practitioners to rethink and represent their existing body of built work through the format of a doctoral study, and this in turn provides them with an opportunity to uncover meaning for their role as architectural practitioners who are designing buildings out there in the 'real world'. The RMIT system has now been extended to satellite courses run in continental Europe and Vietnam, with the former being run initially at the KU Leuven, Faculty of Architecture, Campus Sint-Lucas and subsequently at various other institutions through the EU-funded ADAPT-r network.

There are undoubtedly strong merits for both these doctoral approaches, as well as for other emerging variants, but it is not the aim here to suggest that any single approach holds primacy over others in terms of offering a single paradigm for PhDs by design. Indeed, in attempting to bridge a range of positions between practice and academia, the PhD by design will by necessity probably always be highly varied in tone and structure. As such, it is able to cover a great variety of subject areas including design method, visual representation, textual analysis, social processes, and strategies for action. As noted, any design doctorate needs to contain a substantial

74 *Murray Fraser*

amount of serious and innovative historical/theoretical research as written text, with this being combined with creative propositions realised through a symbiotic mixture of drawings, models and textual analysis. In this regard, the design projects might well be drawn, built, filmed, or reliant upon a range of other investigative media. Yet in all cases a deeper textual analysis absolutely has to be present. Indeed, it is this essential symbiotic interplay between designing and writing which creates the essential framework for a design doctorate in architecture.

The precise nature of this interplay of text and project in the PhD by design model remains a much debated and open issue, something that is of course symptomatic of the conditions that face any newly emerging kind of doctorate. There is also the need to establish a body of knowledge and methodology through actual worked examples, with such studies enabling their authors not just to explore, propose, and reflect upon their specific subject at hand but also to reflect upon the nature of design research in more general terms – thereby allowing others to use them as exemplars or to take issue with them through reasoned critique. In that spirit, this chapter seeks to contribute to the process by discussing two very different yet also representative PhDs by design that have been produced in two schools of architecture in

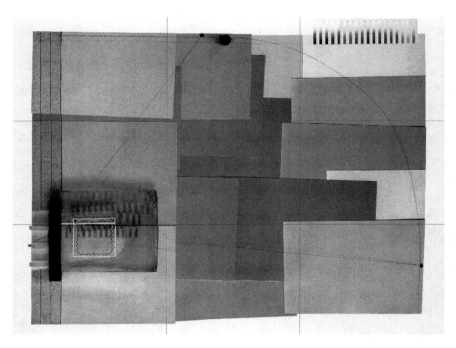

Fig. 5.3 Yeoryia Manolopoulou, site context analysis for the New York pier competition

[Courtesy of Yeoryia Manolopoulou]

the UK, both located in London, over the last decade. These doctorates were created by Yeoryia Manolopoulou at the Bartlett School of Architecture and by Yara Sharif at the University of Westminster, and each will now be summarised and discussed in turn. Both of these PhD theses have also been published in entirety as volumes in the aforementioned 'Design Research in Architecture' book series, so they can be consulted in much fuller detail there (Manolopoulou 2013; Sharif 2016).

Yeoryia Manolopoulou, 'Architectures of Chance' (2005) (Bartlett School of Architecture, UCL – supervisors: Professor Phil Tabor and Professor Jonathan Hill)

In her doctoral thesis, Yeoryia Manolopoulou engages explicitly with the realities of the design processes that are used by architects in their work. It does this by examining the study and practice of chance in architecture. Hence it can legitimately claim to be the first-ever PhD study to theorise and critically frame the concept of chance from an architectural standpoint, and what Manolopoulou suggests thereby is a new area of knowledge in architecture that is able to acknowledge chance as a spatial concept of thought – and, in order to push things further, she also shows how it could be developed as a technique for design action in its own right.

The interplay of necessity and chance is a fundamental aspect of the creative consciousness of the world and as such is a principal form of enquiry in philosophy, science, and the arts. This makes it even more extraordinary that architecture, which directly exposes its artefacts to the indeterminacies of life and the human environment, has so little to say about its relation to chance. Manolopoulou points to the 'aleatory' in the production of spaces and buildings, this term being defined by Lefebvre as the dialectical unity of the necessary and the accidental; as such, he regarded it as an essential characteristic of modernity. But this only makes it even more problematic that architects have resisted the acknowledgement of chance so persistently. Through their everyday interaction with chaos, buildings have rather silently inspired the development of chance-related theories and practices outside the disciplinary limits of architecture. But while artists have methodically recognised the value of chance within their work, especially after the advent of modernism in the 20th century, architectural designers and theorists have tended to suppress the use of the concept. They have instead used other terms to describe the slippage. More productive would be if architecture could redefine its concerns about programme, form, and occupation more radically through the study and use of design *and* chance as a dialectical relationship in architectural practice. If accidents are unavoidable in the way that we experience space, what could be a more creative role of the 'aleatory' in architectural design? How can chance be acknowledged and even used within the drawing process? What can architects learn from art? Or to put it more simply, how can they develop design techniques and strategies that are open to embrace chance during the architectural process?

76 *Murray Fraser*

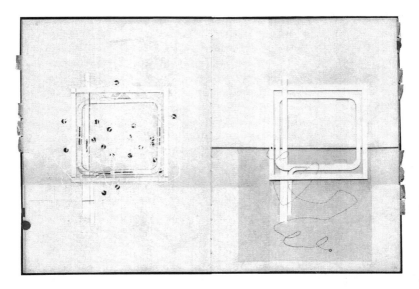

Fig. 5.4 Design models for New York pier competition
[Courtesy of Yeoryia Manolopoulou]

Fig. 5.5 Design models for New York pier competition
[Courtesy of Yeoryia Manolopoulou]

Preserving openness in design research   77

Manolopoulou's PhD by architectural design contains a rich textual and visual study of diverse and multidisciplinary examples that aim to give a critical context for the study and use of chance within the architectural field. The strategies she discusses do not try to offer absolute models but instead suggest that designers ought to pursue a dual dialogue with chance, welcoming and resisting it at once. The thesis seeks to achieve three critical positions: (a) to establish a new area of design research in architecture that systematically studies and develops the practice of chance through drawing, building, and situated spatial action; (b) to expand the scope of architectural research so that it reveals a bigger whole than the building, including the lived experience of space as affected by habits, rhythms, and encounters; (c) to develop a dialogic mode of design research that places the architect in a continual dialogue with other authors, other histories, disciplines, and projects, such that this multiple dialogue is embodied in the making and concrete reality of the architectural project itself. Manolopoulou offers design work in two distinct project portfolios that deal with the themes of *chance in perception* and *chance in design*. In doing so, it identifies three major thematics of chance: *impulsive*, *systematic*, and *active*. These 'species of chance' are open to interaction and evolution. Indeed, as techniques they complement each other and favour collaboration with other working modes, and this is precisely what Manolopoulou demonstrates in her own design projects. As she notes so clearly:

> If chance influences the perception and use of architectural space, this thesis proposes that architecture should value the implications of chance in the process of design. It argues that while architects have dabbled in aleatory manoeuvres, mainly in order to defy the functionalism, rationalism and aesthetics of modernism, architecture can benefit from more radical abandonments to chance. Chance should be one of architecture's main drawing tools.
>
> Chance is mainly favoured as an apparatus that can disrupt determinism and suppress habitual working modes. . . . It should be explored in its own right.
>
> Chance can trigger the mechanisms of imagination in playful and collaborative ways, and release spontaneity, humour and surprise. It can extend rather than eliminate aspects of modernism . . . to the function, logic and aesthetics of indeterminacy.
>
> Whether or not architects intend it, architecture is a producer of design and chance and a product of both. All drawing involves chance, but it can never abolish chance. Chance will always evoke change affecting all architecture. To bring together the last and first lines of Mallarmé's poem *Un coup de dés*:
>
> All Thought emits a Throw of the Dice [but]
> a throw of the dice will never abolish chance.
>
> (Manolopoulou 2013, 221–225)

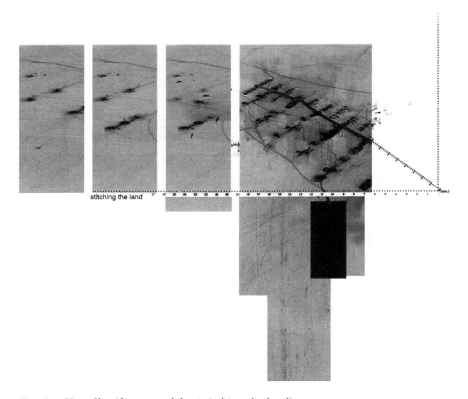

Fig. 5.6 Yara Sharif, proposal for 'stitching the land'
[Courtesy of Yara Sharif]

Yara Sharif, 'Spaces of possibility and imagination within the Palestinian/Israeli conflict' (2012) (University of Westminster – supervisors: Professor Murray Fraser and Samir Pandya)

Yara Sharif's astonishingly original thesis consists of an endeavour to investigate – via the mechanism of the PhD by design – the relationship among architecture, politics, and power by examining the way these factors interplay in relation to the Palestinian/Israeli conflict. In this sense, Palestine is taken as a key testing ground for the intellectual inquiry into the very essence of architecture by looking at the spaces between people, lines, documents, and maps for the meaning of architecture of resistance. Above all, Sharif searches in her thesis for potential spaces of possibilities that can empower a fragmented society and bridge the gap between the divided spaces, working against the deliberate Israeli project of marginalisation of Palestinian residents.

Preserving openness in design research 79

Looking at everything that has already been discussed, proposed, and imposed in relation to the Palestinian/Israeli conflict, it might well appear that there is nothing more left to be said. Sharif believes that we are now faced with two lopsided 'entities' of Palestine and Israel that are superimposed onto one another; neither can be truly integrated, nor can they be separated. The outcome of the various political agreements, summits, and talks from the Oslo Peace Agreement through to the 'Road Map' to the Camp David, Washington, and Sharm-Al-Sheikh Agreements has laid bare the failure of any prospect of finding a 'just peace'. Rather, the result has only been to leave Palestinian people with endless maps, lines, boundaries, and designated areas that mean nothing to their lives, apart from separating and fragmenting and destroying their social and physical space. The urban morphology of the land is thus being pushed to its extreme condition. As a result, Palestine today is left with an absent mental map, no longer making sense of where its spaces start or end.

Stemming from the need for an alternative architectural discourse in such a problematic status, especially with the unbalanced economic and political forces which prevail, the aims of Sharif's doctoral research are thus to explore and propose spatial possibilities through different means. She attempts to re-read the Palestinian landscape from a new perspective by stripping it of the dominant power of drawn lines – including any imagined ones – in order to expose the hidden dynamic topography born from social conditions. Her explicit aim is to redraw the other side of the Palestine/Israel conflict that has been ignored or overlooked by the dominant power structures.

Examining the dialogue of daily Palestinian resistance also shows that within the current Israeli policies of trying to harden the border zones, including the notorious Separation Wall, the quest for counter-spaces is carving out new cultural and urban realities against the hegemonic forces of power. Perhaps the most outstanding outcomes of this reality are the everyday examples of Palestinian spatial resistance that are recasting the geo-political map by displaying creative tools that architecture and planning have so far failed to match. The emergence of small-scale Palestinian social and economic networks appears able to overcome and adapt to the difficult situation, and as a result they are also able to redefine, sometimes invisibly, the meaning of the built environment around them. These collective and informal networks/events are now also drawing up their own lines for a new kind of thinking within architecture. Ostensibly, their task is to subvert spaces of pure oppression and change them into spaces of play and creativity so that social life can be recuperated.

What is so vital in Sharif's research for her PhD by design is her involvement with 'live' design projects and site-specific interventions in various locations in the Palestinian West Bank, such as for the town of Birzeit, which together add a unique dimension to the design process. It also paves the way for imagining new possible moments of spatial stitching inspired and nourished by the matrix of informal Palestinian networks. Here she

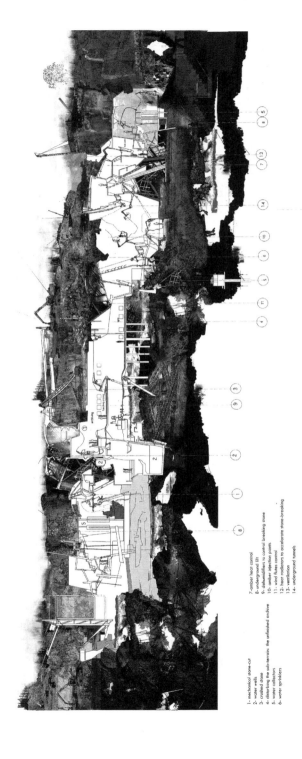

Fig. 5.7 Design proposals for insertions into the Palestinian West Bank [Courtesy of Yara Sharif]

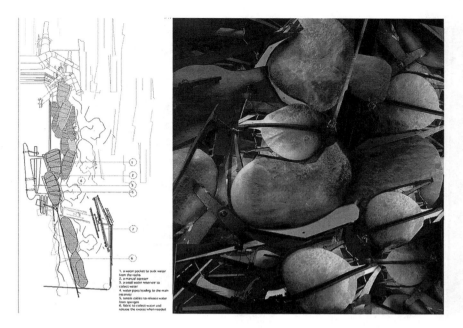

Fig. 5.8 Design proposals for insertions into the Palestinian West Bank
[Courtesy of Yara Sharif]

conceptualises projects that reclaim the airspace above the contested soil and the sub-stratum beneath it as another means to resist hegemonic domination. Sharif intends her outcomes to provoke a deeper and more critical kind of architectural thinking which, in its explicit engagement with political and social realities, can, as I have argued elsewhere, 'move on from Koolhaas' and towards a more truly embedded mode of critical architecture and design practice (Fraser 2007). Design research offers an excellent and open methodology in which to pursue such essential aims, and this is its real strength, and this is what Sharif encapsulates so well in her design research:

> Lying between dream and realism, the series of design proposals need to be seen as moments of slow change for those who are currently unable to fit into the Palestinian/Israeli planet, and who have been forcefully removed from the front line of debate due to political realities. These moments are not meant to enforce themselves onto the map, or onto Palestinian people. Instead, they must be seen as spatial possibilities that are inspired and nourished by everyday social and political events.
>
> The design interventions in the 'live' project for Birzeit's historic centre are intended to be subtle and indeed invisible. They are very

82 *Murray Fraser*

much embedded within local practices and everyday life to create the social and spatial conditions which will allow local citizens to take over. Birzeit's regeneration is seen as a moment of reality that I started from and always returned to.

On the other hand, the 'Underground' and 'Air' chapters offer a tactical critique of the current strategies of Israeli occupation, and indeed offer a sort of ironic and subversive form of reclamation. The two highly speculative design chapters – titled 'Underground' and 'Air' – place an emphasis on the need to step above and underneath the exhausted surface of Palestine to look for possibilities. Both chapters share Lefebvre's quest for a counter-space and re-imagine the 'play and creativity' of the ordinary while inhabiting and recasting space.

By going underground, the design language can be seen as a form of confrontation. It addresses the 'other' while capturing, crushing and excavating their underground territory. This is why the existing machinery that is viciously taking over the Palestinian landscape – cranes, bulldozers, trucks, lifts, etc. – are deliberately retained for my proposed interventions. Their familiar dystopian face is kept as a fake moment of normality, and is then masked by invisible tactics for healing. On the other hand, the 'Air' with its bird machines is a process of 'quiet encroachment' that should be seen as a collective ideology born from the sky.'

(Sharif 2016, 185)

Some future pointers

With this example in mind, it is time to conclude this chapter and suggest some directions for the future. Design research offers a rich approach for architects and academics to develop even more their own kind of knowledge and to establish the necessary approaches and methodologies. Given the open and speculative nature of design, a whole range of topics seems to be able to be drawn into the act of design research, as the essays in this book have shown. These include, for example, spatial morphology, building typology, architectural history and theory, philosophy, performance and performativity, drawn/modelled representations, building materials, construction techniques, sustainability, sociology, psychology, subjective experience, gender relationships, architectural practice, digital social media, and such like.

In terms of envisaging the kinds of characteristics that we ought to be seeking in design research theses, and in particular to establish a level of 'doctorateness' that distinguishes it from lower levels of study, here are six proposed features to consider:

1   Design research in architecture needs to be open ended and speculative in nature and hence self-reflective rather than conceptually fixed;

Preserving openness in design research 83

2 It also seeks to resist economic or political instrumentality;
3 This in turn means that it is often critical of existing social conditions and power structures and prefers to search for newer and fairer ways of organising the world;
4 Design research when properly carried out mixes text, drawings, models, photographs, and so on in what is a fluid, creative, and dialectical process;
5 As such it openly welcomes cross-disciplinary research and blurred intellectual boundaries;
6 And through a combination of these characteristics, it wishes above all to resist easy definitions or normative readings.

Perhaps the main thing to remember is the inventiveness and suppleness of design research, which in turn echoes the sheer fluidity of social and economic relations across the world, especially within the networked conditions that we usually refer to as globalisation. Just as socio-economic systems, or indeed the very patterns of human life, are never written fully in advance, so too does design research offer an astonishing openness. To some this might smack of a lack of rigour, but for that we only need to remember the role of creativity and chance and contingency in even the most supposedly 'rational' scientific research. It is an incredible challenge for architectural practice and academia, and cumulatively the effect could be genuinely substantial. Establishing a profound and creative basis for 'doctorateness' in the pursuit of ever more diverse programmes for PhDs by design offers an exciting way forward, but it is equally necessary to use this innovation to locate more centrally the place of architectural research within the complex and troubling aspects of everyday life that surround us all. If there is to be an underlying intent for furthering the process of design research in architecture, then let it be the aim of redressing (at least partially) some of the most profound economic, social, and cultural inequalities that exist around the world.

Bibliography

Fraser, Murray. 2007. 'Beyond Koolhaas'. In *Critical Architecture*, edited by Jane Rendell, Jonathan Hill, Murray Fraser and Mark Dorrian, 332–339. London/New York: Routledge.
Fraser, Murray. 2013. 'Introduction'. In *Design Research in Architecture: An Overview*, edited by Murray Fraser, 1–14. Farnham, Surrey: Ashgate.
Hill, Jonathan. 2003. *Actions of Architecture: Architects and Creative Users*. London: Routledge.
Manolopoulou, Yeoryia. 2013. *Architectures of Chance*. Farnham, Surrey: Ashgate.
Rendell, Jane. 2013. 'A Way with Words: Feminists Writing Architectural Design Research'. In *Design Research in Architecture: An Overview*, edited by Murray Fraser, 117–136. Farnham, Surrey: Ashgate.
Saarinen, Eero. 1943. *The City: Its Growth, Its Decay, Its Future*. New York: Reinhold Publishing.

Sharif, Yara. 2016. *Architecture of Resistance: Cultivating Moments of Possibility within the Palestinian/Israeli Conflict*. London: Routledge.

van Schaik, Leon, and Anna Johnson. 2011. *By Practice, by Invitation: Design Practice Research in Architecture and Design at RMIT, 1986–2011*. Melbourne: onepointsixone.

6 Design practice research in architecture and design at RMIT University
Discovery, reflection and assessment

Colin Fudge & Adriana Partal

Introduction

This chapter explores the RMIT University approach to practice-based design research at doctoral level and in particular the assessment component of the PhD candidates and their practice-embedded research. In 2008 one of the authors joined RMIT University Melbourne from Bristol and became more directly engaged with the design practice-based PhD programme in Melbourne and subsequently in Europe and Asia. With his background in the Commission for Architecture and the Built Environment (CABE) in the UK, he is positioned to be able to directly reflect on both the national public design review processes within the CABE Design Review System and the more personal design practice review process which is central to the practice based doctoral approach of RMIT in architecture and design. One of the key similarities here being the use of the design 'crit' or 'review' and peer assessment in both the public design review process and within the RMIT PhD model for architecture and design practice research.

First we introduce and explain the RMIT design practice research model including a brief history and context, the underlying philosophy and approach, the experience to date, the current operation of assessment in the model and the internationalising of the design practice research programme.

To understand the process and experience of assessment within the model and to follow the adjustments to the process over time the authors carried out conversations with members of juries and chairs of examination panels, all of whom were external to RMIT. Through these interviews a richer understanding of the nature of assessment became clear and led to further reflections on the nature of the assessment approach, the continuous assessment and peer review experience and views on the RMIT practice-based approach in relation to other doctoral experiences.

In the concluding part of the chapter we summarise what has been discussed before, commenting on the RMIT approach to practice-based PhDs and the assessment process. The authors then move to a second order of reflections and further developmental ideas and questions that surround their earlier findings. Finally we stand back from the discussion and consider

86 Colin Fudge & Adriana Partal

what further research should be considered for advancing the practice-based approach to doctoral programmes and what could be gained from the existing body of work and experience.

RMIT's approach to design practice research PhDs

Origins and evolution

Design practice research at RMIT began in the late 1980s following Leon van Schaik's recent arrival in Melbourne and his delight and fascination with the architecture and the city. He invited practitioners to join him in examining the nature of their work and, as he called it, their 'mastery' demonstrated through their extensive work acclaimed locally through awards, exhibitions, publications and peer review (see van Schaik 2003, 2005, 2008, 2011, 2013).

In addition he was also developing what might be termed a meta-project to acknowledge their work and its contribution in Melbourne, in Australia and in the rest of the world. Up to that time there had been in Melbourne some moves to set up local processes to build local design culture; nevertheless the most significant events 'around which the culture gyrated were visits from architectural stars from the northern hemisphere' (van Schaik and Johnson 2011).

So to counter this van Schaik 'called for meetings of creative innovators and challenged them to research the nature of their innovations' (van Schaik and Johnson 2011). Through these meetings van Schaik also introduced one of the core ideas of the eventual RMIT model, which was 'to inculcate an approach to research that was not "about" design, but was research in the medium of design itself' (van Schaik and Johnson 2011).

Van Schaik argued that together, the practitioners and himself would examine their past and current projects in the light of a new or refreshed understanding and after this reflection speculate through the medium of design about possible futures for their practice, their design work and their approach. This is the core idea in the RMIT design practice research programme. It commenced in the early years as a research Master for practitioners and now operates at doctoral level across three continents. The research programme by 2016 has involved more than 200 practitioners over three continents.

The RMIT practice-based PhD programme now operates in Melbourne, Australia, in Ghent and Barcelona in Europe and in Ho Chi Minh City in Vietnam. The PhD programme for practitioners takes place across three continents with currently (2016) 86 candidates in Australia, 48 in Europe and 13 in Asia. In addition to these figures there are additional students from the School of Media and Communication, School of Fashion and Textiles, and School of Art.

What seems to be clear is that there is interest internationally in the model, that it is translatable in very different cultural contexts and settings and that there is a significant tranche of research associated with the operation of the model itself and to the body of work emerging from the masters and doctoral candidates over the last 30 years.

The move by van Schaik back in the late 1980s can now be appreciated as a highly successful strategy for the School of Architecture and Design and the wider Academy itself, taking both practice and practitioners into the critical frame of the university and building a learning community together. These moves also demonstrate in more contemporary times the motto from the 1887 origins of RMIT, which was and still is, 'A skilled hand and cultivated mind' (Edquist and Grierson 2012). That is a focus on 'practice', an intimate relationship between the academy and practitioners and the creation of an environment to reflect together about the nature and content of practice.

The development of the Practice Research Symposium (PRS)

The architecture 'crit' in its many forms has been central to the study of architecture and other design disciplines from the end of the 19th century through to the present day. There has been considerable observation and writing on the 'architecture studio' and the 'crit'. The history commences with the guilds in the Middle Ages and the apprentice-master model, continues through to the École des Beaux-Arts and to the more contemporary Bauhaus and then was developed further with the broader application in architecture schools across the world. Significant thinkers such as Boyer (1996), Cuff (1992), Dewey (1938), Froebel (1967) and Schön (1983) have pointed to the benefits of the studio and the crit as a way of learning in a community. Boyer and Mittgang (1996, 27), observing architecture education, suggest, 'architectural education is really about fostering the learning habits needed for the discovery, integration, application and sharing of knowledge over a lifetime.'

The success of the crit has varied, but some of the key characteristics include peer review, invited experts, practice and academia coming together, the presentation, explanation and response, the performance, an exhibition and being able to provide an environment in which supportive yet critical learning can take place. This is the ideal but not necessarily always the way crits are conducted or have been experienced!

Van Schaik, when he was thinking about the form of engagement in the early stages of the development of the research symposium, was also confronting the issue of the then lack of resources for supervision. So on reflection, it is not surprising that the model he developed in a sense combines the crit with a broader notion of the learning community in the studio in a mutually supporting device that has come to be known as the **Practice Research Symposium (PRS)**.

The format of the research programme is structured around twice-yearly research gatherings each now known as Practice Research Symposium (PRS).

88   Colin Fudge & Adriana Partal

In the early days there were three symposia per annum, but this frequency did not fit with the vagaries and demands of practice, and it was quickly reduced to two PRSs per annum. This seems to reflect well the needs of the practitioner candidates, but now that the doctoral program operates across three continents it also has to fit with the demands on the RMIT staff, the external academic and practitioner critics and the staging of the events in Australia, Europe and Asia.

The ideas behind the model

In discussing the ideas behind the model it is important to recognise that over time the model has developed and become more refined and integrated as a whole. So to explain it simply is to probably do injustice to the sophistication of its development over many years, different cultures and different actors in key positions. So with recognition of this the RMIT model is founded upon a number of ideas that are both simple and yet deep.

They include the notions and significance of:

Mental space: This component of the model argues that designers of space should be aware of their own histories in space and the 'mental space' they have constructed from that history and interpretation (see Young and Mills 1980). So in the Practice Research Symposia the candidates are encouraged and required to explore their mental space and where it has come from as a key factor in discussing the nature of their practice (see van Schaik 2008).

Research in the medium of design itself: This aspect seems to be distinctive and follows a path to investigate architecture through the practice of design and not necessarily through history or social and/or environmental science. That is to say that the focus is on what is designed and its relation to both the espoused theory and the theory in use and where both of these come from (Argyris and Schön 1974). Our concern here is the development of integrated multi-disciplinary perspectives in indeed an ever-increasing number of practitioners with these attributes and more complex 'enchainments' than in the past and which are needed to cope with the increasingly complex world.

Direct engagement of practitioners: This is crucial to the whole programme and is focused on getting to the heart of the issue of fresh architectural insight into the issues facing designers without what is seen as the blinding or blocking or mistranslation that might come from 'intermediaries' (van Schaik and Johnson 2011). This concern we can see is difficult to avoid; however, there is a very strong intent to keep to the medium of design itself as the vehicle for exploring one's own practice.

Integrated scholarship: This foundational idea stems from the reflection of the 'splitting' of research between academia and practice and even between the research department and the project studios within large

Design practice research at RMIT University 89

practices. Research has come to be seen to be outside of practice, be it in the offices or in the academy. The notion of integrated scholarship comes from an analysis of what the professoriates in universities actually do rather than what they espouse to do (Argyris and Schön 1974). Boyer in his study of architecture demonstrates that practitioners do not research or teach in the conventional meanings of these terms but rather engage in four modes of scholarship, namely, discovery, integration, application and dissemination. And it is to this understanding of Boyer (1996) and others that the RMIT model turns in attempting to avoid the splitting and move to a notion of integration and integrated scholarship.

Public behaviours recognition: This final component is about creating the safe but challenging 'forum' or 'place' where candidates can explore with their peers and the community of practice their own behaviour in relation to their design practice. The creation of this learning community who have to handle the disclosure, unpacking, reconstructing and repositioning through the twice-yearly Practice Research Symposia is clearly seen as crucial to the exploration, discovery and reflection of design practice. It has become, as Professor Kester Rattenbury observes, 'the best crit system in the world . . . allowing architects to develop their work as research'.

(Rattenbury 2015)

Over the years, the use of these foundational ideas has developed beyond the original research masters such that the model now encompasses PhD-level research as seen in the work of SueAnne Ware 2005, Shane Murray 2004 and Jenny Lowe 2002. In their exemplified work the same basic model and sequence is used but at PhD level. As van Schaik explains,

Observe and analyse a body of work. Derive from this a clear understanding of the (provincial) architectural intentions of the work, and of how that work is situated within its national and international (metropolitan) context, thus defining the community of learning capable of engaging it in its best possible metropolitan conversation. Identify the propositions driving your design practice, and analyse the gaps between where you (and your peers) are on the path to a fulfilment of those propositions. Conduct the next tranche of your work in the light of that analysis. Evaluate and redefine the gaps. Conduct another tranche of work. Evaluate and redefine the gaps. Conduct a closing tranche of work in the light of this redefinition. (In the Masters there was just one tranche of work). Conclude by speculating through design on possible future practices ensuing from this investigation.

(van Schaik and Johnson 2011, 28)

Van Schaik also notes that 'consistently this model has revealed hitherto undocumented design practice processes, unmasking intuition and making a major contribution to new knowledge in the domain' (van Schaik and Johnson 2011, 28).

90 *Colin Fudge & Adriana Partal*

The doctoral assessment process

There are three clear stages for all PhDs that were developed and agreed by the School of Graduate Research at RMIT that take place before the final examination for a PhD.

They are:

A *Confirmation Seminar* in which the potential candidate comes through an application process and submission via the Practice Research Symposium, has discussions with potential supervisors and obtains an agreement formally from the university to proceed.

There is a formal *Candidate Mid-Point Review* in which the candidate must prove that they have made sufficient progress including a written component of 5,000 words plus a pin-up exhibition. Again this is taken through the PRS.

There is a *Conclusion Seminar* which takes place at least 12 months before the final examination. This includes a full draft of the dissertation in writing, a very clear idea of the exhibition and a clear explanation of how it will all be presented. In a sense it is a critical rehearsal of the three components that make up the final examination.

The final examination is conducted in front of a three-person jury in public. There are specific rules as to the jurors' roles, the role of the chair, confidentiality and how the decisions are processed and eventually conveyed to the candidate. These are common with all PhDs in RMIT. The candidates have to prepare a written thesis of 40,000 words, an exhibition and an explanation/performance/defence of the PhD and must be able to respond and defend the thesis to the jury and in public. The whole examination is filmed and the record archived.

These are the formal measures which have to be followed. They of course need to be seen in the context of the requirement to have a supervisor(s) and to attend, present and take part as a peer at two practice research symposia per annum for the length of the PhD.

So the candidates who are working in their practices full time, in addition for a period of around four years, take on the demands of the PhD, the requirement to carry out research methods training, to take part in the twice-yearly PRS, to go through the formal stages of confirmation, mid-point review, conclusion seminar and final examination. For a full-time working architect and designer this is a demanding personal and work commitment.

Understanding practice-based research and assessment

As authors of this chapter we were interested in the views of the external jury members in relation to the RMIT model, their own work and positions when assessing the candidates' work, how they carried out their assessments and what value they placed on the approach from RMIT.

We invited the jury members external to RMIT to informal discussions with us around four issues and engaged them in a conversation around these

Design practice research at RMIT University 91

issues. We carried out these conversations during one of the PRS events in Barcelona in 2014. The results of these somewhat journalistic and qualitative conversations are presented here to provide a sense and flavour of their responses and to try to get closer to their views on the RMIT approach.

The first conversation was around what they understood about practice-embedded design research.

'Acknowledges strongly the notion of creativity and that creativity includes both tacit and explicit knowledge. It also flags up the complexity of the interrelationship between tacit and explicit knowledge'.

'What is really created is a discourse around design-based knowledge which is deep and sometimes involves translating the knowledge to another register'.

'It is clearly about the disclosure of one's own practice to peers, and this involves discovery in relation to self and discovery for peers'.

'The assessment component is complex because it is such a public process and far less prescribed than the conventional PhD'.

'Reflection and self-reflection of one's own practice is the core of the programme'.

'The real criticality of this approach is the active doing of design research, i.e. the act of doing as opposed to thinking about doing or writing about doing'.

'It is about interrogating the nature of your practice and communicating this discovery and the new knowledge about your practice to the world'.

'The difference between more conventional research and the more practice-based research is that more conventional research can be:

Research to
Research for
Research about
Whereas the PRS is research **through**'.

'Practice Design Research is in a sense a form of literacy. And even the examination includes this notion in its requirement for a literary component, a material form component and the performance/communication component, which when taken together demonstrate a form of literacy'.

The second issue for discussion was around the design practice research assessment itself.

'From my experience the work is genuine, authentic and original, and I see no difference in this PhD from more conventional ones I have assessed'.

'I think the continuous public peer review throughout the practice-based PhD is in some ways much more demanding than the conventional

PhD. Indeed some of this practice would help in the process of the more conventional PhD'.

'One of the differences is that the diversity of the peer review processes and the diversity of the final panel is both demanding for the candidate but also ensures rigour in relation to the assessment'.

'The genuine fusion of the written document, the exhibition and the performance is unique in this system and is very challenging and rigorous'.

'One of my concerns is how the practitioner places his or her ideas and practice in the history of practice. I think this is somewhat unresolved and needs attention'.

'Traditional Anglo-Saxon PhDs would benefit enormously from the candidates being able to talk together formally, the continuous peer support and challenge and the public nature of the assessment process'.

'The two PhD outcomes are very similar, but how you get there is very different'.

The third conversation involved the question of the particular ways you as a designer appreciate and examine a candidate's work.

'For me it is important to have sensibility, i.e. the ability to be able to understand and put yourself in the other person's place having gone through this whole process'.

'For me I am struck by the accumulation of assessment throughout the whole process and how that is understood and brought to bear in the final assessment. How do we assess adequately the journey the candidate has gone through?'

'For me the key question to be answered from the three interrelated submissions is "Is this a doctorate?"'

'I think that in this approach the discovery process and how the discovery process is made explicit and used is crucial in the final assessment'.

'You are using different methodologies and skills from different disciplines and some are more conventional and some are from conventional design criticism. It is how these are combined that is the strength of the assessment'.

'This is difficult work to assess, and the processes I use are partly perceptive, partly about practice, partly historical and partly from the social sciences and philosophy. We are working on all of these modes and have to apply them to assess the coherent body of work in front of us'.

'In the RMIT model I think that the change processes are often quite demanding and radical for the candidates, and this is a crucial and positive element of the model. So I am often observing with wonder and delight what the candidate has gone through and is expressing in their

Design practice research at RMIT University 93

final submission. However, this does not mean that the assessment is easy, and indeed for me these are more complex to assess than the more prescribed conventional PhD'.

'We are objective as far as I know and often from different disciplines, cultures and experience. This multi-disciplinarity is very important and allows objectivity and different perspectives to be considered in relation to the submission'.

'The assessment is about the depth of investigation and reflection in relation to the intention of the PhD. And the key test is whether this is an original contribution to the field'.

The final conversation was around their own views on RMIT's model/approach and whether it provided added value in the broad topic of design research.

'My own sense is that compared to conventional PhDs in relation to design this is a better way to work, particularly if you are exploring the nature of design through design practice itself'.

'The RMIT model over more than 30 years has made all of us rethink our ways of understanding design practice and design research. It has been very influential in terms of process, assessment, pedagogy and the role of the academy'.

'What has come out of the RMIT model are interesting concepts that surround the process and the work of the candidates. These include: philosophies of design research; exploration through new languages; the significance of peer review and peer support; the development of the public 'crit' and exploring and disentangling the design process'.

'For me the key added values are the notion of search and discovery within the PhD process and secondly the ability to translate the experience to the world of practice'.

'I think this is mostly about how it is done. The crucial added value is the Practice Research Symposia twice a year, how it is done and the culture that it has inspired and developed'.

'The authentic peer review, the openness to criticism and the reality of the practice community are the key value adds'.

'There is significance in the continuous peer-review approach, but perhaps more important for me seems to be the lasting nature of change that comes out of this process and how that translates into future practice. The PhD is not just sitting on the shelf; it is alive and influencing practice'.

'For me the value adds are: first the strengthening of the bridge between the academy and practice; second through the candidate's work the RMIT process contributes to the understanding and translation of what goes on in practice; third what seems to happen if you could add

94 *Colin Fudge & Adriana Partal*

up the 30 years of work is that there has been a large scale translation of personal practice into wider professional knowledge'.

These commentaries from the conversations provide a flavour of the responses and reflections from the international jury members. We will come back to these in the concluding part of the chapter, but we finish this section with a comment from Professor Kester Rattenbury:

> I have just come back from Barcelona, where I was attending my third PRS, the PhD programme for practising architects to develop their real work as research, and on each occasion, I have been aware of an exponential shift in scale. That is, the scale of the actual nature of the work going on; in this vast research into how architects actually think, work, design, communicate, refine, produce, reference, share, criticise and develop their work, individually and collectively. But also a shift in scale in my struggling, feeble attempts to perceive the scope of this extraordinary invention; in the startling step changes in the individual work of the already high level practitioners on this programme; and in the composite growth of intelligence which it is generating throughout its whole booming community.
>
> (Rattenbury 2015)

Conclusions

In this chapter we have tried to explain the origins and background to the RMIT model for design practice research. We have noted that the model in operation today across three continents has developed considerably over the last 30 years, with the foundational ideas remaining at the core of the model. Similarly there is no shortage of demand to participate in the model from practitioners in Australia, Europe and Asia. Indeed there are now issues concerning the management of this interest and demand worldwide and how best to develop the future for this innovative and demanding practice research process.

We have discussed the model and the assessment component of the doctoral process with the external and international jury members. Their qualitative comments provided further insights on the assessment process, the model itself, the value of the model and how their experience on the juries and being part of the peer and learning community fitted with their wider experience of doctoral programmes in architecture and design.

We conclude this chapter with our own reflections on the model, the assessment and a suggested wider research and development agenda that could contribute to the development of design practice research further, expand the thinking in relation to other disciplines, examine applications in wider policy and practice and indeed contribute to the notion and purpose of the contemporary university.

Design practice research at RMIT University   95

It is clear from the discussions with the external jury members, chairs and other non-RMIT colleagues that on balance there is a very positive response to the RMIT model and the role it plays in the assessment of the 'doctorateness' of the design practice research. For many they don't see the assessment as being that different from the more conventional PhD, and they use not dissimilar approaches to their assessment of the work in front of them. They comment positively about the nature of the final examination and particularly about the three components to be assessed, which include the written thesis/catalogue/exegesis, the physical exhibition and the presentation/performance/defence of the doctoral work in public. They comment very positively on the process, the peer review approach twice a year (PRS), the checks in the system at three key points in the PhD process – Confirmation Seminar, Candidate Mid-Point Review and the Conclusion Seminar that takes place around 12 months before the final examination. So in terms of the interviewees they are rather positive about the process, quality, assessment, compared to their experience of more conventional PhDs. Indeed many see benefits that could be translatable to more conventional PhDs and to other very different disciplines like engineering, digital technology, digital media, animation and games.

However, we would like to stand back from the RMIT model and in doing so provide some thoughts and reflections that are more critical, with a view to providing more awareness and possibilities for development of the model and further research. Our personal views on the model concur with those we interviewed, and we applaud both the committed journey of the whole enterprise and the individual doctoral journeys of the practitioners. But what might be the drawbacks or weaker aspects to this approach? And what might be the areas for further development, refinement and research?

First, given that there is considerable new knowledge gained with each candidate's work and a considerable body of knowledge gained over the last 30 years, what is the nature of this knowledge and what is its impact?

It could be argued, and we understand that some do argue this, that whilst there does seem to be quite extraordinary personal knowledge gained through this PhD process, nevertheless this knowledge is relatively closed to the outside world, and the knowledge domains and benefits mostly the individual candidate and their practice, the practice they work for or lead and the design practice community at RMIT. Some people bring forward the notion that this model is quite closed, with difficulties in reaching out and disseminating the new knowledge. Further they argue that the benefits of the approach and the outcomes don't get through to the wider design community nor to other disciplines that might benefit. Is this fair? The answer varies such that in some cases this might have some truth, and the new knowledge is relatively private. However, in many other cases the impact seems to be externalised strongly through new practice, new directions, and these are shared and move the individual and their practice to a new register and direction which in turn influences others and the nature of practice

96   Colin Fudge & Adriana Partal

itself. In some cases, as in all PhDs, there are examples that do make larger paradigm shifts, and these are externalised and form the foundation for new knowledge and suggestions for larger shifts in practice.

Professor C.J. Lim's book from the PhD 'Food City' (2014) is a good example of a strong dissemination to the external world coupled with numerous talks, seminars, workshops and a commitment and campaign to think and act differently about food, our habits, its production, climate change and urban futures across the globe.

Returning to the broader question it seems that this might be true, but isn't this also true for many conventional PhDs? What has been addressed by Leon van Schaik and others are attempts to try to capture the achievements and make sense of them through research and publication; the development of the model and partners participating in it through Richard Blythe's EU ADAPT-r grant and deeper ongoing work funded by the Australian Research Council. Nevertheless there is still a very large body of work over the years that needs documenting, interrogating further and further disseminating.

We suggest two ways forward: first perhaps there should be a strategy developed to ensure that candidates and RMIT jointly disseminate the work and outcomes through the appropriate channels to ensure that knowledge domains are enriched. This could be supported through research councils or foundations or indeed through professional networks and institutions.

Second that looking back over the last 30 years, the knowledge generated is examined again not only in terms of the content and how it develops our understanding of design practice. This is in part in progress through the ARC (Australian Research Council) work of Leon van Schaik and others (van Schaik 2013). But there is also another opportunity that we suggest could be taken to capitalise on the accidental but extraordinary longitudinal study of a professional occupation, that of the 'architect'. So unwittingly alongside the main outcomes from 30 years of experience there is also information to support a large study of the architect and how architectural practice has stayed the same, shifted or has varied enormously within this time frame along with the role of the architect in society. It occurs to us that this opportunity, if taken, would add to the great tradition of the 'understanding of occupations' in the 1940s to the 1960s mostly by American sociologists, for example 'Boys in White', a study of how interns become doctors by Howard Becker, Blanche Geer, Everett Hughes and Anselm Strauss (1961) and the interviews by Studs Terkel (1992) with working people.

Our next set of reflections concerns the application and expansion of the model to other disciplines and indeed to teaching and learning and graduate research more widely.

Within RMIT there are already a number of different approaches to PhDs within the creative disciplines. So although the architecture and design

Design practice research at RMIT University   97

model has been the largest, most influential and the one that has been internationalised, nevertheless there are other approaches. In art, media and communications, fashion and industrial design other models exist that are different from the architecture and design model, but also not so similar to the more conventional PhD model. What is interesting is that some candidates from these disciplines in Australia and Europe have opted to join the architecture and design model and take their practice through the steps and demands of this model. It seems that their decision has been influenced by their attraction to the peer community, the external and international experts that are also part of the learning community, the experience of the Practice Research Symposium, being part of a much wider learning community and the demands on oneself and one's practice (private communications 2012–2015).

Professor Fudge has also discussed the architecture and design model with other disciplines in the academy, with other practice disciplines and with multinational companies. There has been considerable interest in the practice-embedded model for different types of engineers from automotive to aeronautical, from structural to civil engineering and from digital technology to wider electronics. In addition their practices or large-scale companies where they are employed have also been interested as a longer-term benefit for employees as part of their training and development. It is within these two areas we see a very large potential for the expansion and spread of the model into other disciplines and indeed into new partnerships with the academy.

In a more public sense the public crit or review has been used as part of the design review process in certain countries, which has become a relatively standard practice to try to lift design quality in the public domain. This was started at CABE in 1999 and is still maintained in England for most significant projects through the Design Council/CABE process. This has also been rehearsed again recently by Terry Farrell (Farrell 2014). In addition many practices have their own internal design review process or crit process to ensure internal peer review and maintenance of quality. We sense that there could be very fruitful connections and partnership working in relation to taking the experience of the PRS into the wider public domain and influencing public knowledge and practice with a view to lifting design quality.

In terms of further research there are a number of ideas that come from aspects of the RMIT model that would seem to us to form the nucleus of several strands of research benefitting the development of the model itself and expanding the broad notion of the model or its parts to other sectors. Within this we see that the notion of the *learning community* here is something worth trying to understand and capture for the benefit of wider application. What forms the boundaries, motivation, relative equalities, energy and momentum, leadership and maintenance within this model, and can it be transferred to other settings?

98 Colin Fudge & Adriana Partal

Similarly the *Practice Research Symposium* is a very rare forum. It is a space for genuine authenticity and is challenging personally and for the peer colleagues. Further exploration of the key characteristics that make this work so successfully would be useful to tease out. Is there some learning from this approach that could benefit the processes in more conventional PhDs and potentially vice versa? For example does the Scandinavian or Swedish PhD model in architecture, with its structured series of public seminars during the PhD process, already have some of these characteristics, and is there some mutual learning that could benefit both types of models?

Through Professor Fudge's experience with CABE and design review nationally in England and his involvement with the introduction of similar processes, in SW England, Wales, Scotland, Australia and New Zealand we have been intrigued with the notion of the use of the public crit or review outside of the architecture school and the academy for wider public purposes. There is a much larger research agenda here that explores and understands the crit or review both within and without the academy. So this research would examine the rules, settings, motivations, outcomes and complexity of the social processes before moving on to speculate how it could be translatable to other settings. This would continue the earlier work of Argyris and Schön (1974), Boyer (1996) and Schön (1983) and would contribute to the further application of these processes for private and public use.

Finally there is an even wider and further research imperative about exploring the interrelationship between the academy and the world of practice. One of the bigger ideas and sets of values behind the RMIT practice-based PhD model is to seek a connection through a learning community between the academy and the world of practice. This notion, which is far from the so-called ivory tower, is a result of this type of approach and raises the more fundamental questions about the recognition and meaning of practice, the generation of knowledge, the co-production of knowledge and indeed the purpose and work of the contemporary university.

Acknowledgements

The authors gratefully acknowledge contributions and assistance from Professor Leon van Schaik, Professor of Architecture and Innovation Chair, Design Practice Research, RMIT University; Professor Richard Blythe, Dean, School of Architecture and Design, RMIT University; Professor SueAnne Ware, Head, School for Architecture and the Built Environment, University of Newcastle; Professor Martyn Hook, Dean, School of Media and Communication, RMIT University; Professor Laurene Vaughan, Professor in Design and Communication, School of Media and Communication, RMIT University; Professor Nat Chard, Professor of Experimental Architecture, Bartlett School of Architecture, UCL; Associate Professor Felicity Scott, Associate

Professor of Architecture, Columbia University; Professor Ayse Sentur, Professor Faculty of Architecture, Istanbul Technical University; Professor Michael McGarry, Professor of Architecture, Queens University, Belfast; Professor Kester Rattenbury, Professor of Architecture, University of Westminster; Professor Branden W. Joseph, Frank Gallipoli Professor of Modern and Contemporary Art, Columbia University, and numerous candidates enrolled and completed in the design practice research PhD at RMIT University.

Bibliography

Argyris, Chris, and Donald Schön. 1974. *Double loop learning: Theory in practice – Increasing professional efficiency*. San Francisco: Jossey Bass.

Becker, Howard Saul, Blanche Geer, Everett C. Hughes, and Anselm Strauss. 1961. *Boys in white, student culture in medical school*. Chicago: University of Chicago Press.

Boyer, Ernest, and Lee Mittgang. 1996. *Building community: A new future for architectural education and practice*. Princeton: The Carnegie Foundation for the advancement of teaching.

CABE. 2002. *The value of good design*. London: Thomas Telford.

CABE. 2006. *Design review: How CABE evaluates quality in architecture and urban design*. London: CABE.

CABE. 2009. *Design review: Principles and practice*. London: CABE.

Cuff, Dana. 1992. *Architecture: The story of practice*. Cambridge, MA: MIT Press.

Design Council / CABE. 2013. *Design review: Principles and practice*. London: Design Council.

Dewey, John. 1938. *Experience and education*. New York: Macmillan.

Edquist, Harriet, and Elizabeth Grierson. 2012. *A skilled hand and cultivated mind: A guide to the architecture and art of RMIT University*, 2nd edition. Melbourne: RMIT University Press.

Farrell, Terry. 2014. *Our future in place*. In the Farrell Review of Architecture and the Built Environment. www.farrellreview.co.uk

Froebel, Friedrich, and Irene M Lilley. 1967. *Friedrich Froebel: A selection from his writings*. Cambridge: Cambridge University Press.

HMSO Urban Task Force. 1999. *Towards an urban renaissance*. Final Report of the Urban Task Force, Chaired by Lord Richard Rogers of Riverside. London.

Lim, CJ. 2014. *Food city*. London: Routledge.

Rattenbury, Kester. 2015. 'The imagination game.' *RIBA Journal*. 5 January. https://www.ribaj.com/culture/the-imagination-game

Schön, Donald. 1983. *The reflective practitioner: How professionals think in action*. New York: Basic Books.

Terkel, Studs. 1992. *Working: People talk about what they do all day and how they feel about what they do*. New York: The New Press.

van Schaik, Leon. (ed.). 2003. *The practice of practice: Research in the medium of design*. Melbourne: RMIT University Press.

van Schaik, Leon. 2005. *Mastering architecture: Becoming a creative innovator in practice*. Chichester: Wiley-Academy.

van Schaik, Leon. 2006. *Design city Melbourne*. Chichester: Wiley – Academy.

van Schaik, Leon. 2008. *Spatial intelligence*. Chichester: Wiley.

van Schaik, Leon, and A. Johnson. 2011. *By practice, by invitation: Design practice research in architecture and design at RMIT 1986–2011*. Melbourne: Onepointsixone.

van Schaik, Leon, SueAnn Ware, Geoffrey London, and Colin Fudge. 2013. *The practice of spatial thinking – Volume one*. Melbourne: Onepointsixone.

Young, Ken, and Elisabeth Mills. 1980. *Public policy research: A review of qualitative methods*. London: SSRC.

7 Doctoral scholarship in popular music performance

Tor Dybo

Introduction

Many forms of musical styles and expressions included in the term 'popular music' are characterised by the oral transmission of musical knowledge with reference to musicianship in general, rehearsing, composing, arranging, recording and so on. This is about decision making among musicians, composers, arrangers, sound engineers and producers then and there, which often occurs in spontaneous oral settings when songs are created during rehearsals or recording sessions. This contrasts with many forms of Western art music, which in past times have traditionally been preserved and transferred in the form of written scores and printed music. In contrast to the orality within popular music, musicology has traditionally focused on this part of the musical heritage by studying sources about composers and their works based on their written scores. Moreover, the interpretation and dissemination of these kinds of written sources have traditionally been an important aspect of both executive classical music education and research in the field.

The orally based creative processes within popular music mentioned earlier have been discussed for many years in research fields such as jazz studies, popular music studies, ethnomusicology and music education (e.g. Berliner 1994; Dybo 2008; Green 2012; Gullberg 2002; Johansson 2002; Lilliestam 1995; Monson 1991, 1996). Much of the focus of these publications has been on the oral character of popular music; thus the challenge for research and doctoral educational programmes is to capture this orality and tacit knowledge. The establishment of educational programmes in popular music, even at the doctorate level in music education, has been thematised and discussed (e.g. Tønsberg 2013).

This challenge of orality and tacit knowledge within popular music has also been reflected in doctoral education within the field. What are the challenges for the development of an appropriate assessment system for this kind of education? How best to evaluate the outcome of artistic work, in which many decisions leading to the creative artistic results are based on orality and tacit knowledge? How best to handle tacit knowledge in a doctoral education? How do PhD candidates meet such methodological challenges in their education? Last, how have PhD graduates resolved the tension between the artistic work and scientific requirements of a PhD methodologically? The purpose of this chapter is to discuss this type of doctorateness within popular music educational programmes.

The empirical basis for this chapter is largely based on my background as the leader and creator of the ongoing PhD programme and PhD specialisation in popular music performance at the Faculty of Fine Arts, University of Agder (abbreviated UiA), Kristiansand Campus.[1] Although this PhD programme is oriented toward popular music, I believe that it is relevant to the overall challenges and questions within the theory and philosophy of science which also characterise other artistic subjects. For this reason, it may say something about the common distinctive features of such subjects.

About the term 'popular music'

The term 'popular music' has a long history, and the conceptual content has developed and changed as a result. In the 1800s, the term 'popular music' was used in relation to folk songs and music in popular use, while in the first half of the 1900s this term was used for work songs, music in restaurants, jazz and the like.

After World War II, the term 'popular music' has primarily been used to represent orally transferred musical traditions such as rock, pop, reggae, folk songs, world music and so forth. In this way, the concept of popular music encompasses many musical genres and styles, and it is such an understanding of the term that forms the basis for this article.[2]

Artistic works and the Norwegian system of doctoral education

As in many other countries, a Norwegian PhD dissertation has traditionally mostly been a written work, consisting either of a collection of three or four articles plus an extensive framing chapter or a monograph based on three-year, full-time study including doctoral courses.

Until recently it was not normal in the Norwegian educational system to include artistic works as a part of a doctoral study, despite the fact that since 2008 the doctoral programme in popular music performance at UiA has allowed for combined artistic-scholarly dissertations. In parallel, there is an artistic third-cycle education in Norway that is equivalent to a doctoral degree but which currently cannot use the title of doctor. In this programme, each student is expected to produce an artistic work over a three-year full-time period, including courses supported by a written critical reflection about their respective artistic investigations. The candidate also has to defend this artistic work – similar to a PhD candidate – in an open public disputation, with a judging committee discussing the results from the final work with the candidate. This programme is called the Artistic Research Programme

Doctoral scholarship: music performance   103

(http://artistic-research.no), in which the candidate does not receive the doctoral title, although they do achieve the same accreditation as PhD graduates when it comes to academic positions at Norwegian universities and university colleges. This programme is broad in terms of the artistic disciplines it includes, and many of the graduates or research fellows in music have undertaken artistic research projects related to popular music performance (e.g. Aase 2009, 2013; Brandtsegg 2008; Duch 2011; Kleppen 2013).

Opening up the doctoral title to areas other than the traditional ones at universities has created considerable debate in various forums related to higher education in Norway, and there are very many different attitudes to it from universities that do not have artistic education in their study portfolios. My overall impression of this debate is that many representatives from universities argue that a doctoral dissertation should be a written work exclusively based on a traditional study subject.

For this reason, we still do not have a PhD in artistic works (e.g. DMA, the abbreviation for a Doctor of Musical Arts), as can be found in the UK, where one can obtain a PhD through a portfolio of artistic works. Such a PhD or DMA shows a clear development from the start of the doctoral study until they finish three years later with a large final work. In my opinion, it is only a matter of time before the doctoral title will be adopted in the Artistic Research Programme mentioned.

Artistic doctoral studies in music on the Continent

The PhD programme in popular music at the University of Agder therefore facilitates the integration of artistic work on a high international level into the dissertation. But our doctoral candidates usually have a musicological focus on artistic processes, often viewed from the performer perspective. That is to say that the PhD candidate discusses his or her own artistic work in the written part of the dissertation in relation to similar research within popular music studies in musicology. In this sense, the programme has approved PhD projects that have been methodologically based on, for example, action research on creative artistic processes (e.g. Bråthen 2013). This will be discussed later in this chapter.

As mentioned, in Norway we have no tradition for the kind of artistic dissertations that one finds, for example, on the Continent in countries such as the UK, where several higher education institutions offer almost exclusively artistically aligned doctoral studies. In these studies, each of the PhD candidates has a professor with artistic expertise appointed as a supervisor who will act as a mentor to the candidate's artistic development. The results are documented in the form of artistic products such as recordings, compositions and the like, plus a reflective text about the artistic research during the doctoral study.

To be admitted to a portfolio doctoral programme in the UK (e.g. the University of York and the University of Huddersfield), the candidates must

104   *Tor Dybo*

document their high artistic level (equivalent to a completed master's degree in music performance) by the submission of a specified number of work samples that can be compositions, studio recordings or the like. The portfolio must demonstrate that the PhD candidate has undergone an extensive artistic development during the three years of the doctoral study. In other words, a well-established performer at a high international artistic level is normally not permitted to submit previously written compositions or previously released CDs from a former career in his or her doctoral portfolio. Everyone must show a clear artistic development over the three years' duration of their PhD study.

The judging committee expects a high international artistic level as a result of such PhD studies, and reports from British educational institutions that offer these kinds of doctoral studies reveal that this is a very demanding way of doing a PhD. In this context, it may be mentioned that the relevant universities require regular supervision meetings between the candidate and supervisor, in which continuously submitted work samples must show good progress in the implementation of the PhD study. It may be worth noting that residency at the university is required of the doctoral candidate.

In my view, this type of doctoral study will also become a part of the academic portfolio at Nordic higher education institutions in due course, although today there is no tradition of it. As already mentioned, this has been solved in Norway by the establishment of the artistic research programme, in which the candidate achieves academic competence as an associate professor after the completion of the artistic fellowship programme, similar to that obtained in the traditional doctorate. This opens up a more fundamental discussion about doctoral education and whether the title is exclusively reserved for print media or whether other forms of documentation in the form of audio and video media can offer alternative options.

The PhD education in popular music performance at the University of Agder

How can we address this challenge to our PhD education in popular music performance? In 2008, UiA established this study as a PhD programme at the university.[3] In accordance with the changes to the overall structure of doctoral studies at the university in 2011, it was changed to a PhD specialisation in popular music performance on the doctoral programme at the Faculty of Fine Arts.

This PhD education in popular music performance offers a combined artistic-scholarly dissertation that contains both a written and an artistic performing part. On average, we have 15 PhD candidates enrolled on this programme. The first doctoral defence was undertaken in January 2013, and to date five PhD candidates have graduated with a PhD degree. Two of the graduates (Bråthen 2013; Ellingsen 2014) completed a combined artistic-scholarly dissertation, while the other three (Askerøi 2013; Djupvik 2014; Rolfhamre 2014) completed a traditional scholarly dissertation.

As mentioned, we also give the opportunity to do a more traditional text-based doctoral study, but here too, we focus on the performing part of popular musical practices and performances. This includes not only musicianship but also other important areas of research regarding performance, such as the studio recording process and the roles of the music industry.

The structure of the PhD study in popular music performance

The PhD specialisation in popular music performance was established in 2008 by the board of the University of Agder, in accordance with the national rules for the establishment of such studies in Norway given by NOKUT (the Norwegian Agency for Quality Assurance in Education). This initiative took place as part of the strategy to build the new University of Agder in southern Norway, which opened on 1 October 2007. The wish of the university board was that we develop a doctoral programme that was as closely related to the performing practices in today's popular music as possible so far as was permitted by NOKUT.

As with all Norwegian PhD studies, the length of the study is standardised to three years of full-time work with a total of 180 ECTS (European Credit Transfer and Accumulation System) credit points (60 full-time ECTS each year). This specialisation consists of a training component totalling 30 ECTS credit points, as well as a thesis study with a total of 150 ECTS points under supervision.

Each PhD candidate has to choose between two dissertation variants:

1   A combined dissertation that contains both a written and an artistic performing part
2   A more traditional scholarly dissertation in which the entire dissertation is either a text-based monograph or a collection of articles and where the focus is on the performing part of popular musical practices and performances

For PhD candidates who select a combined thesis (variant 1), the extent and distribution of the written and practical part of the thesis work are decided in each individual case. The supervision partly takes place individually and partly through a regular thesis seminar.

The aim of this specialisation is to develop candidates' qualifications for research in the field of popular music performance and other work in the field, in which there is a need for a high level of scientific knowledge and methodology.

106   Tor Dybo

Oral and tacit knowledge as research areas within popular music performance

In the following the strategic academic thinking that formed the basis for the creation of this PhD programme and later PhD specialisation in popular music performance at the University of Agder will be discussed. This PhD specialisation is based on sub-disciplines within musicology such as popular music performance, popular musicology, music technology (electronic music), the music business, the music industry and world music studies, all of which have the common feature that they are oriented towards oral-based cultures with little tradition of writing down music in the form of sheet music and scores. This often generates types of scholarly theoretical challenges other than simply musical performances based on written traditions in terms of written down compositions and their accompanying material (notes, sheets, etc.). The challenge is to capture the unexpected during orally based events such as improvisation and the intuitive decision making during recordings and concerts that can produce unexpected – yet exciting – musical results. Amongst other things, one challenge is to further capture the creation of musical grooves and a sound world in which music technology in recording studios and onstage is of a great importance.

The peculiarity of doctoral studies within popular music

As indicated in the introduction, the discussion of orality among musicians, sound engineers and record producers in their professional work has revealed that tacit and intuitive forms of musical knowledge characterise much artistic expression and other skill areas, especially within popular music performance. Such knowledge indicates that professionals at an executive level use their skills in an intuitive way. Examples of such expert knowledge include topics affecting studio practice and the music industry (e.g. the producer's role, the recording engineer's role, the recording studio as a music cultural arena, etc.), popular music and multimedia (including film music and music videos), the rock festival as a cultural phenomenon, the rock concert seen from the stage and so forth.

Relevant research questions within these topics might affect aesthetic choices and creative processes among the performers and sound engineers. Similar examples can also be retrieved from most artistic areas (theatre, arts and crafts, etc.), and some will mention this as an 'expert doctrine'. This is often knowledge that is orally delivered and is acquired through long-term practice and testing, thereby resulting in the practitioner being intuitively on top of the situation and using this expertise here and now in a given situation.

Methodological challenges

How can one explore such areas of knowledge? Many of these skills are insider knowledge, learned in an oral and tacit way that can be challenging to document in a doctoral dissertation. One example is when a PhD

Doctoral scholarship: music performance 107

candidate wants to examine the artistic choices and creative processes that occur during a recording session. Another example is when PhD candidates with a professional background as musicians want to examine their own artistic works: how can one document one's own artistic process during a performance and further analyse the same processes in a PhD dissertation?

When PhD candidates from the University of Agder have presented their dissertation projects in seminars, facing researchers from other educational institutions, they have often been confronted with questions such as: is this research? Is it not rather artistic development? It is difficult to set up clear definitions of what constitutes research and what constitutes artistic development in such cases. In response to this, an important argument is that artistic work is very much about artistic recognition. And such realisations are important to document in the written part of the dissertation in the form of a critical reflection and analysis of their own artistic work. But at the same time – regarding the discussion of doctorateness – the PhD candidate is expected to place their research at the forefront of international research in the field, in this case the broad area of popular music studies. Stated differently, we expect them to show artistic skills in their PhD work at the international level while at the same time also placing their doctoral work at the forefront of research in the field.

Understandably, there have been a few objections to such claims in doctoral education from other higher education institutions in Norway, where among others these issues have been raised: Is it possible to be at the same time on a high international level both artistically and scholarly? Our answer to this is that the PhD candidates admitted to such a combined artistic-scholarly PhD study are initially expected to hold a high international level as musicians, composers, sound engineers and producers. In other words, we expect an active background as a professional in the artistic areas mentioned. For such candidates, the PhD education will further develop their personal artistic signature as performers.

How does one judge and evaluate such combined scholarly and academic processes? Our PhD candidates encounter both scientific and artistic professors in our thesis seminars throughout the study. These seminars focus on both the scholarly and artistic questions regarding the PhD programme in popular music performance, and the candidate has ample opportunity to present their project in all its different variations, from rough drafts to completed chapters and studio productions. In the debates relating to these seminars, active participation is expected from both the candidates and the professors involved. In addition, each candidate has two supervisors, one scientific and one artistic.

Documentation and the research outcome of artistic research in popular music

Regarding documentation and outcome the following questions arise: Does research only have to be presented in written form? What about audio and

108 *Tor Dybo*

video media as documentation? The documentation and publishing of artistic research is a challenge that brings up a basic question: Do the final results from research only have to be in a written form, or are there other arenas or types of media for the presentation of final results? In my opinion, other arenas such as home pages, podcasting, downloads and the like, in which one can combine artistic presentations with scholarly analytical thinking, are a way forward. However, there remains a big challenge regarding future responses to the question of doctorateness.

By adopting media such as audio, video, websites among many others, we have today more opportunities and options than hitherto for documenting the results of research. Previously, the written documentation of the research was the dominant way of publishing, but digitisation has made it much easier to store and distribute sound and visual expressions, hence opening up a range of possibilities for publishing research results. Nevertheless, my experience of being a member of judging committees at many final doctoral presentations (disputation) in Norway gives me the impression that the research world responds slowly to such alternative digital opportunities. Many do not dare to take up the challenge of documenting research in alternative ways.

Recently, the new common PhD rules at several Norwegian universities and colleges specified the following about alternative forms of documentation (in this case from the University of Agder):

> The main component of the thesis may consist of a new product or a systematised collection of materials or be presented in another manner (for example sound, image, video electronic presentation) where the thesis' theoretical and methodical basis is not evident from the product itself. In such instances, the thesis, in addition to the main product, must include an additional part. The additional part should consist of a written presentation of the problem, choice of theory and method and assessment of results according to international standards and the professional level of the field.
>
> (regulations related to PhD at UiA [2016])

Regardless of documentation of artistic exploration, a number of basic scholarly and methodological requirements of research could be satisfactorily met through a supplementary text. In this context, it is important to note that several scholarly journals are now online, with the editors and editorial boards inviting researchers to use the opportunities provided by sound and image media. However, copyright and ethical questions are challenging in such contexts.

Doctoral education in popular music performance

In the doctoral specialisation in popular music performance at UiA's Faculty of Fine Arts, we attempt to capture more of the afore-mentioned topics and

Doctoral scholarship: music performance 109

questions, including those affecting alternative forms of documentation of research results. The curriculum allows for both dissertations with a familiar musicological focus on performing practices in popular music and dissertations with an artistic focus, in which the text contains a scholarly reflection on one's own artistic practice and/or analysis of his or her artistic practice.

Our aim is to offer a PhD study that lets a candidate include his or her professional artistic background experiences – as musicians, singers, producers and so on – into a dissertation. This is an artistic background characterised by a tacit and intuitive knowledge. Regarding the assessment of the final result, the doctoral candidate must connect this artistic experience in his or her dissertation background to the international field of popular music research.

In a research political context, we find it important to focus on such artistic experience backgrounds. In other words, our ambition is to develop research expertise in tacit experience backgrounds, for example to identify aesthetic values and insider codes. Put differently: artistic expression is seen from the inside, which among other things enters the informal decision-making structures and aesthetic values of performers, sound engineers and so forth, which in turn focuses on the artistic choices based on what feels right in the moment. In that context, an important challenge has been to train the PhD candidates to recognise and verbalise their oral and tacit knowledge in their respective professional artistic works and, in so doing, to develop transparency in the presentation of their research results.

Examples of completed artistic doctoral dissertations in popular music performance

Elin Synnøve Bråthen completed the first combined artistic-scholarly dissertation at UiA in 2013 (Bråthen 2013). In the following, her dissertation is used as an example of how a combined artistic-scholarly degree can be achieved within our PhD programme. Bråthen is an internationally profiled popular music artist (singer and composer within styles such as pop, ballads, jazz and world music) with three CD releases thus far. Besides her music education in popular music performance at all levels from a BA to a PhD at the University of Agder, she also has a BA degree in linguistics from the University of Tromsø in Northern Norway.

In both her master's thesis and doctoral dissertation, she used the theoretical foundations of linguistic research to analyse the conversation during the rehearsal process of her own band (the master's thesis) and the recording process in connection with her latest CD release (the dissertation). An important point for her is to show that musicians, singers, sound engineers, producers and others in popular music styles have not established a terminology for musical expression as is the case in the classical musical tradition. In the latter, a number of Latin terms have been established for the musical expression of timbre variables, strength, tempo and so on. Instead, in

110 *Tor Dybo*

popular music styles one is either using linguistic metaphors for sound or such metaphors will depend on the style of popular music being talked about.

By this means, the conversations in the studio were the empirical part of her dissertation, whereas her CD release accounted for the artistic part of her dissertation. Consequently, this work is an example of a possible way to handle a rather complex methodological challenge. The biggest challenge was that she was both an artist and a scholar during her PhD study. She was in the studio and doing research on her own studio production. Again, one important question in this context arises: Is it possible to undertake such a project within the frame of a doctoral degree? In other words, can you be a scholar or an anthropological fieldworker in a recording studio while at the same time being a performing artist and composer on a high international level?

At our dissertation seminars, the best advice we could give her before she started her studio work was to have a digital recorder with her in the studio and by this means to record everything. 'Do not think about this recording unit; be an artist, be a composer, be in your normal cooperation with the sound engineer and the producer and the other musicians in the studio during the recording session' was our best advice to her. And furthermore: 'Do not think that you are a scholar at the same time as you do your studio work. Afterwards, you can listen to the talk and conversations and have it transcribed, and then find tendencies about the communication strategies between the musicians, and between the musicians and the sound engineer, and the producer.'

Another interesting example of combined artistic-scholarly dissertations within the research field of popular music performance is Michael Howlett's doctoral work, *The Record Producer as Nexus: Creative Inspiration, Technology and the Recording Industry* (Howlett 2009), at the University of Glamorgan in Wales, UK. This work is interesting in the way Howlett combined his professional background within the music industry – mainly as a bass player and record producer – with a scholarly investigation on his professional role as a producer in previous decades. Before he became an internationally renowned record producer in the 1980s, Howlett was a professional bass player for many years in the British-French 'hippie-cult' band Gong.[4]

How then to address the question of doctorateness in this case? Or, in other words, how to solve the crossing point between a record producer's artistic work and background and the scholarly demand that is needed to include this professional background into a doctoral work? Howlett based his dissertation on artistic work he previously carried out as a producer, and he conducted an auto-ethnographic doctoral work on his role as a producer in earlier years. An important method in this respect was to recheck studio logs from the selected studio recordings he produced in the 1980s and in this way recall the selected recording venues.

Howlett's dissertation was presented as a PhD by portfolio, in which the final result consists of a written text and a portfolio of six studio recordings that he produced. Hence, the portfolio consists of his artistic works and a written text that contextualises his dissertation in the field of popular research and his role as record producer.

Some final thoughts and concluding remarks

Why did we build up this new PhD programme and later PhD specialisation in popular music performance? One important reason is that popular music musicianship is about decisions taken then and there, both in the studio and on stage. As a result, this is about oral-based processes between musicians, sound engineers, producers, the concert crew and the audience. Therefore, not much of it is written down in the form of scores as would be the case in a classical music tradition.

This in turn raises the following question: How does one create a song or composition in such an orally distinguished setting? A member of the band will often first introduce the melody line – or a vamp – orally to the other band members by playing it, singing it and so forth. Next, the melody line will be collectively arranged while rehearsing, and often the producer and the sound engineer will be involved in this compositional process. This is a culture that recognises both oral and tacit knowledge. Regarding the question of doctorateness and assessment, the challenge is to capture this in a PhD programme. For this reason, candidates at our PhD specialisation are challenged to verbalise and thus describe what takes place in such processes. This analysis in the written part of the thesis, the location of the project at the forefront of international research in popular music research and the artistic presentation of the project will be evaluated together.

All in all, our attention will be focused on what is going on in the studio and the stage. One important research question is to ask what is going on during such artistic processes, a situation that could be characterised by very small cues between the actors during a performance or recording session. In other words, this is an important part of many PhD projects within our PhD specialisation.

Such an approach has also created some methodological challenges within this type of research. One of the most important questions that has been actualised: Is it possible at the same time to be both a critical scholar at a high international level and a professional musician? This topic has been discussed at many of our dissertation seminars. One important aspect regarding such a question is that we only accept to this combined dissertation variant PhD candidates with a professional background as a musician, studio engineer, producer and the like within the popular music industry.

This combined artistic and scholarly approach to a PhD study makes our profile different from an artistic PhD, as for example we know it from the

112 Tor Dybo

UK. The latter one is profiled as an artistic PhD based on a portfolio of smaller artistic works together with a larger final one. Our profile is based on the PhD candidates having a professional background as an artist at a high level when they start. In this way, they use their artistic background as the basis for a PhD study, in which a critical examination of their own artistic practices is included in the written part of the dissertation. Thus, this becomes his or her artistic activity presented as the second part of the dissertation, such as a CD release.

I argue that this is an important way to go regarding research on insider knowledge within such professional areas, with the aim of building up a practice-related approach to popular music research from a music industry perspective, a musician perspective and a sound engineer perspective. This says that each PhD candidate must research artistic expression within his or her profession. At the dissertation seminars, the PhD candidates will encounter professors with both artistic and scholarly backgrounds, thereby giving each candidate the opportunity to discuss the standards expected of the dissertation.

Notes

1 The University of Agder has approximately 13,000 students and is located on two campuses, respectively, in the cities of Kristiansand and Grimstad in Southern Norway. The principle is one PhD programme at each faculty with its related PhD specialisations. This means that the University of Agder currently has six PhD programmes (five faculties and one business school) and 14 PhD specialisations. The Faculty of Fine Arts has one PhD programme in fine arts and currently one PhD specialisation in popular music performance.
2 For a more detailed discussion of the term 'popular music' I refer to e.g. Dybo (2013), Frith (2007) and Middleton (1990).
3 The PhD specialisation in popular music performance at the University of Agder started up as a separate doctoral programme on 1 October 2008 as a part of the strategy to build up the new university that was established on September 1, 2007.
4 See http://www.planetgong.co.uk

Bibliography

Aase, Andreas. 2009. *Improvisation in Scandinavian Traditional Guitar*. Artistic Dissertation. Trondheim: Norwegian University of Science and Technology.

Åse, Tone. 2013. *The Voice and the Machine – And the Voice in the Machine*. Artistic Dissertation. Trondheim: Norwegian University of Science and Technology.

Askerøi, Eirik. 2013. *Reading Pop Production: Sonic Markers and Musical Identity*. PhD Dissertation. Kristiansand: University of Agder.

Berliner, Paul F. 1994. *Thinking in Jazz: The Infinite Art of Improvisation*. Chicago: University of Chicago Press.

Brandtsegg, Øyvind. 2008. *New Creative Possibilities through Improvisational Use of Compositional Techniques*. Artistic Dissertation. Trondheim: Norwegian University of Science and Technology.

Doctoral scholarship: music performance 113

Bråthen, Elin Synnøve. 2013. *Metaphor as a Communication Strategy within a Pop Music Recording Setting.* PhD Dissertation. Kristiansand: University of Agder.

Djupvik, Marita Buanes. 2014. *King of the Rhythm – Slave to the Beat: Representation of Black Masculinity in Hip-Hop Videos.* PhD Dissertation. Kristiansand: University of Agder.

Duch, Michael Francis. 2011. *Free Improvisation: Method and Genre.* Artistic Dissertation. Trondheim: Norwegian University of Science and Technology.

Dybo, Tor. 2008. 'Jazz som etnomusikologisk forskingsfelt'. *STM Online*, 11. Available from: http://musikforskning.se/stmonline/vol_11/dybo/index.php?menu=3 (Retrieved 7 March 2016).

Dybo, Tor. 2013. *Representasjonsformer i jazz- og populærmusikkanalyse.* Trondheim: Akademika Forlag.

Ellingsen, Odd Fredrik. 2014. *"Fra Kithara til Les Paul": En undersøkelse av gitarens historie, utvikling og teknologi: Endringer sett i et organologisk perspektiv.* ["From Kithara to Les Paul": A Survey of the Guitar History, Development and Technology: Changes Seen in an Organological Perspective]. PhD Dissertation. Kristiansand: University of Agder.

Frith, Simon. 2007. 'Is Jazz Popular Music?'. *Jazz Research Journal* 1(1): 7–23.

Green, Lucy. 2012. *How Popular Musicians Learn: A Way Ahead for Music Education.* Aldershot: Ashgate.

Gullberg, Anna-Karin. 2002. *Skolvägen eller garagevägen: Studier av musikalisk socialisation.* Fil. Dr Dissertation. Piteå: Luleå tekniska universitet.

Howlett, Michael J.G. 2009. *The Record Producer as Nexus: Creative Inspiration, Technology and the Recording Industry.* PhD Thesis. Treforest: University of Glamorgan.

Johansson, K.G. 2002. *Can You Hear What They're Playing? A Study of Strategies among Ear Players in Rock Music.* PhD Dissertation. Piteå: Luleå tekniska universitet.

Kleppen, Mattis. 2013. *Bassgriotism.* Artistic Dissertation. Trondheim: Norwegian University of Science and Technology.

Lilliestam, Lars. 1995. *Gehörsmusik: Blues, rock och muntlig tradering.* Göteborg: Akademiförlaget.

Middleton, Richard. 1990. *Studying Popular Music.* Milton Keynes: Open University Press.

Monson, Ingrid. 1991. *Musical Interaction in Modern Jazz: An Ethnomusicological Perspective.* PhD Dissertation. New York: New York University.

Monson, Ingrid. 1996. *Saying Something: Jazz Improvisation and Interaction.* Chicago and London: University of Chicago Press.

Regulations related to PhD at UiA. 2016. Available from: http://www.uia.no/en/research/phd-programmes/regulations-related-to-phd-at-uia (Retrieved 3 March 2016).

Rolfhamre, Robin. 2014. *The Popular Lute: An Investigation of the Function and Performance of Music in France between 1650 and 1700.* PhD Dissertation. Kristiansand: University of Agder.

Tønsberg, Knut. 2013. *Akademiseringen av jazz, pop og rock – en dannelsesreise.* Trondheim: Akademika forlag.

8 Exploring, enhancing and evaluating musical 'doctorateness'

Perspectives on performance and composition

Karen Burland, Michael Spencer & Luke Windsor

Compared to their traditional counterparts, practice-based doctoral programmes are a relatively recent development, emerging in the early 1980s (Candy 2006). Whilst their value is not disputed, a lack of clarity about how they are described (research-led/research-based), as well as their purpose, structure and assessment across different fields of study means that understanding the characteristics of 'doctorateness' in relation to the creative and performing arts is complicated (Candy 2006, 3). Previous research investigating practice-based research degrees (RDs) in music suggests that there needs to be more discussion of the 'practices and issues surrounding them' (Draper and Harrison 2010, 1), with reports that students feel 'ill informed' (Draper and Harrison 2011, 97) about the written document which supports the portfolio of practice, and there is general uncertainty about what constitutes 'good practice in supervision and assessment' (Hannan 2008, 128). Studies investigating practice-based RDs in the fields of art and design also have relevance for understanding musical 'doctorateness'. Work by Collinson (2005), for example, portrays a view of a RD in which the student commences his/her studies with a strong foundation of 'the creative self' (Collinson 2005, 716) with 'considerable expertise in making' (Collinson 2005, 721). Collinson suggests that there are two aspects of this expertise which characterise research students working in art and design:

> First, there was a haptic facility (Rose 1999) that allowed them to manipulate materials and constructed objects, a capacity based on an appreciation of the qualities and limits of the materials with which they worked. . . . Second, and intimately connected to this manual dexterity and sensitivity, was a particular way of seeing (Goodwin 1994, 1995), developed to a high degree of sophistication, and attuned to features such as the synthesis of colours, the relationship between objects, the configuration of different shapes, the complexities of light etc.
>
> (Collinson 2005, 721)

It is clear that there are parallels here with the technical expertise required of musicians embarking upon a practice-based RD in composition or

Exploring musical 'doctorateness' 115

performance, and Collinson's work suggests that these qualities underpin success as a doctoral student. The link between music and self-identity is also likely to be of relevance to doctoral students in music. It is well documented that performers and composers have musical identities which connect closely with their conceptions of self (Burland 2005; MacDonald, Hargreaves and Miell 2002), and therefore it is likely that practice-based doctoral students will undergo a 'transformation of the self' (Hockey 2003, 90) during the process.

Collinson's (2005) work does, however, highlight the unease created by the constraints of an RD 'that in a sense are the antithesis of the creative freedom previously experienced' (Collinson 2005, 718), and this concern is based on the perceived threat of 'routines of creativity being laid bare' (Collinson 2005, 720). Despite some of the challenges associated with the current implementation of practice-based RDs, there is general agreement that by the end of the process, the successful candidate will 'begin to conceptualise research itself as a creative process . . . similarities between their making and this new endeavour gradually became evident' (Hockey 2003, 89).

With this broader context in mind, practice-based RD candidates in performance and composition provide a useful lens through which to examine the meaning of 'doctorateness' in the creative and performing arts: such students must immerse themselves in their chosen field, acquiring awareness and competency in order to produce performances/works that are novel or contribute to knowledge (Dunin-Woyseth and Nilsson 2012); they must satisfy both academic demands as well as those relating to professional practice (Dunin-Woyseth and Nilsson 2012); they must focus on both product and process (Dunin-Woyseth and Nilsson 2012) and at the same time consider professional or personal identity. This chapter considers practice-based composition and performance RDs exploring, first, the characteristics of successful students and projects and, second, the process of preparing a practice-based PhD – using the voices of students and supervisors to characterise 'doctorateness' in music.

In order to contextualise the thematic discussion of the data which follows, a brief overview of practice-based RDs at the University of Leeds is provided. The development of practice as research at the university is considered before a more detailed discussion about what practice-based PhDs mean for those who already have a professional background as a performer or composer.

Practice as research: PhD programmes at the University of Leeds

In 2003, the Schools of Music and Performance and Cultural Industries (PCI) at the University of Leeds developed protocols specifically for practice-based RD programmes. While it had been possible to do relatively ad hoc PhDs in music composition and performance before this point, these protocols were more nuanced and brought practice directly in line with other thesis-based

PhD programmes at the university. These protocols now allowed for theatrical performance, dance and installation artworks as well as music composition and performance, including improvisation. The word count stipulated for the accompanying critical commentary was set at 15,000 words. Several years later, changes were made to the protocols to allow for larger commentaries of between 15,000 and 50,000 words (reflecting ranges reported in Hannan 2008), a flexibility that in part reflected student requests for more space to expand on often complex methodological background discussion and also to accommodate certain types of artistic practice that involved a significant quantity of audience questionnaires in the form of appendices, which at Leeds are counted within the word count.

It is clear at local and institutional levels that the portfolio of practice/document of practice is the central focus of assessment at the University of Leeds and that the critical commentary is supporting evidence. This is not to say the latter is unimportant, but it allows the postgraduate researcher to further justify their creative decisions and, to some extent, potentially set the agenda for the final examination viva. In certain instances, a PhD viva can be preceded by a presentation of some of the practice (for example, with a performance of a 20-minute 'conference paper-cum-music composition' for the examiners prior to the viva). All PhD examination vivas at Leeds are conducted by an internal examiner, normally from the same school, and an external examiner from another institution, and they are closed examinations. Unlike some other UK institutions, Leeds does not use independent chairs for these examinations except in exceptional circumstances (usually where an internal examiner has little experience or is new to the process). It is possible for the postgraduate researcher to request that one of their supervision team attend the viva: in instances in which this is the case, the supervisor is not permitted to speak or take part in the proceedings. Culturally, it is quite common for PhD students in art theory and practical arts areas to make this request, whereas it is unusual to find this practice in science/technology/engineering/medicine areas.

The types of artistic practice that constitute postgraduate research projects in the Faculty of Performance, Visual Arts and Communications (PVAC) are extremely varied and can include significant levels of interdisciplinary working; for example, one PhD student in the School of Fine Art, History of Art and Cultural Studies (FAHACS) focused on the intersection of his visual art with music. Similarly, another student recently completed a PhD concerned with ideas of 'the voice and the lens'. There have been other examples of cross-faculty supervisory arrangements, for example, a current project looking at music and autonomic control of the heart is supervised across the School of Music and the School of Biomedical Sciences, and there have been instances of collaboration between practice postgraduate researchers in different schools, for example the opera *Green Angel*, which was submitted by a composition student as part of her PhD portfolio in the School of Music and which she collaborated on with a postgraduate researcher in the School of PCI.

Postgraduate researchers with a professional background

Since the mid-2000s, the School of Music has received a relatively steady intake of performers with a professional background applying to undertake PhD study, in part due to the expertise of staff in areas of Baroque and Romantic music performance practice. In the last three years, there has been an increase in interest from professional composers and contemporary music performers. In part, this interest is due to what John Hockey calls 'forms of adaptation'. That is

> students [who] had been attracted to the prospect of three years funding enabling the further development of their creative practice. This was an attractive proposition, particularly in the context of the financial difficulties that normally face most artists and designers in the UK . . . To these individuals, pursuing a research degree was to some extent incidental. In a sense they did not take seriously their formal involvement, what one might term their institutional contract. Their objective was to push the boundaries of their creative practice as far as possible in the time in which they received funding and resources.
>
> (Hockey 2003, 86–87)

There are other less cynical reasons for professionals to apply for PhD programmes, of course. One student currently studying with Spencer had been intending to write a book about his creative practice for some years, but his professional career as a composer prevented such an undertaking: the discipline of a three-year PhD offered him a practical framework for collating his ideas about the compositional process.

Hockey also finds that there can be issues with the critical commentary component of the PhD:

> Developing the craft of academic writing is a difficult enough task for students whose disciplines demand a high facility in writing at undergraduate level, but for art and design students it constitutes a particularly daunting task, which produces a reality 'shock' to their artistic identity.
>
> (Hockey 2003, 85)

To some extent this is a valid differentiation, and postgraduate researchers who have been undergraduates and master's students at the same institution do have a better understanding of the expectations of academic writing. On the other hand, professional practitioners are aware of these expectations at the start of the programme through discussion with potential supervisors.

Collinson's (2005) discussion of the tension between 'institutional processes and academic demands' and the 'autonomy and control' (Collinson 2005, 718) emphasised by those working in the creative arts is reflected amongst practice-based research students across the Faculty of PVAC and advice at school level as well as faculty inductions focuses on developing strategies for managing these types of responses, primarily by outlining the 'academic contract' expectations of becoming a research student. Collinson (2005) rightly points out that, as Bourdieu states, the student 'constructs and inhabits a form of synthesized *habitus*' (p. 25), one which her respondents suggest is a constantly changing space, both positively and negatively.

Draper and Harrison's (2010) reflections on practice-based doctorateness in music raise many interesting questions that are more relevant to conservatoire systems than university contexts. However, importantly, they note that the 'temporal nature' of music practitioners requires careful consideration of how these practical elements might be documented. Perhaps of more relevance is Blom, Bennett and Wright's research about how artists in academia view artistic practice (2011), which states at the outset, 'often [. . .] recognition of their artistic research requires the underpinning process and thinking to be documented in traditional written format' (p. 360). In the UK, this aspect has arguably not been properly outlined or clarified for academics submitting to the national research audit (Research Excellence Framework), nor has it filtered down to postgraduate research student projects. In general, Blom, Bennett and Wright's (2011) findings chime more with experiences of University of Leeds practitioners; one of their conclusions is that

> [w]hen combined with an understanding of how artists in academia move fluidly between different roles, this calls for recognition, by universities with visual and performing arts courses, of the multi-faceted identity of the artist in academia and the need to educate students about this likely identity.
>
> (Blom, Bennett and Wright 2011, 370)

This should be a key expectation and goal of any higher education institution offering PhD programmes in artistic practice, but it seems that there is still some work to do in this area. It is clear from this context that conceptions of doctorateness are still undergoing some development and that they vary widely between institutions and across Europe. In the next section we describe an interview study with two supervisors and two practice-based RD students in order to gain a richer insight into the experience of studying an RD in music composition or performance and to understand more about the process and experiences of such degrees.

Exploring doctorateness: perspectives from students and supervisors

In order to explore perspectives on musical doctorateness, a series of semi-structured interviews were conducted with two supervisors (Spencer and Windsor, the two co-authors of this chapter) and two successful practice-based doctoral students – one performer/improviser (Max) and one composer (Alan). Max was supervised by Windsor and Alan by both Spencer and Windsor. The data discussed here are therefore centred on the specific context of the University of Leeds outlined earlier, which allows a focused consideration of musical 'doctorateness' within one particular institutional environment. This facilitates a rich discussion and provides a detailed insight into the experiences and processes associated with studying a practice-based RD in composition or performance.

The interviews with the students explored motivations to study as doctoral students alongside their choice of supervisor; the development of the practice throughout the RD; their experiences of the process (including key milestones, successes and challenges); and the personal characteristics that helped them succeed. The interviews with the supervisors explored experiences of supervising practice-based research, their roles in the development of the students' practice (here they reflect on a range of students supervised, although the focus is on Max and Alan) and the way in which it develops over time, the views about the personal qualities of successful projects and students, the link between practice and academic requirements and the nature of the student-supervisor relationship. Each interview lasted between 60 and 90 minutes and was subsequently transcribed verbatim.

The interviews were analysed using Interpretative Phenomenological Analysis (IPA), which is a technique that explores an individual's perception of his/her experiences whilst acknowledging that it is never entirely possible to gain an 'insider's perspective', as the researcher's own conceptions both complicate and inform the process (Smith, Jarman and Osborn 1999). Analysis develops from simple summaries of the data to more interpretative activity, which results in a series of themes and associated sub-themes which provide the structure for the following section.

The current careers of the two students are also worth noting here as context for the discussion which follows. Max is now a successful performer-improviser who performs and records regularly. Alan is a freelance composer, conductor and arranger who also works in arts administration at a reputable music college in the UK.

Results

Four main themes arise from our data which characterise the process, experience and success of practice-based RDs in music. These relate to the personal characteristics of the doctoral students, relationships with supervisors, the ways in which practice is defined and processes are established and factors relating to assessment. The themes emerge from all interviews and represent the views of students and supervisors; despite the range of experience represented by the participants, there was remarkable internal consistency in their responses. It is also worth noting that whilst the supervisors' experiences associated with our two student respondents were discussed in the interviews, we did also consider their extensive and broader experience as supervisors of practice-based research degrees. The four emergent themes are now discussed in the sections which follow.

Personal characteristics

It was clear from discussion with the supervisors that successful practice-based RD students studying performance or composition had unusual or special characteristics that made them well suited to the degree. Max, for example, worked with Windsor, who remembers his interview:

> It was very, very clear that we wanted him to do a PhD at Leeds. We listened to him play, we talked to him, I'd heard various things about him and I think there was a sense that 'this guy's an . . . award winning performer, but he's not typical, he's unusual'. There was something about the fact that he had some credentials in a sense but also [he] didn't fit the mould [which] was very attractive.
>
> (Windsor, 4)

Max was obviously an excellent musician, demonstrating the 'haptic facility' described by Collinson (2005, 721), but something about his approach to his playing sparked initial interest in his supervisor – it was the fact that he 'didn't fit the mould' that was appealing, and indeed, as the discussion that follows highlights, Max's approach to his PhD built on his independent and critical approach to his performances. The ways in which an individual's interests and experiences combine also seems to indicate potential to study a practice-based PhD:

> [Paul] presented to us as [being] very unusual, he had an interesting background, [he was an] incredibly talented performer but he was clearly a thinker, he had read some interesting literature about music and phenomenology and all this kind of thing and he had a bit of a background in philosophy from his schooling . . . so he was an interesting character. And I think what we aimed to do was . . . if people had interesting ideas we tried to get them on board and then kind of shape what they were doing into a PhD.
>
> (Windsor, 2)

Finding a balance between knowledge and practice is perhaps the typical expectation for a practice-based PhD student (cf. Dunin-Woyseth and Nilsson 2012), but there is a suggestion here that, for musicians, there has to be something more than this, that there needs to be 'something unusual about them to offer, there's something of quality that is about them' (Windsor, 10). This also suggests that practice-based RDs in music rely on the connection between the individual and their practice; in the instances described

Exploring musical 'doctorateness' 121

throughout the interviews, the practice was already in development (and of a high quality) before the PhD commenced. The decision to apply for a practice-based PhD also indicates an open-mindedness and willingness to engage critically with practice, and it is such qualities which enable the research to progress (cf. Collinson 2005), as Alan explains: 'having a natural inclination toward trying things in practice rather than "settling" for the theory also made me well-suited [to studying a practice-based PhD]' (Alan, 3). Indeed, as the discussion indicates, openness and adaptability are central features of practice-based RDs in music.

One final characteristic of the practice-based PhD students is their passion and drive for their practice. This is perhaps unsurprising, since the relationship between musical practice, identity and motivation has been reported widely in the literature (cf. Burland 2005, 2012; MacDonald, Hargreaves and Miell 2002), but in this particular instance, it seems that passion and drive emerge from a hunger to explore and explain:

> I think it is all about how you engage, and about latching onto something that you don't understand but are hungry, yet there's an appetite for, for discovery and of investigation . . . I think that's key to all PhDs 'cause if you don't have that, you obviously can't, won't be able to sustain the work' . . . I think that's it, I just think it's down to appetite really.
> (Max, 4)

Max's comments reflect Draper and Harrison's research, which suggests that 'imagination and commitment have been engaged by ideas of personal growth, intellectual pursuit and knowledge transfer' (2011, 92) and are reminiscent of theories of intrinsic motivation associated with high levels of musical achievement (cf. McPherson and McCormick 1999). The passion with which Max describes his thirst for knowledge suggests that the ways in which performance/compositional practice combines with critical self-reflection and impacts on individual identity is vital to the success of practice-based PhDs in music. Indeed, the interaction between *practice–self-reflection–identity* underpins the way in which the RD develops and culminates (cf. Collinson 2005).

Defining practice, establishing process

Across the board, the participants discussed the ways in which their definitions of practice emerged and transformed during the degree as part of an organic and adaptable process. Exploration and reflection were central processes but were grounded in inherent high quality and clear research aims.

> If there's nothing to come back to, there's no 'big idea' you just end up going all over the place; and I think with all the practice-based PhDs that I've had that I felt comfortable with, I've had a clear idea what that

122 *Burland, Spencer & Windsor*

[big idea] is and I've felt I can allow that to develop away or back to that central idea as long as it's there, as long as you can find that [big idea] in maybe the first year.

(Windsor, 4)

One of the risks associated with practice-based RDs in music is that without a clear understanding of the scope of the research it can drift and lose its focus. In many ways, the process of developing a practice-based research project should be 'explored as a process akin to experimental forms of research' (Schippers 2007, 35), and a clear rationale for the development of the research is therefore vital.

One of the central aims of Max's research related to making the processes surrounding his improvised performance more transparent:

One of the things in my agenda was to make the work understandable and available to other improvisers, for people also wanting to try and unpick what they're doing and why they're doing it and to draw conclusions and to help that inform their future works and to be, I suppose, quite confessional about it.

(Max, 6)

As discussed, Max did not have the same academic background as some of the other practice-based PhD students he studied alongside, but he saw his PhD as an opportunity to develop and enhance his practice, using 'the rigour of it, the self-reflection, the kind of the critical reflection . . . I was really trying to learn from what I did' (Max, 2). Max's desire for processual transparency are in direct opposition to the concerns expressed by art and design students (Collinson 2005) but are not unusual amongst students in music. The two quotes highlight the importance of his identity as a performer to the emergent RD, but more significantly, perhaps, the refinement of his skills of critical self-reflection became integrated into his identity, such that they still play a vital role in his practice:

I found that I suppose throughout my course of study I was able to challenge my insecurities and I suppose it's a bit like being in therapy [laughs] in that . . . within the framework of the PhD . . . anything goes, you're permitted to go wherever you want, you can, you've got this conceptual space in which to think and to be insecure and to work through problems and to conclude and to lay, to put things to bed or to justify things or to . . . And I think that's ultimately what to me the point of doing a PhD is, it's the beginning of an approach which hopefully doesn't, I mean you're still writing and being inquisitive and looking at things and, and so I think if you, if one gets it right, they'll find themselves, you know, it's like having a companion for the rest of your life.

(Max, 21)

Exploring musical 'doctorateness' 123

Practice-based RDs in music offer the student opportunities to explore and to take risks, and in so doing, they are forced to reflect on their practice in ways that will help them develop their ideas (cf. Hockey 2003). In discussing his two highly established and reputable composition students, Spencer highlights how such opportunities are as useful for those with established careers as they are for younger students:

> For [an already professional composer] it's probably the starting point of a book about his practice; and if they get a scholarship it's time, it's time and money to do something that they haven't had time and money to do before because they've had to earn a living. So I think . . . it's a reflection, a self-reflection.
>
> (Spencer, 9)

Time and space seem vital to allow for practice to develop; more than this, however, it is important that the way in which the PhD develops responds directly to the individual's skills, experiences, identity and needs. As Windsor stated, 'it's very individual; my student has to – with the supervisor – discover something that is useful to them' (9). The individualistic nature of practice-based RDs in music is clearly essential, but, as we discussed, this can create problems, particularly in terms of the scope and focus of the project. The role of the supervisor and the nature of the student-supervisor relationship are therefore critical for ensuring that the research has rigour, purpose and integrity.

Relationships with supervisors

Since practice-based RDs in music seem to be closely connected to the individual's identity, it is unsurprising that the student-supervisor relationship is vital to the success of the research. The students spoke of their supervisors highly, extolling their virtues and positive working relationships. For example, Alan valued the positive impact of Spencer's supervision on the quality of his work as well as his wider opportunities:

> I knew him well and trusted him enormously. We worked very well together, which allowed us to get some amazing projects going. As I said, being given the freedom to seek private tutelage with some highly regarded professional composers was a very generous bonus, too.
>
> (Alan, 1)

For Max, on the other hand, Windsor's approachable style and their shared interests benefited the working relationship: 'I already found Luke to be very amenable and approachable and we had a lot of common listening and a lot of common . . . I mean it was almost like we agreed on everything all the time' (Max, 9). These two examples demonstrate that the

124 *Burland, Spencer & Windsor*

student-supervisor relationship must be individualised and therefore it is the supervisor's responsibility to ascertain the nature of each student's needs. In likening the student-supervisor relationship to that of 'a kind of traditional kind of Chinese model with a master and an apprentice' (Windsor, 11), Windsor summarises his perceptions of supervisor responsibilities:

> You have to kind of get into the student's world, and not be fully in, but you have to be critical, but you also have to believe because as soon as you stop believing in them you've lost it, you can't carry on, you can't because it is potentially stoic, you have to have faith.
>
> (Windsor, 11)

Trust between supervisor and student is key; since practice-based RDs in music are so closely connected to the individual's identity, shared goals and respect are important in order for the student to have the confidence to take risks and explore or challenge their practice (cf. Draper and Harrison 2011, 94). This is not necessarily straightforward or simple; on the one hand being too comfortable with a supervisor can result in a certain amount of complacency (Alan, 3), whilst on the other too much crossover can cause the relationship to break down (Spencer, 8). In a system which values a close connection between the research interests of the student and supervisor, Spencer's experience highlights how this may be a risky strategy, perhaps particularly when either party loses trust or confidence in the other.

Whilst the supervisors generally spoke enthusiastically about their supervision experiences, Windsor in particular highlighted that practice-based PhDs in music can feel quite risky:

> I did not find him difficult to supervise . . . I was terrified that everything was going to go wrong, not necessarily because of him, just because of the music that he was doing and it was . . . challenging . . . I found him incredibly exhilarating to supervise.
>
> (Windsor, 9)

The freedom to explore and to question practice can result in unpredictability; the individualistic nature of practice-based RDs in music also means that the experience of supervising each student is quite different because individual student needs and goals need to be accommodated. As the scope of practice-based RDs in music can vary widely, clear articulation of their limits and requirements is very important; however, experience of the assessment and examination of these research degrees is inconsistent and can cause uncertainty and frustration (Draper and Harrison 2011).

Assessment, contexts and commonality

As discussed at the beginning of the chapter, the role of the commentary in a practice-based RD is that of supplementary evidence. Discussion about the

Exploring musical 'doctorateness' 125

relationship between the portfolio of practice and the commentary revealed the diverse range of approaches that this could take. Alan expressed frustration at the limited word count, stating that 'keeping the whole thing together with so few words allowed for my thesis element, I actually thought the result was too dense a read. There was a lot to cram in!' (Alan, 3). However, other students took a more flexible approach to the commentary, choosing to write more extensive commentaries regardless of the guidelines. Spencer describes how Lola approached hers:

> I think [she] was the first one who said 'I'm doing 50,000 words and I'm doing this enormous portfolio which includes an opera'. So, I think that was a bit of a game-changer because I don't think that was the intention at all to have the same size of portfolio.
>
> (Spencer, 6)

The content of the commentary also varies widely, from philosophical or psychological theorisation to a more self-reflective and personal account of the practice.

> I was becoming aware that it could easily slip into a memoir, a diary account, really easily, and I think as I was writing about sort of the pre-concert conditions for one of the performances, I wrote it and looked at it and thought 'hang on a minute, no this is too informal', there was something wrong. And so I stripped it right back and . . . got rid of this sort of poetic description of the weather . . . or whatever it was . . . even early on I felt that whatever written documentation there was, I wanted it to be understood by the average Joe on the street, or somebody who had a vague interest in music and could listen to it, pick it up and go 'oh you know, that's interesting'.
>
> (Max, 13)

Given the data discussed so far, it is unsurprising that there is such diversity in the nature and scope of the commentary submission (and in the portfolios too, though this was discussed much less by all respondents). Since the practice develops gradually and in direct response to the individual and his/her self-reflections and desired outcomes, the commentary must necessarily be flexible and adaptable too. However, it seems from the data that a lack of clarity on the role of the portfolio and commentary can cause broader institutional confusion and, at times, cause frustration (cf. Draper and Harrison 2011). Max described a conversation with a fellow practice-based PhD student:

> [H]e was relaying a conversation he was having with somebody who argued that us guys who were doing a practice-based PhD weren't . . . required to submit as much written work and therefore should justify more why . . . we had to provide further, it was as if what we were doing

126   *Burland, Spencer & Windsor*

wasn't valid because there wasn't enough written material . . . he said 'no well, we're making new work, so if anything, it's you who is sitting writing books [laughs] that actually . . . why should we, but you're writing about music and yet we're making music, so why should we be made to justify in extra . . . so why can't we be academic *as* practitioners, why should we have to turn into musicologists?'

(Max, 16)

This suggests that even in a music department there is uncertainty about the scope and nature of practice-based RDs, especially in relation to the work which is submitted. The respondents shared tales of being told 'you should be doing an ethnomusicology PhD' (Windsor, 8) and that 'certainly we've had external examiners come in who have not understood the relationship between the commentary and the practice, and getting externals to talk to the practice is very difficult' (Spencer, 7). This clearly highlights that there is a need for wider discussion about the value of practice-based RDs in music – an argument articulated clearly by Hannan (2008). A community of practice-based PhD students can be useful for providing clarity about the nature of the degrees in a musical context and can ensure some internal consistency in the scope and nature of the work submission; perhaps institutions should also consider sharing practice across the organisation in order to foster a more open and flexible approach to this kind of postgraduate research degree. The ultimate goal is for the focus of the viva to be on the portfolio of practice, with explanation provided by the commentary, as described so positively by Max:

[T]he good thing about the viva was that we spent, well an hour and a half at least . . . discussing music, and the stuff about the actual writing and what you've written was almost like an endnote . . . [the examiners were] talking about the actual music and so it was great because they'd actually listened to it.

(Max, 10)

Conclusions

This chapter highlights the diverse ways in which practice-based PhDs have been recently implemented at the University of Leeds. Despite the fact that Leeds made early strides in developing the research degrees, it seems that approaches to their design and examination are not unified. This is partly due to the necessity that practice-based RDs in music are individualised according to the needs, goals and current practice of the students. The interaction of three factors – *practice–self-reflection–identity* – underpins the shape and progress of the project, and this is supplemented by positive working relationships with supervisors. Expectations of supervisors are extremely high, and their skills of empathy and understanding are of

Exploring musical 'doctorateness' 127

paramount importance; mutual trust provides a supportive environment in which the student has the freedom to take risks and to explore their ideas in full. At Leeds there seems to be clear understanding that the PhD is awarded on the basis of the portfolio of practice; however, the extent to which that is understood within the institution and beyond is negligible. Practice-based RDs in music are occasionally viewed with suspicion and misunderstanding; perhaps their conceptualisation as different from more traditional experimental research projects exacerbates this problem (Schippers 2007). Cross-institutional communities of students and supervisors may go some way to developing shared understanding, but clearly a broader debate about practice-as-research is still required. Hannan's (2008) call for greater dissemination of practice-based music research (and the accompanying commentaries for RDs) is certainly justified by the data reported here. It shouldn't be a surprise when a viva focuses on the practice, but our data suggests that a consistent approach is still some way off. Practice-based RDs should celebrate individualism and originality; practice is usually fully integrated with the individual's identity, and to ignore that would mean overlooking what makes the practice special in the first place. Finding a way to ensure consistency with the required flexibility is the challenge which now needs to be considered.

Bibliography

Blom, Diana, Dawn Bennett, and David Wright. 2011. 'How artists working in academia view artistic practice as research: Implications for tertiary music education'. *International Journal of Music Education*. 29(4): 359–373.

Burland, Karen. 2005. *Becoming a musician: A longitudinal study investigating the career transitions of undergraduate music students*. Unpublished PhD Thesis. Sheffield: University of Sheffield. http://music.leeds.ac.uk/files/2012/04/Burland-PhD.pdf

Burland, Karen. 2012. 'Transition and identity in collaborative creativity: Musical success, collaborative failure'. *Society for Education, Music and Psychology Research 40th Anniversary Conference*, 14–15 September, London.

Candy, Linda. 2006. *Practice Based Research: A Guide. CCS Report: 2006-V.1.0 November*. Sydney, Australia: Creativity and Cognition Studios, University of Technology. https://www.mangold-international.com/_Resources/Persistent/764d 26fd86a709d05e8d0a0d2695bd65fd85de4f/Practice_Based_Research_A_Guide. pdf

Collinson, Jaquelin Allen. 2005. 'Artistry and analysis: Student experiences of UK practice-based doctorates in art and design'. *International Journal of Qualitative Studies in Education*. 18(6): 713–728.

Draper, Paul, and Scott Harrison. 2010. 'Reflecting on reflection-in-action: Supervising practice-based doctorates in music'. *Proceedings of the 29th International Society for Music Education (ISME) World Conference*, 1–6 August 2010, Beijing.

Draper, Paul, and Scott Harrison. 2011. 'Through the eye of a needle: The emergence of a practice-led research doctorate in music'. *British Journal of Music Education*. 28(1): 87–102.

128 *Burland, Spencer & Windsor*

Dunin-Woyseth, Halina, and Fredrik Nilsson. 2012. 'Doctorateness in design disciplines: Negotiating connoisseurship and criticism in practice-related fields'. *FORMakademisk*. 5(2): 1–11. Available: http://www.FORMakademisk.org.

Hannan, Michael Francis. 2008. 'Unruly rules: Guidelines for Australian practice-based doctorates in music'. *Proceedings of the 28th International Society for Music Education (ISME) World Conference*, 20–25 July, Bologna, Italy.

Hockey, John. 2003. 'Practice-based research degree students in art and design: Identity and adaptation'. *International Journal of Art and Design Education*. 22(1): 82–91.

MacDonald, Raymond A. R., David Hargreaves, and Dorothy Miell. 2002. *Musical Identities*. Oxford: Oxford University Press.

McPherson, Gary E., and John McCormick. 1999. 'Motivational and self-regulated learning components of musical practice'. *Bulletin of the Council for Research in Music Education*. 141: 98–102.

Schiffers, Huib. 2007. 'The marriage of art and academia: Challenges and opportunities for music research in practice-based environments'. *Dutch Journal of Music Therapy*. 12(1): 34–39.

Smith, Jonathan A., Maria Jarman, and Mike Osborn. 1999. 'Doing interpretative phenomenological analysis'. In *Qualitative Health Psychology*, edited by M. Murray and K. Chamberlain, 218–240. London: Sage Publications Ltd.

9 Constructing publics as a key to doctoral research

A discussion of two PhD projects engaging in societal issues with artistic and design-based methods

Liesbeth Huybrechts & Marijn van de Weijer

Introduction

Shortly after the first 47 PhDs in art and design were defended in the Flemish Universities, it became clear that the range of PhDs is too broad to be organised and evaluated by one single model (Crombez 2015). The idea of doctorateness in art and design fields (Dunin-Woyseth and Nilsson 2012) has in Flanders been largely inspired by the ideal of the autonomous design and artistic researcher. Accordingly, PhDs that question this autonomous position of designers and artists are often labelled as 'applied' by traditional scientists or 'not artistic enough' by practicing designers. Among other factors, this discussion closely relates to the perceived divide between art and design (see e.g. Darras 2006). As in many other countries, the discussion in Flanders on PhDs in art and (architectural) design has also been dominated by contrasting these disciplinary practices to science. These dichotomies have often obstructed a constructive exploration of how to define doctorateness in art and design.

This chapter describes a type of research that transcends prevailing dichotomies. More specifically, it makes explicit some contradictions of conducting this research when addressing the complex situations of contemporary society. It questions what we can define as doctorateness in this type of research. The research discussed here stands out by constructing publics around societal issues, so that people might take action on those situations (DiSalvo 2009; Latour and Weibel 2005). Here, we discuss two Flemish PhD trajectories that construct publics on societal issues. We start with a brief literature overview on the concepts of doctorateness in art and design in relation to the form of research we address. Both PhD projects deal with everyday issues, employment and housing respectively, and centre on spatial aspects of these broad societal concerns. These trajectories have inspired us to formulate pointers for nurturing a more nuanced debate on the richness and diversity of ways in which doctorateness in art and design, actively engaged with societal issues and publics, can be understood.

Doctorateness and research through design

Dunin-Woyseth and Nilsson (2012, 3) define doctorateness in design disciplines based on two sets of criteria related to the final product (Frayling et al. 1997) and the process of a PhD (based on the European Framework for Qualifications, 'Dublin Descriptors'). This second set describes the doctoral competences PhD candidates need to develop during the process of doctoral studies. Dunin-Woyseth and Nilsson relate these skills to the roles of the connoisseur and the critic. They explain (2012, 7–8) that a connoisseur's skills are marked by 'a systematic understanding of a field of study including mastery of the skills and methods of research'; 'the ability to conceive and pursue a substantial process of research with scholarly integrity' and 'a contribution through original research'. Skills related to the critic are the 'capacity of critical analysis and evaluation' and an 'ability to communicate with peers, the larger scholarly community and with society in general'. These skills provide a framework for structuring our conception of doctorateness in art and design addressing societal issues through constructing publics. It also serves to point out the pitfalls for PhD candidates in determining a pathway between design-based and scientific disciplines, each having its own set of values and principles which cannot always be reconciled.

It is important to understand some contradictions that characterise 'research through art and design'. In Dutch-speaking regions the term is widely used, including outside of academia, where it mainly refers to the practice of producing art or design as a means to study complex issues (e.g. art, design or spatial challenges). The argument for such an approach is that these complex issues resist scrutiny from one singular, disciplinary perspective and require a projective approach, in order to unveil artistic, design and spatial potential and the quality of a specific situation or location. This type of projective research does not necessarily have the intention to be implemented or built as such: art and design are used as levers to incite the complicated development process and to breach impeding barriers. The undefined boundary between academia and practice leads art- and design-based researchers not to work 'cleanly' within the borders of academia or society, which often results in confused reactions in both these domains. In the continuous back and forth between science and practice, scientists might find the research value of the art- and design-based process too limited. In the same way, the design and art world might find the material qualities of the research too little elaborated upon because of the extensive focus on the scientific process. In searching for a compromise between doing research through art and design in science and practice, researchers – and certainly early-stage researchers – risk weakening both the process and result.

In art, design and architecture in the Dutch-speaking countries, most researchers have made academic research careers in the domains of artistic or engineering research, thus distinguishing themselves from traditional

Constructing publics as key to research   131

doctorates in art history or architectural theory. Overarching these interests, we categorise a group of researchers in a third domain, namely determined by direct interaction with society itself. With artistic researchers, this group shares the artistic ethos of wanting to function independently of a market logic, but it does not necessarily identify this position with an autonomous position. It deliberately engages with the 'real world' and the different publics that populate this world. Papanek's *Design for The Real World* (1971) was one of the first books that made a plea for designers to take such an explicit position outside of the market, through involvement in the 'real world'. Also the Scandinavian participatory design (PD) research community that developed in the 1970s was characterised by this activist attitude and practice. They worked closely with the unions in designing for/with skilled workers, emancipating them from the oppression of structures and technologies introduced by management (Ehn 1988).

The rise of the post-Fordist era during the economic crisis in the 1970s made this relation between academic research and society more complex. Post-Fordism is characterised by the fast development of new technologies, a highly diverse and competitive market, globalisation and the privatisation of previously public infrastructures (Graham and Marvin 1994). This condition inhibits contemporary art- and design-based researchers simply functioning inside or outside the market. Indeed, the socially embedded type of research on which this chapter focuses might be best characterised by its continuous crossing of borders between – on the one hand – academic research and art and design practice and – on the other hand – the public and the private realms. This entails, as is argued by van de Weijer et al. (2014), seeking exchange across disciplinary boundaries, taking on input such as theoretical frameworks from sciences or social sciences, and coupling this with design and artistic methods and paradigms to return specific feedback which is determined by an artist's or designer's perspective. Hence, the finality of the research is shifted to serve a mode of questioning, in order to engage with publics and to generate data.

Devising an inquisitive approach to projective thinking, design and artistic ambition thus emerges as a form of 'minor activism' (Lenskjold et al. 2015). This kind of activism does not work against but from within hegemonic public institutions and agendas to challenge and reconfigure them. We distinguish certain forms of this minor activism. In contemporary participatory planning research, interaction is sought with both built-environment experts and non-professional users by means of investigating developmental strategies and their consequences. These strategies are visualised, discussed with respondents, feedback is collected, and this feedback is rigorously analysed in order to revise and readjust the initial strategies (see e.g. van de Weijer 2014). Alternatively, contemporary PD is highly involved in the setting up of living labs as social innovation labs where new ideas can evolve from bottom-up, long-term collaborations amongst diverse stakeholders operating in public, private, academic areas and/or design practice (Björgvinsson

132 Huybrechts & van de Weijer

et al. 2012, 41). In the domain of human-computer interaction (HCI) and interaction design, DiSalvo (2012) has pointed to the potential of conceiving research through design as being adversarial, embracing the positive aspects of political conflict instead of 'acting against'. The socio-material configurations that are created as a result of these practices demonstrate possible futures, while being modest, situated and particular without having ambitions to be universally applicable but, most importantly, are developed for interaction with and feedback from relevant stakeholders.

Two case studies with a joint theoretical framework

Both research projects discussed in this chapter share an approach of minor activism, thus illustrating how the researchers choose to reconcile frictions between practice and research. The first PhD trajectory, *Design as Public Practice. How interventionism can give design [back its] public character and social relevance*,[1] addresses the closing down of the traditional automotive manufacturing industry in the city of Genk – as well as the historical precedent of the mines. It questions how design (interventions) can contribute to constructing publics around the challenge of the city of Genk to create alternative spaces for work. This is a contested subject because different groups in society have different views on and stakes in how work should be organised and developed in the future. This particular case helps explore the question on a more reflective level, namely if and how interventions can be used by design-based researchers to construct publics around contested societal issues in long-term participatory design-based research processes in order to build sustainable impact in the local context.

The second PhD project, *Reconfiguration, Replacement or Removal*,[2] enquired into the performance and sustainability of detached dwellings in low-density suburban neighbourhoods in Flanders. Having been built for young families of the baby-boom generation, many of these houses are now inhabited by ageing households. Demographic data point out that housing needs have changed in the past decades and will most likely continue to evolve under the influence of developments such as ageing, a decreasing average household size and increasing concerns for economic and ecological sustainability. A transformation of the existing patrimony is in order, but is also contested because of the social construct of housing codes, design and build processes, and in relation to the cost-benefit analysis of intervening in a strongly determined housing pattern.

Both PhD processes have been positioned at the heart of societal concerns without clearly defined solution spaces. Rather, partial solutions might fit the needs for one concerned group but fail at servicing the needs of another concerned group. Furthermore, both PhD processes study the built environment as a locus where social and technological aspects co-determine the mode of production, of which design (architecture, industrial design) is part. This led in both projects to the consideration of science, technology and society studies

(STS) as a support in giving form to this highly complex and dynamic research processes (Jasanoff et al. 1995). STS studies are closely related to a social constructivist approach of research, hence acknowledging the social construction of technology (or design) as the effort of very diverse social groups who are involved in modelling, testing, using, discussing or criticising such products. In this view it is thus not the practice of the expert alone who determines the development of a certain technology (see e.g. Bijker 1995, 273). One of the known approaches in STS, which is explicitly addressed in the *Design as Public Practice* project, is actor network theory (ANT). ANT goes as far as to propose a 'symmetry' between human and non-human (buildings, benches or information systems) factors in studying a given issue, establishing an even more extensive network of decisive actors (Latour 2005; Latour and Yaneva 2008, 81). ANT approaches also contribute to an understanding of a design (e.g. a building) as being contested, controversial, a 'thing', which brings objects and subjects together and in which actors (agree to) disagree (Huybrechts et al. 2015; Latour 2005).

STS thus enables both PhD trajectories to think about design as a tool for mapping change and dynamics. However, the decision to engage in STS equally induces paradigmatic frictions between the worlds of practice and social science. In design practice, the practitioner is obliged to formulate a position vis-à-vis a design problem, and in general, clear and unambiguous decisions support the development of a high quality design response. Social constructivism, and especially as practiced in ANT, takes on a descriptive guise and is uneasily combined, as argues Madden (2010) with a critical stance common to urban studies. This critique might be extended to research through art and design in general. Secondly, design-based research inspired by ANT centres on discourse, underexposing the traditional tools of designers as instruments for analysis and argumentation (Heynen 2013). This descriptive approach and the focus on discourse dissolves the significance of certainties inherent to the practice of art and design. Hence, the PhD researcher faces decisive choices in mediating between practice and socially engaged research.

Design as public practice

Research design

The PhD *Design as Public Practice* is built on one Belgian anchor case study under the project name 'The Other Market' (TOM) and some smaller case studies abroad. TOM addresses changing work spaces over time, in parallel with the ways in which PD and design-based research dealt with this topic. In the early days of PD, design-based researchers organised participatory workshops wherein workers, managers and designers could negotiate how, for instance, machines entered the workspace (Ehn and Kyng 1987). Although the democratic goals have not changed, changing work models

134 *Huybrechts & van de Weijer*

have altered PD's approaches to work. As argued earlier, participation and its activist program have become more interwoven with daily life, extending flexibly throughout time and space.

Concretely, interventions are explored as flexible instruments of inquiry in this particular process. The PhD candidate in collaboration with other more experienced members of the TOM research team enter public space with a cargo bike, asking people to share their skills and imagine how they can be used in future workspaces for their city. The preparations, the design interventions and the analysis of the data are all exhibited publicly on the walls of a shop front also named TOM, on the project blog and Facebook page and via public co-design workshops wherein data is collaboratively reinterpreted to support new research and design steps. Citizens who encounter the bike are invited to use a printing press mounted on it to create a poster that expresses their skills and to hang it in their own personal space to create visual cues of the skills present in the city (Figure 9.1). The process of making the sign is recorded, as well as the conversations about how the skills of the participants contribute to the city's visions on the future of work. To tackle the potential superficiality of the data generated through the short interventions, the TOM research team pays attention to high-quality documentation and iterative repetition of the interventions, allowing for a snowball effect. The main participating researchers in TOM independently conducted qualitative analyses of the documentation collected during the process by carrying out an open coding of the different data to look for patterns. These analyses were regularly brought together to conduct a selective coding to discuss the limits and possibilities of the role of design (interventions) in constructing publics around future work spaces as a societal issue.

Socio-material dimension

This research builds on an STS view allowing a dynamic view of what kind of workspaces and skills are already present with the inhabitants of Genk and bring these to the surface, as a means to open a conversation on, and to start changing the future of, work in the city via a PD approach. Complementing STS with a PD approach allows the introduction of change by intervening in the context that is the object of study and accepting the researcher as part of the context. It is a change-oriented practice, in which knowledge is generated through collective action and critical reflection: it attempts to understand the world by trying to change it and goes beyond the descriptive level.

The setup of the design interventions is – in line with the STS idea that design is influenced by many social groups – designed to be as open as possible for individuals of all ages, genders, cultures and communities and conceived as a way to develop closer relations between the citizens, the design-based researchers, daily policy making and city infrastructures. The interventions are handled as 'prototypes' of relations among researchers, citizens and policy, changing in

Fig. 9.1 Visual cues of skills, created during 'TOM' interventions exploring the future of work

Picture: Boumediene Belbachir

136 *Huybrechts & van de Weijer*

character, intensity, depth and depending on the changing needs of the context and research questions over time. The main mediating objects in the process are the shop, the cargo bike, social media and the posters/signs made by the citizens. The shop front is a way of building a program and a long-term partnership of trust between the actors while leaving the shop's activities and people's roles in exploring work relatively open. This open approach provokes uncertainties and renegotiations (Huybrechts et al. 2015) among citizens who are used to being anonymous, policy makers who have to adapt to a more transparent way of working and designers/researchers who are used to handling field data confidentially and working behind closed doors until they come up with finished artefacts (nicely detailed maps, models, products, systems, spaces).

Concluding the project

This PhD trajectory aims to use design interventions to understand and change daily engagements with a public matter of concern: space for work. As we learn from STS, it becomes clear that all the knowledge that is generated throughout this PhD process is highly situated, contextual and partial. The engagements with the participants developed as a snowball: interventions in some parts of the city generated interest by some other actors, inviting us to develop interventions in other spaces of the city and co-design further trajectories on work. Together with local youth we quickly discovered a need for spaces for youth to openly share and experiment with their talents: music, design, knitting, gardening. The shop front has become a meeting place for many young talents, an incubator for small initiatives to grow (e.g. a sewing atelier for refugees to learn knitting and communication skills) and has developed interactions with other research initiatives centred on the urban development of Genk.[3] The PhD trajectory has been struggling with – on the one hand – being very engaged with developing and reflecting on infrastructure and interventions as an approach, wherein the design artefacts are just one of the actors, and – on the other hand – the expectations of the design and policy 'field' to present design artefacts as results, demonstrating the achievements of the project. However, this struggle appears especially difficult in the starting phase, because through the iterative engagements with the field the relations between the design artefacts and the reflections slowly become clearer for all parties involved. Another struggle with which this research deals is the eclectic nature of this interdisciplinary endeavour, which is critically addressed by peers and evaluators. Composing an interdisciplinary research team and ensuring strong guidance of this team, mixing more and less experienced researchers, answers this critique.

Reconfiguration, replacement or removal?

Research design

In this research project, the design instrument of sketching was used with respondents and built environment professionals to render visual overviews for communicating multiple strategies, targeting low-density neighbourhoods consisting of detached dwellings. This approach was chosen for two main reasons, primarily because of the expectation that a combined verbal and visual account of possible futures as a part of qualitative data gathering would result in rich data, since visualisation brings detailed information in a compact manner that can be read at a single glance. Second, the proposal of abstract sketches rather than detailed plans for the neighbourhoods of respondents was intended to reassure them that no concrete plans were in the pipeline for their neighbourhood, in order to be able to discuss the concepts more freely and without a sense of threat. Hence, design has been used as an instrument for documenting the spatial, social and technological factors that obstruct or inhibit the implementation of innovative spatial patterns (Hommels 2005) and to discover parameters that could point out an overarching, common interest that could serve as a foundation for redesign. It relates generic concepts through drawings and discussions to place-specific conditions and draws out the un-espoused positions of relevant stakeholders.

Socio-material dimension

In accordance with the STS perspective the residential neighbourhoods in the study are considered as urban artefacts and, as such, in the words of Aibar and Bijker, 'can be interpreted as remarkable physical records of the socio-technical world in which the city was developed and conceived' (Aibar and Bijker 1997, 23). The exploration of this socio-technical dimension led to the coupling of the study of built form with the viewpoints of involved professional actors. This reformulation process sought to balance the technical and social aspects of the issue at hand. Both of these aspects were used to find arguments for and against the possibility of transformation; in other words, a certain project brief and spatial analysis were brought together. Hence it was acknowledged that a technological object or a system of objects acquires a certain meaning within a certain societal context, which is coloured by specific ways of using and interpreting these objects (Bijker 1995).

Where a social constructivist perspective would hold on to a descriptive stance, the ambition of this project was to contribute to a project of transition. The discussion of strategies with inhabitants can therefore also be seen as a process of creating awareness. The influential social theorist David Harvey explains how changing one's perception of the world is like a 'chicken-and-egg problem' of determining what comes first: either the world (construed out of diverse societal dimensions) changes first, and the individual adapts, or an individual's perception of the world (the individual being a socially constructed entity) changes first, which incites the individual to change the world (Harvey 2004, 341). In the case of this project, the interaction with inhabitants and professionals directly resulted in awareness; the actors were confronted with the problem field of the low-density residential environment, and the researchers took an active role intervening

Fig. 9.2 Sketches used in discussions with inhabitants. The drawings abstracted 'recognisable' streetscapes (above) and proposed diverse interventions, e.g. densification (middle) or removal of built structures (bottom)

Drawings: Marijn van de Weijer

in social reality. The discussion of transformative strategies with inhabitants inevitably included disapproving as well as approving reactions. Especially when there was no present interest among inhabitants in retrofitting strategies or in diversifying housing types and functions in the neighbourhood, inhabitants clearly expressed their arguments against the three strategies. This allowed for the documentation of weak spots and risks of these strategies and also demonstrated the persistence of spatial configurations.

The architectural viewpoint of this research contributes an analysis of the built environment in itself to Harvey's perspective, in order to determine what transformations could be possible: here, the researcher acts as an 'insurgent architect' (Harvey 2004) in trying to uncover such possibilities as could facilitate transformation. Thus it complements the social constructivist perspective by means of a critical architectural analysis of mono-cultural building patterns. In so doing, the dissertation follows the argument of philosopher Andrew Feenberg, who, seeking to mediate between the perspective of philosophy of technology and the social-scientific perspective, argues that both an understanding of the properties of a given technological system and an understanding of its constructed meaning in a societal context are necessary (Feenberg 2000).

Concluding the project

This project has developed a role for design, which has taken shape as a mode of communication and as a mode of enquiry, resulting in scenario narratives. There was no one single clear project brief or programme to this research project. The scope of the project to search for diversity and density was deemed to be both too ambitious (for example by satisfied inhabitants) and not ambitious enough (by engaged designers). As a result, design developed as a contribution to methodology by documenting arguments for and against transformation. Opting for this interpretation of practice-based design led to a certain hiatus, owing to a discrepancy between its approach and common interpretations of (architectural) design. Commonly, a finished design in architecture provides a clear statement of a solution for a problem, which was set in the project brief or as a result of a (designerly) analysis. Although not all aspects of a stated problem will be resolved in an equal way – design, after all, also involves a continuous problem definition process, which is run by every designer in his or her own way (Dorst and Cross 2001) – the end result is usually a product which a designer stands by and which is considered a valid response to the stated or redefined problem. Furthermore, the chosen approach allowed for comparison of arguments on an abstract level but also proved to have its limitations, especially when discussing design strategies with spatial designers who are used to basing their decisions on a deep understanding of a specific site or condition.

Discussion

This comparison allows us to outline an in-depth and diversified image of the PhD trajectories described earlier, leading to an appropriate conceptualisation of doctorateness in art and design fields that is firmly embedded in society. Both projects show how such research into societal concerns lack clear-cut solutions and that doctorateness is determined by weighing the result and the process according to diverging measures. Principally, both trajectories exemplify how doctorateness cannot be measured in terms of mastery of a field of study, its skills or methods. Both projects rely on the combination of instruments across disciplinary boundaries and are steered by interdisciplinary juries. Hence, this form of research has to satisfy very diverse criteria. In both projects, a substantial research process was designed and implemented by referencing a diversity of theoretical concepts and methodologies. This is less common for scientific research than for practice, because a contemporary artist or designer more than ever takes the role of integrating diverse tranches of disciplinary input to bring a complex process to a unified end. Individual jury members assessing the end result and the intermediate results, bringing in their own disciplinary viewpoints and theoretical frameworks, review such an approach as eclectic and address controversies in how theories can be combined. In response, strong interdisciplinary supervisory teams should be formed, and teamwork with more mature researchers is encouraged.

Furthermore, considering the shared usage of STS theories, we assert that this theoretical framework has proved productive to a certain extent in developing significant and original contributions in art and design fields. However, at some point, the boundaries of the descriptive social sciences need to be stretched in order to allow the researcher to voice normative conclusions. In our cases, designers moved beyond the task of a social scientist by rephrasing a design approach in order to overcome such resistance and in order to strive for development on the basis of a normative framework, for example, the belief in art and design as a facilitator for a more democratic work environment or a more sustainable residential environment, using his or her own disciplinary instruments rather than fully and exclusively engaging with discourse analysis, for which ANT studies are criticised (Heynen 2013).

Moreover, with regard to the capacity of critical analysis and evaluation, STS as applied here in art and design fields grows awareness among those who conduct the research that one is intrinsically part of a field of research and is not hovering outside and above it. Outstanding practicing artists and designers develop a form of critical analysis in their professional careers, and usually this grows as a result of being immersed in the issues at hand. Equally, for academic researchers in design, being immersed in the societal complexity of an issue leads to the cultivation of a critical capacity related to experience, empathy and normative choices. In the first period of the PhD

Constructing publics as key to research 141

trajectory this capacity is needed to critically deal with an experience of complexity when constructing publics around societal issues that are often overwhelming. In relation to this complexity, the artist or designer iteratively develops the different phases of the fieldwork as ways of prototyping relations between the different human and non-human actors instead of striving for results.

Both projects have interacted with many publics, not least outside academia. While in some PhD trajectories the interaction with diverse publics is considered a surplus, in these projects it is of central importance. The *Design as Public Practice* project has gained interest from many Genk citizens through online media, its physical presence in the city and a growing international network of design and artistic researchers dealing with topics of participation, public space and work. Also, policy domains of spatial planning, social affairs, work and economy, and participation have developed a great interest in the project. *Reconfiguration, Replacement or Removal* had its impact in the civil domain (governmental bodies, trade unions, health organisations), among built-environment experts (housing developers, lawyers, research organisations) and in news media because of the cultural importance given to privacy, laissez-faire and freedom in the Flemish housing question. With regard to communication with peers, the scholarly community and society in general, these results illustrate the extent to which doctorateness in art and design does not exist solely within these fields but allows for valid contributions to broader scientific discussions, filling in gaps between traditional scientific and professional fields. This means that the value of such PhDs can only be determined in relation to these different aspects.

Conclusion

This contribution has proposed an alliance between STS studies and art and design disciplines in constructing publics around complex societal concerns without a clear-cut solution space, because diverse stakeholders in society have diverse – and often conflicting – interests. It drew out a number of points where research involving art and design instruments provides a surplus but where traditional notions of doctorateness are being put to the test as a consequence of transdisciplinary interaction and of the candidate's search for balance between immersion in society and scientific detachment, allowing for reflection. This association with STS studies has proven productive as a theoretical framework for the two PhD trajectories, and this shared theoretical context provided the necessary level of comparison to draft our argument.

In concluding this contribution, we emphasise how this comparison points out in what way elements of methodology, supervision and peer communication deserve significant attention in the context of such PhD projects. It became clear that because of the demands of balancing

142 *Huybrechts & van de Weijer*

academia and the 'outside world' in a specific manner, PhD students needed to build critical capacity in understanding, reflecting and acting in a highly complex context. The students do not develop this capacity alone, but it is relational and constructed in a mutual learning process with many actors. The comparison also showed that the productive inclusion of theoretical frameworks from external scientific fields in a PhD originating in a design discipline – in this case an STS framework – relies strongly on a critical review of its key concepts by the PhD candidate. This review is necessary to understand which elements are consonant with art and design disciplines and entails a partial inclusion of concepts. Candidates need significant scientific maturity in order to be able to find a productive interaction between such theories and their design discipline. Last but no less importantly, a clear vision needs to be developed on the position a candidate takes with their contribution in relation to the professional design field, because the candidate, in contrast to professional peers, develops an unconventional portfolio and unconventional standards.

Notes

1 This section describes one of the six PhDs framing within the European Marie Curie ITN TRADERS (Training Art and Design Researchers for Participation in Public Space) project (www.tr-aders.eu).
2 This section describes one of two PhDs resulting from the FWO- (Research Foundation – Flanders) funded project *Large Underused Dwellings in Flanders*. The discussed PhD research (van de Weijer 2014) was conducted at KU Leuven and Hasselt University.
3 The city of Genk is, for example, developing plans for rethinking an old coaltrack, and a lot of our research investment went into understanding work initiatives along this track (urban farming, gardening, sports, transport and restoring of cars, bikes and motorcycles) while connecting the many smaller initiatives with each other and larger initiatives to create design proposals for future workscapes/spaces.

Bibliography

Aibar, Eduardo, and Wiebe Bijker. 1997. 'Constructing a City: The Cerdà Plan for the Extension of Barcelona'. *Science, Technology & Human Values*, 22(1): 3–30.

Bijker, Wiebe. 1995. *Of Bicycles, Bakelites and Bulbs: Toward a Theory of Sociotechnical Change*. Cambridge MA: The MIT Press.

Björgvinsson, Erling, Pelle Ehn, and Per-Anders Hillgren. 2012. 'Design Things and Design Thinking: Contemporary Participatory Design Challenges'. *Design Issues*, 28(3): 101–116.

Crombez, Thomas. 2015. 'Het doctoraat in de kunsten, tien jaar later'. *Recto Verso*, 66, May 2015. Available at: http://www.rektoverso.be/artikel/het-doctoraat-de-kunsten-tien-jaar-later (accessed 2 March 2016).

Darras, Bernard. 2006. 'Artists and Designers: Can the Divide Be Overcome'. *7th Congresso Brasileiro de Pesquisa & Desenvolvimento em Design*. Curitiba 9–11 August 2006, 1–17.

Constructing publics as key to research   143

DiSalvo, Carl. 2009. 'Design and the Construction of Publics'. *Design Issues*, 25(1): 48–63.

DiSalvo, Carl. 2012. *Adversarial Design*. Cambridge MA: The MIT Press.

Dorst, Kees, and Nigel Cross. 2001. 'Creativity in the Design Process: Co-Evolution of Problem-Solution'. *Design Studies*, 22(5): 425–437.

Dunin-Woyseth, Halina, and Fredrik Nilsson. 2012. 'Doctorateness in Design Disciplines: Negotiating Connoisseurship and Criticism in Practice-Related Fields'. *FORMakademisk*, 5(2): 1–11.

Ehn, Pelle. 1988. *Work-Oriented Design of Computer Artifacts*. Stockholm: Arbetslivscentrum.

Ehn, Pelle, and Morten Kyng. 1987. 'The Collective Resource Approach to Systems Design'. In *Computers and Democracy: A Scandinavian Challenge*, edited by Gro Bjerknes, Pelle Ehn, and Morten Kyng, 17–57. Brookfield VT: Avebury.

Feenberg, Andrew. 2000. 'From Essentialism to Constructivism: Philosophy of Technology at the Crossroads'. In *Technology and the Good Life?*, edited by Erik Higgs, Andrew Light, and David Strong, 294–315. Chicago IL: The University of Chicago Press.

Frayling, Christopher, Valery Stead, Bruce Archer, Nicholas Cook, James Powel, Victor Sage, Stephen Scrivener, and Michael Tovey. 1997. *Practice-Based Doctorates in the Creative and Performing Arts and Design*. Lichfield: UK Council for Graduate Education.

Graham, Steven, and Simon Marvin. 1994. 'More Than Ducts and Wires: Post-Fordism, Cities and Utility Networks'. In *Managing Cities: The New Urban Context* edited by Patsy Healey, Stuart Cameron, Simin Davoudi, Stephen Graham, and Ali Madanipour, 169–190. London: John Wiley.

Harvey, David. 2004. 'The Insurgent Architect at Work'. In *Readings in the Philosophy of Technology*, edited by David Kaplan, 337–353. Lanham MD: Rowman & Littlefield Publishers.

Heynen, Hilde. 2013. 'Space as Receptor, Instrument or Stage: Notes on the Interaction between Spatial and Social Constellations'. *International Planning Studies*, 18(3–4): 342–357.

Hommels, Anique. 2005. *Unbuilding Cities: Obduracy in Urban Sociotechnical Change*. Cambridge MA: The MIT press.

Huybrechts, Liesbeth, Katrien Dreessen, and Selina Schepers. 2015. 'Uncertainties Revisited: Actor-Network Theory as a Lens for Exploring the Relationship between Uncertainties and the Quality of Participation'. *International Journal of Actor-Network Theory and Technological Innovation (IJANTTI)*, 7(3): 49–63.

Jasanoff, Sheila, Gerald Markle, James Petersen, and Trevor Pinch, eds. 1995. *Handbook of Science and Technology Studies*. Los Angeles: CA: Sage Publications.

Latour, Bruno. 2005. *Reassembling the Social: An Introduction to Actor-Network Theory*. New York NY: Oxford University Press.

Latour, Bruno, and Peter Weibel. 2005. *Making Things Public: Atmospheres of Democracy*. Cambridge MA: The MIT press.

Latour, Bruno, and Albena Yaneva. 2008. 'Give Me a Gun and I Will Make All Buildings Move: An ANT's View on Architecture. In *Explorations in Architecture: Teaching, Design, Research*, edited by Urs Staub and Reto Geiser, 80–89. Basel: Birkhäuser.

144 *Huybrechts & van de Weijer*

Lenskjold, Tau Ulv, Sissel Olander, and Joachim Halse. 2015. 'Minor Design Activism: Prompting Change from Within'. *Design Issues*, 31(4): 66–77.

Madden, David J. 2010. 'Urban ANTs: A Review Essay'. *Qualitative Sociology*, 33(4): 583–589.

Papanek, Victor. 1971. *Design for the Real World: Human Ecology and Social Change*. New York NY: Pantheon Books.

van de Weijer, Marijn. 2014. *Reconfiguration, Replacement or Removal? Evaluating the Flemish Post-War Detached Dwelling and Its Part in Contemporary Spatial Planning and Architecture*. Leuven: KU Leuven and Hasselt University. PhD Thesis.

van de Weijer, Marijn, Koenraad Van Cleempoel, and Hilde Heynen. 2014. 'Positioning Research and Design in Academia and Practice: A Contribution to a Continuing Debate'. *Design Issues*, 30(2): 17–29.

Section 3

Doctorateness to come?

Non-observational research: a possible future route for knowledge acquisition in architecture and the arts.

Nel Janssens & Gerard de Zeeuw

When will it thunder?

Rolf Hughes

Precision: the compositional accuracy of artistic judgement

Catharina Dyrssen

10 Non-observational research

A possible future route for knowledge acquisition in architecture and the arts

Nel Janssens & Gerard de Zeeuw

Introduction: the past, the future and the gateway to knowledge acquisition

Knowledge is not what it used to be. This statement is both trivial and deep. It is trivial in that the number of people who have access to knowledge has increased tremendously – involving nowadays a huge number of people involved in the production, the teaching and the use of knowledge. And it is trivial in that the concept of knowledge has turned into a dragnet – it may be used to refer to anything, such as knowing that we consist of and live among atoms, as well as knowing it is Granny's birthday and knowing what people are experiencing across the globe, decades ago, hours ago or in real time. At the same time it is deep in that knowledge is now a commodity of high economic value and of strategic importance in a competitive world. It is also deep in the sense that our society faces important challenges that require the production of knowledge in order to find a way out of our present difficulties and to continue to improve the quality of life on our planet. At an early stage it was realised that the acquisition of sound knowledge faced many threats, so over time quite robust forms of assurance had to be introduced. These include highly structured processes of accumulation and dissemination as well as socially recognised exams, patents and other gateways to its use.

One of these gateways is the doctorate. Over time the meaning of the doctorate has changed probably as much as that of knowledge. A relatively recent definition is encoded in the Bologna Declaration of 1999, the Dublin Descriptors and the Bologna-Berlin Communiqué of 2003, in which training for the doctorate has been defined as the third cycle of higher education. This implies that 'doctorateness' has now become a *learning outcome,* which arguably requires a curriculum that is designed to help students achieve particular *competences* within a set time frame of study. In this third cycle students have to learn to shift from learning knowledge to producing knowledge. The Bologna process also required that areas that formerly were not primarily driven by research, notably creative fields like architecture and the arts, had to articulate how they produced knowledge and had to invest in developing genuine research communities.

148 *Nel Janssens & Gerard de Zeeuw*

In all fields, achieving doctorateness implies being admitted as a member of what is called the community of researchers. In principle, members can be anyone, but there are restrictions. One prepares to become a member by being guided by an established member, usually called a supervisor, by engaging in a doctoral education program, by producing so-called original work or by embarking on a journey of publishing in certain journals. This constitutes the *past of membership*, that is, what one has done to acquire the necessary competences. There is also a *future of membership* in that one is expected to autonomously develop activities of new knowledge-production, contributing as a member of the community of researchers. And there is a *gateway of membership*. It may consist of a formal event such as an examination and/or a less formal one such as a public celebration. These distinctions – past, future and gateway – classify three ways to protect the process of acquiring knowledge as part of what is basically a social organisation. Each implies an advantage as well as a risk. This raises the question of when 'doctorateness' can be assessed: is it a moment – the individual candidate passing through the gateway – or is it a more continuous process reaching from the past to future research and as such involving both the individual as well as the community of researchers? The changing of the meaning of the doctorate also raises the question how one may reform, if necessary, the route to membership (third-cycle education), the nature of the community (with the new academic fields) and the adequacy of the gateway. New academic fields, like architecture and the arts, have started to claim their right to be members while bringing along a meaning of knowledge that appears to be predominantly *situated* knowledge for *action* and *change*. They experience the gateway as difficult to pass, especially when it emphasises the production of *explanatory* knowledge based on systematised *observation*. This situation has challenged the authors to consider how the one may help the other in extending the process of knowledge acquisition, that is, look at the past knowledge-production process and see how we can build on this to develop a possible future extension to knowledge-production but of a different type.

To understand the observational focus of traditional canons of research we need to go back to its 'initial position' (Rawls 1999). Over a few nights in November of the year 1609 Galileo observed an unexpected event. Some lights next to the planet Jupiter moved (Kuhn 1957). He realised they might belong to the class of known planets, like Venus and Mars, and hence was able to recognise them as planets or moons of Jupiter. This procedure can be summarised in the manner of Pearson (1892), who refers to it as 'scientific' (Suppes and Zinnes 1963). It involves collecting observations or data, usually reported by more than one individual, and putting them into a preliminary category, which is then mapped onto or, as we will say, framed by a theory. Next, one attempts to modify the theory or the data until their framing is considered to be of high quality (sometimes referred to as 'true'). This process is referred to as testing. Its aim is to increase the quality of the framing until it is independent of personal biases or intentions. When this happens it allows any person to recognise new observations as either belonging to or remaining outside the theory (i.e. one recognises the light as a planet or not).

This kind of research is called *observational* – given its focus on and its use of observations. Since its inception in the 17th century, it has become the best known as well as the most developed and diversified form of research. It is valuable, because this knowledge is stable and its quality is independent of the purpose for which it is to be used (e.g. the same knowledge may serve in building atom bombs as well as in curing cancer). This stability and independence from biases and purposes requires continuous effort to check for deviations and hence, testing is considered an integral and essential part of the research procedure. It protects knowledge acquisition and hence is sometimes referred to as 'organised scepticism'. Built-in checks and inherent criticality are essential to warrant that research is self-protective and self-maintaining so its results are trustworthy. In that respect, anyone not checking for deviations can even be assumed not to be a member of the community of researchers. The procedure also protects against authority dependence (also called mind dependence), that is, against those who impose theories even when deviant observations are still ubiquitous and the quality of the frame linking data and theory weak. Both types of protection have proved strong enough to consider the procedure unique and sufficient to serve as gatekeeper to differentiate who is or is not a researcher (Popper 1959). In what follows we refer to this procedure as the protected research procedure (PRP); it is also referred to as traditional research.

While one will obviously wish to adhere to procedures that have proved to work in the past, one wouldn't want to exclude those based on other types of knowledge and other ways of framing. In other words, heeding the past to protect the present should not make one conservative but help one strive to explore new forms and procedures of knowledge acquisition. The past should enrich the future, not fixate it. This type of openness seems especially relevant when one tries to explore what constitutes knowledge building in the creative fields. Here one may extend or rather *augment* the meaning of the concepts of high-quality framing, theory and data, for example, while retaining the principle of self-protection in research (De Zeeuw 2006, 2007). Such an augmenting of knowledge acquisition, we suggest, might be found in extending the traditional observational research, producing stable, explanatory knowledge with what we call *non-observational research*, producing situated knowledge for action and change.

There are many reasons why, next to observational research, forms of research might be considered that take experiences other than observation as their input. In the 17th century the focus on observation seemed quite reasonable. Later on many issues one would like to find out more about proved to be outside research, precisely because of the 'dictate' of observation. For instance, in the 1950s and 1960s complaints increased that the

150 Nel Janssens & Gerard de Zeeuw

social world had become too observational and was forgetting and omitting its affective, ethical and intentional content. People need not only explanatory knowledge of the phenomena in the world but also knowledge to structure processes that generate purposeful and transformative interactions to create diversified life worlds. In recent times, therefore, we notice more and more attempts to go beyond the observational. Individual emotions, preferences and purposes are increasingly recognised as necessary resources for the understanding of our interaction with the world. This holds for fields such as politics and business management but is especially apparent in artistic and design research. However, preferences and intentions have never been part of scientific research (except as categories that could be observed).

We intend to develop non-observational research as the equivalent of PRP. This requires the establishment of forms and procedures of knowledge acquisition that may differ in both resources and use but nonetheless are equivalent to PRP. In some of the new academic fields it was decided to design the gateway experimentally, thereby to determine how far its practitioners might extend research principles and still have their work accepted as equivalent of PRP and be eligible as members of the community of researchers. An example of this approach is the PhD programme in the Sint Lucas School of Architecture, now a Faculty in the University of Leuven (further referred to as 'Sint Lucas'). In the rest of this chapter we take the journey as well as the contributions of one participant in this programme (co-author of this chapter) as the base to explore the concept of non-observational research. We will refer to her as the 'candidate'. By developing aspects of her work that she had left open we aim to determine doctorateness in her field as the ability to systematically extend the knowledge required for high-quality architectural design. This ability should allow researchers to continue extending and augmenting what supports the work of knowledgeable architects.

Exploring the notion of an 'instruct' as part of the knowledge-production process in architectural design

When starting the PhD programme the candidate had already had many years of experience as a designer. She had participated in a number of projects with an urban and landscape scope. They had a conceptual-artistic character and weren't part of a commission-driven building practice. Their aim was to critically question and clarify how to improve people's 'ways to inhabit their environment', for example in unsettling conditions of coastal areas under threat from climate change (Janssens 2012, 8). These visionary, utopian projects were evaluated as inspirational and as contributing to the societal debate on future needs. However, their investigative quality was less clear. The candidate decided to embark on the doctoral process offered at Sint Lucas to improve that aspect of the projects and to address what she called their 'action-deficit'. She imagined that conceptual design projects could be made part of systematic inquiry and thereby increase

Non-observational research 151

their relevance for the wider field of architecture (Janssens 2012, 9). This led her to ask what might determine the deficit she saw in the projects' general agency in urban planning practice. Why weren't the results of her design projects unequivocally accepted as high-quality theories? In her doctoral study she explored the transition from a designer's perspective (design without PRP) to a researcher's perspective (design embedded in PRP), both as a way to pass through the gateway as well as to identify failures that might affect her future work. We reflect on her trajectory as the prequel to the presentation of an approach that is shown to constitute a form of research – even though it focuses on action and change instead of on observations.

To facilitate our attempt three types of effort may be distinguished to identify what architects do or wish to do and how this relates to what they call practice-based research. The first is that a number of design *projects* are made – using skills and techniques that have been known for a considerable time. The second is that the results are *evaluated* against obvious criteria such as overall design qualities and the objectives of the projects. This belongs to the practice of the designer. The third effort refers to how designer-practitioners may be recognised as researchers. A number of routes have developed. Some PhD programmes adhere to the principle that researchers are expected to reflect on their design projects and to contextualise them in the field of architecture. Other PhD programmes (research by design) claim that making design projects as a method to investigate certain issues is a way to become a member of the community of researchers. Although the work of the candidate started out as an example of the latter, eventually another approach seemed needed to move the investigative issue forward. This approach aims to extend traditional research by allowing for a non-observational input.

The core issue of the candidate's study revolved around enabling processes of collective future-oriented sense making regarding our urbanised way of inhabiting the environment. Projectivity, imagineering and prefiguration, resulting in visionary, utopian urbanisation models, are deemed central to this process. The focus is not on the creation of the single best urbanisation model; the aim is instead to systematically include material (in the form of various utopian projects) for the exploration of future ways to inhabit the environment. With this procedure she attempted to search for the inclusion of preferences, values and intentions – utopia being considered a very value-laden design type. As such, the projects were to constitute an exercise in finding preferences, translated into spatial concepts, regarding urbanisation (Janssens 2012). The result of developing such projects was believed to stimulate patterns for renewal and generate a favourable state of mind for change.

Individuals' visions and dreams (in this case of future ways of inhabiting the environment) depend on what each of them intends and prefers to do or achieve, not on what others deem they should intend collectively in a top-down manner (a criticism that has been raised against utopia many times).

152   Nel Janssens & Gerard de Zeeuw

One would have to search, therefore, for collective preferences that derive from those of individuals, so no such preferences would have to be imposed. Unfortunately, according to Arrow's 'impossibility theorem', no procedure exists that might be successful (Arrow 1950). He proved that it is 'impossible' to construct a collective preference out of individual preferences such that the individuals involved will permanently accept it as better than their own individual preference. In other words, individual preferences (as data) cannot be *generalised* in a stable way. This goes against the core of observational research, which is that individual observations can be successfully replaced by observations constructed from them, that is by theories. If the construction of a stable, universal, collective preference is indeed impossible, what then can we achieve when dealing with preferences? We might say that preferences (and the related values) derive from both past and future anticipated experiences (and the related emotions) that people have inhabiting an environment. To investigate this we might want to design something that has the capacity to allow for many possible, evolving and improving experiences by offering a structure to interact – we call this an *instruct*.

Instructions work by providing a structure (from the Latin *'in'-'struere'*) in which interactions can take place. It assumes an active process-with-a-purpose that cannot exist without people (and their values, experiences etc.). Instructions function as constraints because they suggest boundaries to the interaction. However, the boundaries set by instructions create an *open* collection of events. What is confined nonetheless remains open because instructions refer to *possible* experiences in the *future*. They don't predict what will be experienced, but they anticipate experiences that might happen with the aim of making many different experiences possible, to improve these experiences and to prevent effects that are less desired. So how might this notion of instruction work for design and making disciplines? Given the definition or rather working of 'in-structing' we might say that a design such as a building is a kind of materialised instruction. It offers a structure in which a variety of experiences are made possible through the interactions between people and between people and the material structure. Through the precise position of its boundaries it also aspires to the reduction of unwanted experiences. Furthermore, acting as a kind of channelling device of experiences, the building as an *'in-struere'* also facilitates a quality of interactions between people and between people and the instruct. In this way they augment or extend each person's resources to act. This is not to say, of course, that all buildings instruct positively, and so one would wish to know which instructions help avoid unwanted experiences. Therefore, in addition to the instructs in material or immaterial form, one needs to support not only 'how to make' but also how to create a suitable 'what for', such that something made (such as a building) supports an open field of possible high-quality experiences.

If we consider the notion of an instruct as helpful for research as one that involves preferences and that produces knowledge for change (non-observational research), can we then detect its presence in current architectural design research? To explore this a bit further we return to the candidate's doctoral study. Insisting on the role of preferences and values as the core of the study (Janssens 2012), we might assume that the candidate undertook a non-observational approach without, however, articulating it as such. This creates a tension in her study: it does not comply with the observational type of knowledge-production, and at the same time it seems unable to be explicit about and develop non-observational searches. For instance, she did not recognize the relation between instructs and the design projects she developed and studied, nor did she identify high-quality instructs as the intended outcome of her work. However, the candidate did succeed in formulating one instruct that is important. She introduced the notion of 'worlding' as an approach to sense making that acts both on the level of goal setting and on the level of creating a navigational frame (Janssens 2012, 83). Each such 'world', part of and identified within what she considered her design-based approach, she considered as imbued with and formed by values, desires and preferences. Each world was seen as supporting its inhabitants in stimulating interaction with each other and with the (un)built environment.

Although the candidate had already intuited the value of the notion of 'world', it wasn't yet clear how it could be made to work. Nonetheless, the community of researchers, as represented by her examiners, recognised that she had journeyed sufficiently far to pass through the gate. Passing it challenged her to continue the search for a procedure to acquire knowledge concerning the way preferences and intentions may be improved and become resources for PRP. Indeed, when it comes to defining doctorateness, the challenge remained to identify details that help recognise what procedure to follow to acquire situated knowledge that involves preferences and intentions. To take this a step further we will dig deeper into the notion of worlding and instructs in the following section and discuss how they can be positioned in a knowledge-production process suited to the creative fields.

The improvement of activities by means of a high-quality instruct to interact

Instructs are considered the base of every social (inter)acting. They provide structures through which people can interact and improve their experience of inhabiting a world. We might say that instructs form the basis of worlding. Worlding is understood here as a strongly creative action, requiring continuous testing of possible new contributions that might or might not support new interactions. It refers to a dynamic process that produces realities out of an unformed but generative flux of forces (Law 2004, 7). The world historian William McNeill (2006) emphasises that this process should be understood not only as something that already exists (and even may serve as the subject of observational research) but as an 'event' that is a coming into being: 'it forms itself, it is intrinsically poetic, transformative' (and this way constitutes the core of non-observational research). Worlding thus

154 *Nel Janssens & Gerard de Zeeuw*

provides an approach to knowledge that is inextricably linked to productive interaction. It is not about neutral knowledge but about creating 'things with a purpose' or, more precisely, searching for instructs to help people interact to implement their purposes and improve their activities (De Zeeuw 2010). Nelson Goodman states that many different world-versions are of independent interest and importance and that there is no requirement or presumption of reducibility of these world-versions to a single base (Goodman 1978). In our view, he suggests here that worlding is not based on mapping observations but rather on channelling values and preferences into a high-quality intentional interaction.

To return to the start of our chapter for a moment, there seems little doubt that experiences form a substantial and important input to what architects do. We argued, however, that the protected form of research (PRP) – still dominant although strongly diversified after more than four centuries – does not include them. As a consequence, acquiring knowledge to support architectural design is still limited to searching for observations that link to a theory so it can be used as a resource to any action. While this might not be problematic in fields such as architectural history and building technology, it does impede the development of architectural design research. Even today much of the work that takes emotions and preferences seriously is limited to exploring observational categories. This appears a serious loss. In recent years a number of attempts have been made to prevent such loss, including PhD programmes such as the one in which the candidate participated. The challenge is then to create high-quality instructions that allow situated knowledge to be generated in everyone who is acting freely within the constraints of the instruct.

The variation and improvement of interaction within the constraints of an instruct creates a continuously evolving world. A world is here to be understood in Jean-Luc Nancy's terms of 'that which allows something to properly take place. [. . .] A world is a common place of a totality of places: of presences and dispositions for possible events' (Nancy 2007, 42) – that is, the results of actions in the world. What is meant may be more clearly shown by an example. When two people dance, such as to a waltz by Johan Strauss, they create the type of 'world' we envision. It is the result of a sophisticated instruct that allows varying and improving interaction between those participating in the instruct, the dancers. The constraints of the dance world, including style and type of music, channel the interactions such that the experiences of movement can achieve high quality. It leaves space for each dancer to vary as in an open space of possibilities while still interacting in the world of the dance. Dancing further exemplifies the notion that worlds are 'situated'. Any dance takes place at a particular place and time and involves particular people – and also starts and stops at particular times. However, its music may be played at other times with other dancers and in other places. It can be transferred so as to engage others who are ready, willing and presumably able to dance. The waltz appears to have an especially strong structuring, that is instructional value, within the class of

Non-observational research   155

dances, each with different individual constraints and attracting different people who are ready to choose and adhere to them in their dancing. Every action (or move) performed by the individual dancer becomes a resource for the partner to continue the dance and improve the experience from which the preferred interaction derives. In this way dancers 'know' how to achieve what they want. It is clear from the example of the dance that, as said, the boundaries set by instructs create the possibility of variation and in that sense create an *open* future. They don't fixate (like stable, universal knowledge) what will happen, but they support activities that may happen with the aim of making many different experiences possible, to improve these experiences and to make them self-propelling. The importance of the openness of the instruct can be noted in dance competitions, where a strict, repetitious adherence to the structure of the dance is often evaluated by the jury as being too technical and emotionless and in that sense of low quality. Although the roles of the body, the music and the space are indispensable to extend and augment the experiences, it is ultimately the quality of the instruct that makes the extension possible. Part of that quality is that new instructs may develop out of old ones. Dancers may stretch their performance to a point at which their interactions (with the space, with the music) no longer follow the instruct. At that moment either a new instruct (dance) is born, that may yet reach high quality, or the dancers are considered to have left the world of the dance, for example the waltz. It is the development and improvement of the instruct that we consider the core of non-observational research. This is something that can be detected in many creative fields. Buildings play the same role as dance, as do streets, books, paintings, bicycles, cities – and also the utopian designs that the candidate contributed.

Doctorateness in non-observational research

While limited to the improvement of observations, the research procedure that was conceived in the 17th century has a number of important and useful properties. The knowledge it helped acquire serves as a powerful resource for the technologies that now make it possible for an increasing number of people to live increasingly well on our small planet. These advantages have stimulated the search for knowledge in other areas that were not considered in the 17th century but may have a similar positive impact. Observational research aims at empirically evidencing knowledge that is sufficiently stable and certain to predict phenomena in the world. However, the certainties achieved are not the only ones people want and need. They also search for the certainties of the emotions and values that allow them to make sense of and give significance to the world they inhabit as well as to interact meaningfully with others. However, presently the most highly protected form of research (observational) does not support this search. We argued, however, that there is another approach that serves as a similarly powerful resource. It helps explore the instructs that structure our *(inter)actions* and help to improve

156   *Nel Janssens & Gerard de Zeeuw*

our *ability to act* – in the same way as observational research improves our *observational* abilities. It operates on our preferences and values rather than on our observations. We called this non-observational research.

According to this research approach doctorateness involves first, moving from the study of 'things' (observationally, explanatory, in themselves purposeless) to that of interactions among humans and among humans and environment that are supported by 'things with a purpose' (transformative, engaging, resulting in the ability or competence to augment one's resources) (Shoham and Leyton-Brown 2008). Second, it is linked to observational research in that 'people' take the place of 'data' in PRP. Such people contribute activities that are guided by preferences, emotions and values. They are expected to act, not report on their observations. Third, this suggests an equivalence: that the process of searching for interactions so they link their resources (experiences, preferences etc.) serves the same role as searching for links between data and theory that can be shared by anyone (to avoid biases).

The interactions are based on instructs. When they are of high quality, they constitute knowledge that is comparable to knowledge conceived as a link between data and theory. The former type of knowledge has been referred to as 'situated' – that is, relevant to specific persons in a specific context and with a specific purpose (instead of valid universally – for all people, in any context and independent of the purpose). The more stable the interactions become, the higher the quality of the links and the more able those involved become to resist threats to their interactions and actions. The search for instructs allows knowledge to be acquired with an input of intentions, preferences and emotions. The results serve as resources to extend activities and to become resilient – rather than to merely describe what exists. For this reason we believe such a search will help move projects and their evaluations to the investigative level in fields such as architecture and the arts. It is intended to increase the quality of instructs to create interactions that permit extended abilities; they are not expected to help evaluate an individual's work. Non-observational research thus means searching to increase the quality of the instructs implicit in their design – such that addressees would become able to deal with the issues and threats that led to its design. Candidates for the doctorate may wish to demonstrate how they recognise the relation between instructs and the design projects they develop and study and identify high-quality instructs as the intended outcome of their work. This further implies that they generate (inter)actions of various kinds through which instructs and their materialisation can gain quality. Achieving doctorateness on the individual level thus implies that candidates have been taught what to do in third-cycle education and how to vary their efforts and that the individual candidate has successfully completed this programme. Research education should include being embedded in a strong research environment, a 'world' in which experienced researchers already act and interact, according to the non-observational research paradigm.

Conclusion

We have explored what might help protect or rather self-maintain a type of research that should serve as an effective alternative to the type of research referred to as observational research. The latter is designed to mould events in the world into the form of the visible part of a mechanical process model that does not include individual preferences or intentions which are considered the reason for unwarranted biases. Such moulding or modelling has proved effective when those experiences can indeed be excluded. However, excluding preferences and experiences does not appear possible in the case of design, in particular architectural design. Taking preferences, emotions and experiences as resources requires different yet equivalent forms and procedures to knowledge acquisition, and we referred to these forms as non-observational research. We explored a recent PhD as to whether it implemented such a procedure, but we found that it fell short of identifying what would be needed for it to constitute a full equivalent of observational research. We introduced the notion of an instruct in non-observational research as the equivalent of the notion of theory in the observational form and identified how the search for high-quality instructs raises both the investigative nature of the doctorate as well as that of research embedded in the community of researchers. Further work is planned to demonstrate the procedure's practical value, its translation to serve in PhD programmes and its potential to become a culture of knowledge for communities of researchers in (some of) the creative fields.

Bibliography

Arrow, Kenneth J. 1950. 'A Difficulty in the Concept of Social Welfare'. *The Journal of Political Economy* 58 (4): 328–346.

de Zeeuw, Gerard. 2006. 'A Forgotten Message? Von Bertalanffy's Puzzle'. *Kybernetes* 35 (3/4): 433–441.

de Zeeuw, Gerard. 2007. 'The heroes and the helpers'. In *Gordon Pask's legacy*, edited by Ranulph Glanville, 143–151. Vienna: Remaprint.

de Zeeuw, Gerard. 2010. 'Research to Support Social Interventions'. *Journal of Social Intervention: Theory and Practice* 19 (2): 4–24.

Goodman, Nelson. 1978. *Ways of worldmaking*. Indiana: Hackett Publishing Company.

Janssens, Nel. 2012. *Utopia-driven projective research: A design approach to explore the theory and practice of Meta-Urbanism*. Doctoral dissertation. Gothenburg: Department of Architecture, Chalmers University of Technology.

Kuhn, Thomas. 1957. *The Copernican revolution*. Harvard: Harvard University Press.

Law, John. 2004. *After method, mess in social science research*. London and New York: Routledge.

McNeill, Will. 2006. 'Design and the enigma of the world'. In *Design philosophy papers, issue 2*, edited by A.-M. Willis. Available at: http://www.desphilosophy.com/dpp/dpp_journal/paper2/body.html [Accessed August 16, 2006].

Nancy, Jean-Luc. 2007. *The creation of the world or globalization*. Albany: State University of New York Press.

Pearson, Karl. 1892. *The grammar of science*. London: Dent & Sons Limited.

Popper, Karl. 1959. *The logic of scientific discovery*. 2nd ed. London: Routledge.

Rawls, John. 1999. *A theory of justice*. Oxford: Oxford University Press.

Shoham, Yoav, and Kevin Leyton-Brown. 2008. *Multi-agent systems: Algorithmic, game-theoretic and logical foundations*. Cambridge: Cambridge University Press.

Suppes, Patrick, and Joseph Zinnes. 1963. 'Basic measurement theory'. In *Mathematical psychology*, edited by R. Duncan Luce, Robert R. Bush and Eugene Galanter, 1–77. New York: London.

11 When will it thunder?[1]

Rolf Hughes

> *"They had heard that we were great Philosophers, and expected much from us, one of the first questions that they asked was, when it would thunder."*
>
> Joseph Banks, *The 'Endeavour' Journal*[2]

Introduction

How do we prepare our students for futures we currently lack the imagination to envisage?

As hitherto seemingly impermeable boundaries dissolve under the force of the free (market) movement of capital (and with it, supposedly, ideas) in a globalised economy, are concepts such as *universities, disciplines, national identities* – with their logics of borders, and therefore exclusions – sustainable? What (if any) career paths exist for an artist-researcher – a choice between varieties of economic insecurity, entrepreneurship, or the fate of continual professional shape-shifting in response to the unpredictable modulations of deregulated economies? If 'Generation Y' is better educated than their forbears but condemned to dimmer prospects than their parents (a 2014 report[3] revealed that almost half of Europe's young adults are still living with their parents), does the concept of 'career' need to be consigned to the scrap heap of twentieth-century detritus for 'Generation Z'?

What are the consequences of ongoing employment uncertainty? Michael Denning writes that under capitalism the only thing worse than being exploited is 'not being exploited'. He depicts 'wageless life' as a state of calamitous invisibility:

> Since the beginnings of the wage-labour economy, wageless life has been a calamity for those dispossessed of land, tools and means of subsistence. Expelled from work, the wageless also became invisible to science: political economy, as Marx noted in the earliest formulations of his critique of the discipline, 'does not recognize the unemployed worker': 'The rascal, swindler, beggar, the unemployed, the starving, wretched and criminal workingman – these are figures who do not exist

160 *Rolf Hughes*

for political economy but only for other eyes, those of the doctor, the judge, the gravedigger, and bum-bailiff, etc; such figures are spectres outside its domain'.

(Marx and Engels cited by Denning, 2010)[4]

Such questions are implied in the question of to what *doctorateness* – the focus of the present collection – might lead. What does this transitional zone facilitate? The particular challenges of developing appropriate learning resources for doctoral candidates in artistic research, such as finding the balance between a common curriculum and individually tailored research resources, can only be configured on a case-by-case basis. The generalisable sits alongside the particular and distinct. Reduced standardisation implies greater resources, of course, but potentially higher-quality results. This is why the challenge of evaluating *quality* must also be addressed.

In 2014, the Stockholm University of the Arts came into being, the latest materialisation of Sweden's on-going commitment to artistic research. It is intended to be a dynamic driving force in the advancement of artistic knowledge as well as a leading international artistic research milieu. Accordingly, it represents the promise of a new kind of pedagogical space, one that may link artistic research to the future learning institutions of our increasingly performative and mediated society.

It is an interesting question, but outside the scope of this chapter, to ask why Sweden, a nation earlier recognised for innovative engineering, design, and social sciences, has become an early adopter of artistic research, investing significant resources in supporting its development and infrastructure as evidenced in initiatives such as a dedicated artistic research committee within the Swedish Research Council, a national artistic research school, and now a Stockholm University of the Arts. What is the assumed relation between artistic creativity and the 'transformational' economy? What is the role of a new university of the arts in relation to the ethics, politics, and epistemologies of *learning*? And will its doctorates become better artists, researchers – or both (or, as cynics might claim, neither)?

The role of communication

The pairing of the terms *practice* and *research* – not infrequently through Christopher Frayling's oft-cited prepositions (1997) research *into/through/for* practice; but also *research by practice, practice-led research*, and so forth – implies a central role for *communication*. In staking a claim that artistic practice is capable of articulation as a form of research, we are forced to confront the consequences of our chosen mode(s) of expression, its material, technological, political, and epistemological assumptions, its generic, grammatical, and philosophical implications – and, not least, its *appropriateness*. Thus if we must consciously design our modes of communication, communication itself becomes a core consideration in undertaking artistic research.[5]

When will it thunder? 161

Yet communication can be said to be central to *all* research activities – without appropriate articulation and effective *dissemination*, research *results* would have little or no *value*. Why, then, should communication be particularly challenging in artistic research?

Performing doctorateness

Knowledge today resides less in a collection or archive (library or database) than in how a person *actualises* – performs or expresses – their knowledge *in practice*. There is both a private (silent, reflective) and a public (expressive, performative) dimension to this performance.[6] It may include an element of interpreting, adapting and applying the information stored in various collection systems (historical, methodological, educational, or technical archives), but it equally involves a range of emotions related to our desires to connect and communicate while simultaneously acknowledging the unavoidably partial, limited, or situated nature of our cultural, disciplinary, biological, and historical perspectives.[7] This (emphasised through the use of the spatial term *perspective*) reminds us that research is typically *purposive* and thus *positional* – we set out to *investigate* or *explore* from a particular point of *origin* (or set of origins), orienting ourselves *towards* a particular concern, with particular *goals* (*outcomes* and *audiences*) in mind. So the ways we choose to conduct our inquiry, the nature of our questions and ethical purposes, as well as our behaviour towards colleagues and collaborators in the research process, all influence our research perspective.

Knowledge is thus not only situated, embodied, personal, but also (being communicated) *connective* and *performative* in a particular kind of way. These aspects cohere within the concept of *experience*. 'To be knowledgeable,' Churchman writes, 'one must be able to adjust behavior to changing circumstances' (Churchman 1971). The capacity to adjust behaviour to uncertain or changing circumstances arises from familiarity with a repertoire of practices. As Thomas Kuhn has shown, for science to advance, emerging scientists must acquire not merely a methodology but also a 'way of seeing' – an ability, that is, to identify the salient features of a problem situation and evaluate their significance in the appropriate context. What is acquired is the ability to directly discern the parameters of a situation in a manner analogous to what is involved in the appreciation of a work of art. Kuhn's analysis of the role of 'exemplars' in effective scientific problem-solving illustrates the centrality of reliable judgment, acquired through practice, to scientific inquiry and research (Kuhn 1970, 187–191). Trained judgment involves the ability to recognise the relevant features in a situation, the appropriate combination of operative factors and patterns, their harmony or disharmony, and the weight they should have in a particular context. This 'way of seeing' is thus a skilled performance achieved only after exposure to a range of problems and the types of strategies employed for their resolution. It shares much in common with the Aristotelian notion

162 *Rolf Hughes*

of *phronesis* (practical wisdom); like phronesis, it is acquired through training and practice, and the development of a given level of skill creates the conditions for still more skilled performances in the future. And as practical wisdom becomes second nature to the *phronimos*, so good judgment – an essential attribute of a successful designer and researcher – becomes second nature, or so we hope, to the person who can reason in an innovative and useful manner.

But is 'problem solving' (with its associations of intervention in localised situations of intellectual spillage or accident) an adequate description – or even a desirable goal – for artistic researchers? The problem solver works within prescribed limits – *fix it and be gone!* Yet artistic research typically involves synthesising a broad range of information from a diverse range of knowledge traditions. Even a 'simple' architectural project, for example, would likely involve research-related activities spanning behaviour that can be classed as teleological ('goal seeking'), explorative, conceptual, analytical, evaluative, quantitative, qualitative, hermeneutical ('interpretative'), generative, explorative, and so forth. Each activity produces its own class of outcomes which needs to be synthesised without damaging the integrity of the findings or the coherence of the research project as a whole.

Representing the practitioner's knowledge

If the practitioner's knowledge is partly or largely rooted in *experience*, then the consequences of adopting an inappropriate form or inauthentic language for *giving an account* of such experience (out of insecurity, perhaps, or an ill-conceived desire to rhetorically construct an authoritative tone of voice) are potentially damaging.[8]

Michael Biggs has characterised practice-based research as (1) prioritising some property of experience arising through practice over cognitive content arising from reflection on practice and as (2) able to be communicated or disseminated ('this being more desirable than research that cannot be communicated or disseminated, because it will have greater impact in its field') (Biggs 2004).[9] It follows that practice-based research involves an experiential component that is communicable to others; the core of the problem, Biggs claims, is precisely this communication of experiential content – the meaning of an experience, its significance, and how it might be related to a shared context. It is a problem inseparable from considerations of *representation* and thus of *form* (Biggs 2004).[10] For Biggs, the 'most intractable problem' of research in this area underpins exactly this – the representational challenge of experiential knowledge:

> The problem is that the experiential feelings that represent experiential content are private to the experiencing individual. Experiences must be expressed in the first person; 'I feel . . . '. While they remain private experiences they cannot reasonably be regarded as research because

When will it thunder?   163

they do not meet the criterion that research should be disseminated (assumption 2). But the problems of identifying and communicating first person experiences to second and third persons is notoriously difficult. For example, it has come under sustained attack from Wittgenstein in his so-called private language argument.

(Wittgenstein 1953, §§243–315 cited in Biggs 2004, 10)

Hybridisation

The development of any field of research or professional practice involves privileging particular cultural metaphors and analogies, references, and examples, and, in the process, cross-pollinating, hybridising (or repressing) existing assumptions and methodologies (Hughes and Monk 1998, 2003). We might explore forms of practice that demand more than the formal properties of reason alone by appropriating strategies, methods, and concepts from other material and discursive regimes. This places particular emphasis on our capacity to discern connections across diverse discourses, changing language games, shape-shifting input, and material or non-linguistic data. Herbert Simon writes of Method being replaced by 'variable, creative, non-algorithmic' methods, of generalised laws being displaced by 'contingent, historically situated truths, reflective of values and interests, and found more or less useful by cultures and communities which are themselves symbolically constituted'. Furthermore, he writes:

> there are faint suspicions that scholarly communities are no less influenced by 'fuzzy' logics than by formal, deductive, 'closed-fisted' logics: by arguments from sign and analogy, by anecdotes and exemplars; and even by appeals to authority, tradition, convention, intuition and aesthetic goodness-of-fit.

(Simon 1990, 12)

This is particularly the case in contemporary contexts of interdisciplinary or transdisciplinary ways of working. The many convergences taking place today – between biology, technology, economics, and the arts, for example – are symptomatic of a more generalised reconfiguration of cultural, national, and political boundaries, all of which contribute, as Klein argues, to reversing 'the differentiating, classificatory dynamic of modernity and increasing hybridization of cultural categories, identities, and previous certainties. [. . .] All cultural categories, identities, and certainties have undergone de-differentiation, de-insulation, and hybridization. All boundaries are at risk' (Thompson Klein 2004, 8). Since there are as a result a growing number of problems 'without a discipline', this skill in _seeing connections_ – a skill that blends creative and critical (or design and hermeneutical) modes of inquiry (or curiosity) – will become increasingly important for our doctoral candidates.

164 *Rolf Hughes*

It may be that artistic research similarly acknowledges alternative, competing, or even contradictory belief systems that nonetheless organise diverse and variable (culturally, professionally, and historically) conceptions of reason. In this sense, artistic research may serve not merely to *deconstruct* systems of logic which depend on a process of self-validation for their support but also to *reconstruct* the question of how we might investigate, make reasonable comparisons, judgements, and evaluations, and use language in contexts where there can exist no 'proof' as such. If this is so, the need to explore forms of argument appropriate to identifying and representing the elements of our practice and the expressions of our shared and evolving professional knowledge becomes for artistic researchers a central challenge, if not *the* central challenge. Accordingly, we arrive at an account of artistic research as an architectonic strategy for orchestrating, enacting, or curating the interplay of discourse, material practices, and experiential content in forms that represent arguments for artistic and scientific significance beyond the relatively narrow concerns of an audience (or readership) limited to fellow practitioners.

And so to the collective concept of 'doctorateness'.

Open-textured concepts

I start with a proposition: *doctorateness* is not something we need seek to define, but rather we should treat it as an *open-textured concept*. *The Blackwell Dictionary of Western Philosophy* defines both 'open texture' and 'open concept' as follows:

> Open texture is the possibility of vagueness, because vagueness arises when a word is actually used in a fluctuating way while open texture exists because there are always possible gaps in determining the meaning of a term.
>
> [. . .]
>
> The notion of an open concept, which is derived from open texture, is a concept that has an incomplete intension and needs to be modified in order to deal with unforeseen situations. It does not admit of a precise definition. The necessary and sufficient conditions of its application are not fixed. An open concept is not a vague concept but is the basis of the possibility of vagueness.
>
> (*The Blackwell Dictionary of Western Philosophy* 2004, 492)

One way of exploring this 'possibility of vagueness' is by considering Wittgenstein's remarks on the notion of 'game', for these, according to Morris Weitz, provide a model of an open-textured concept that can equally be applied to the concept of 'art'. In both cases, the concept contains 'blurred edges', is not 'closed by a frontier' and not 'bound by rigid limits'. 'Art' is thus, for Weitz, a family resemblance concept in the same way as 'game' is for Wittgenstein (Weitz 1956, cit. Sclafani 1971, 333).

When will it thunder? 165

The term 'open-textured concept' – originally coined by Friedrich Weisman in his 1945 article 'Verifiability'[11] – is relevant for our discussion because we can never anticipate all the possible circumstances in which a concept such as *doctorateness* can be applied. There will always be the possibility of certain cases (certain candidates, behaviours, backgrounds, demands) for which no rules exist for applying our pre-existing criteria. A performance artist might advocate the claim that live performance can be considered a form of live documentation in itself, thereby challenging conventions of research publication, archiving, and dissemination. Both Wittgenstein and Wassman agree, according to Sclafani, that 'a concept can be said to be open in texture if it is possible for cases to arise for which we have no rules to determine the applicability of the concept, cases which are characterized by the feature of being possible to anticipate' (Sclafani 1971, 335).

The advantage of such a formulation for doctoral students is that their work will be evaluated on a case-by-case basis, requiring supervisors that are agile, empathetic, and artistically informed as well as intellectually proven and critically astute.[12] This will not be an exercise in verifying 'ease of fit' between individual theses and pre-existing models. Significant new knowledge is arguably more likely to emerge by colliding new methods and designing more flexible formats for their exposition. The disadvantage for research managers is that the journey from enrolment to graduation is therefore a relatively resource-intensive one.

Building support structures for doctoral students involves the strategic deployment of *resources*. As such, we are invariably engaging with different types of politics – what we might call the *politics of enrolment*, the *politics of legitimisation*, versus the *politics of contestation*. The first two, with their anointed gatekeepers and measurement systems, are not particularly interesting in this context. The latter – the concept of a university where learning occurs by values being debated and contested – strikes me as a more desirable learning environment, or at least one that corresponds more closely to the original purpose of the university as a site of knowledge creation. So we will take a moment to consider the origins of the university, how its founding ideas have evolved over recent centuries, and whether they are capable of resisting contemporary pressures.

An evolving university

Kant, Schiller, Fichte, and subsequently Humboldt were dedicated to the notion of the university as a site of idealistic progress, during a period witnessing the rapid secularisation of Western culture. As a result, the modern idea of an institution developed as the distillation of Enlightenment values 'dedicated to the infinite growth of knowledge, and the fostering of citizenship and social bonds' (Ruin 2014, 164). The concept of *freedom* became the central organising principle, around which related concepts such as

166 *Rolf Hughes*

reason, knowledge, truth, critique, and *Bildung* were organised to reinforce Enlightenment philosophy:

> The university is a place that should make possible the growth of knowledge, in a communal spirit of critical analysis, free of all presuppositions; it is in this way that the university should promote and embody the very idea of freedom.
>
> (Ruin 2014, 165)

Although theological, legal, and medical faculties would dominate in terms of student numbers, securing the production of civil servants to maintain a well-functioning society, for Kant in *The Conflict of the Faculties* it was *philosophy* that guaranteed a *more free* and *exploratory* knowledge process – that is 'a mode of research that is free from assumptions and that makes possible a mutual critique' (Ruin 2014, 165).

The modern university has developed three core concepts in relation to its function: the concept of *reason* (after Kant), *culture* (after Humboldt), and the techno-bureaucratic pursuit of *excellence*. With increasing disciplinary specialisation come recurring warnings about the risks of channelling knowledge into separate silos. As early as 1945, the economist F. A. Hayek was writing in 'The Use of Knowledge in Society':

> [C]ivilization rests on the fact that we all benefit from knowledge which we do not possess. And one of the ways in which civilization helps us to overcome that limitation on the extent of individual knowledge is by conquering ignorance, not by the acquisition of more knowledge, but by the utilization of knowledge which is and which remains widely dispersed among individuals.
>
> (Hayek 1945)

D. T. Campbell warned of the emergence of an 'ethnocentrism of disciplines' already in 1969:

> The pursuit of research within university departments has given rise to the ongoing specialization of disciplines and thematic fields with fuzzy, somewhat arbitrary, shifting boundaries. The high degree of compartmentalization of scientific knowledge is due to two interacting factors. Institutional structures and incentives in academia result in an 'ethnocentrism of disciplines'.
>
> (Campbell 1969)

Thirty years later (1999), knowledge remained highly compartmentalised within our universities. Noting that environmental problems require interdisciplinary approaches which the conventional knowledge institutions have been 'unable, unwilling or slow to provide,' Gerry Brewer poignantly adds,

When will it thunder? 167

'Or, as cynics have stated it: "The world has problems, but universities have departments"' (Brewer 1999, 328).

Today, however, the founding ideals of the university are being rapidly dismantled by neo-liberal processes. When the Citizen Artist team at Goldsmiths asked themselves in 2012 the question 'What is a university?', they arrived at the conclusion that the university answers today not to an Enlightenment ideal of human progress and perfectibility but to a "moral vacuum":

> Historically, the twin pillars of a Nation State have been the government (the legislator) and the University (the educator of its legislators and citizens). Out of the Enlightenment, the University was a space within which individuals 'came into being'. The University fostered 'criticality', 'investigation', 'study', underpinned by a notion of the self in relation to the public sphere where learning was understood and pursued as a value in its own right and/or for the formation of a good citizen, thereby constituting a 'nation'.
>
> [. . .] For the past thirty years, the 'public' (sphere) has been shredded under the aggressive implementation of neo-liberal policies. Coupled with technological developments, the rise of the internet and social networks, the economic fallout from the rampant negligence of bankers and wayward financial markets, the idea of a 'society' – even if we reconceptualise its form and character and coin new terms for it such as a multitude, a rhizome, an assemblage, or a network, etc. – without a state that sees its role as more than a panopticon, is but a moral vacuum to which the University is subject.
>
> (Plessner 2014)

As part of an exercise to rethink the purpose of the university, I co-organised during 2013 a series of workshops at Chalmers University of Technology, Department of Architecture, at the end of which the group co-authored a 'Manifesto' for a post-graduate course, conference, and eventual publication on 'transvaluation'. The manifesto (a genre hitherto alien to me) is reproduced in full in the endnotes.[13] It advocates a future university as 'the site where values are forged and contested, the place where materials, energies and ideas are invented and transformed [. . .] a *U-topos:* the kind of space *Bologna* dreamt of, but immediately forgot upon waking'.

Central to this ambition will be broadening core constituencies active inside the university. The integration of artistic methods and sensibilities may be seen as one step in this direction. Having worked at various points in my professional life as a creative and critical writing tutor in universities and prisons, a lecturer in literature and drama, a researcher into the epistemology of skill and practical knowledge, a theatre director and prose poet, a professor of design theory and practice-based research, a supervisor of design-led and artistic PhD dissertations, an expert advisor to the national research council, and, more recently, head of research and professor of artistic research at the

168   *Rolf Hughes*

newly created Stockholm University of the Arts, I have a long-standing interest in the accounts given by artistic professionals attempting to articulate a *way of looking* at their work and, through it, at the world. Such an account is not exclusively verbal – typically a presentation fuses a spoken narrative of inquiry with prototyping materials such as slides, sketches, photographs, partly built models, demonstrations, performances, pedagogic interactions, diagrammatic abstractions, material investigations, examples of inspiration, and so forth. The search for an appropriate mode of expression is an integral part of these early stages in the formulation of a researcher's sensibility – a reflective account of a series of cases, supported by the standard props of PowerPoint or Keynote, is sometimes followed, somewhat dismayingly, by a series of generalised theoretical postures. At such times, an ill-conceived pursuit of legitimacy (the *politics of enrolment*, the *politics of legitimisation*) tramples nascent explorations of wherever curiosity or wonder leads. Between presenter and listener, there is also, of course, an urgent question of 'literacy' – or, better, *literacies* – we do not understand a sketch the same way as a text, nor are there single, unwavering hermeneutic procedures for engaging with either form (and their myriad sub-genres). But we can usually understand each other, with a minimum of resources, should we wish to do so – a *sympathetic engagement* is often more important than linguistic or technical facility in this respect. We can, for example, slip the constraints of verbal/visual representation altogether and attempt to understand a concept through movement, interaction (such as a game or performance), demonstration, improvisation, sensory experience (such as eating), or embodied rhythms (such as dance). We discuss our research not infrequently through spatially challenged settings, as if bodily comfort, accessibility, or acoustic efficiency were optional extras in this supposedly bloodless 'life of the mind'. Rarely do we stop to consider how a redistribution of the furniture, for example, or hacking the imprisoning logics of the presentation technologies we use so nonchalantly might change the sort of conversation about our work that we have or might wish to have. The conversation itself, in other words, is there to be supported by artistic and design practices in a variety of different ways. Artistic researchers possess already the qualities needed to make a difference – for example, a preference for creative *problem setting* over efficient problem solving. *Quality*, another open-textured concept, is here not merely an abstract ideal for weighing and measuring results but rather a principle for arriving at a form of (provisional) closure for processes that would otherwise tend to the open ended.

Concluding remarks

How is a practice changed by investigation into that practice? The artist who becomes a doctoral candidate is promised that there are advantages in *making assumptions visible*, the better to facilitate a conversation about the strengths and pitfalls of chosen *perspectives*. Thomas McLaughlin writes,

When will it thunder? 169

Practitioners of a given craft or skill develop a picture of their practice – a sense of how it is or ought to be practiced, of its values and its worldview – and many are quite articulate about this 'theory,' aware for example that there are competing theories, that not all practitioners work from the same premises. These practitioners' theories may contrast sharply with the theories of their practice constructed by academic theorists. . . . It would be possible to find the nurse's theory of disease, the musician's theory of audience, the computer designer's theory of interpretation, the athlete's theory of sport, the bookstore designer's theory of reading, the casting director's theory of character.

(McLaughlin 1996, 22)

Such theories are rooted in experience but may not be the ones that gain ascendency in the lottery of research applications and funding.

The artistic research doctoral candidate is charged with the imperative of severing the umbilicus between practice and habit. Research, in exposing habits and the implicit assumptions that support them, brings the artistic researcher's own sensibility into play as a legitimate area of research. This is sometimes called nurturing the capacity for critical self-reflection.

But reflection and criticality belong to the universes of *understanding* and *explaining*, these being central activities to the university's historical mission. 'So, again, what is a University?' Plessner asks,

What is it if it no longer nurtures citizens and their 'coming into being'? Are they places for the formation of self-selecting elites within a multitude? Again, whom do the elites serve? Other elites, such as our powerful neo-feudal corporate masters? Or are universities autonomous communities? In which case, (1) are they not then superfluous, subject to the populist pressures of celebrity culture where rhetorically skilled professors provide intellectual entertainment or 'edu-tainment' for their network of fee-paying acolytes? Or (2) is it simply a space within which intellectual fads are played out and then fade out?

(Plessner 2014)

Alternatively, we can end on more optimistic questions. What is the name of the practice for those who pursue *unknowing*, or *not* knowing, a pursuit that is rigorous and demands refined skills and reflective methods? Is it a discipline of 'respect' in front of questions before they have fully emerged? And, if so, might this also be one analogy to the doctorate's experience in undertaking a period of training during which one respectfully acknowledges the limitations of our own forms of understanding – the certainties that formerly sustained us – and with this acknowledgement, a dawning sense of greater agility, poise, and increasing degrees of imaginative and creative freedom?

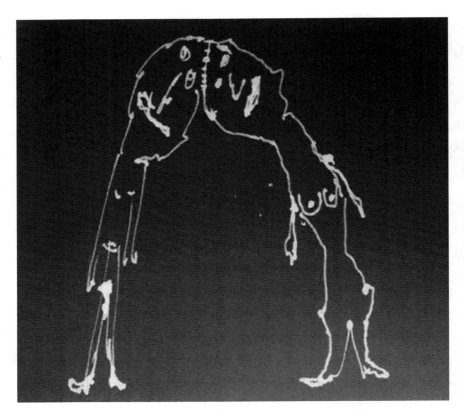

Fig. 11.1 The temptations of the non-linear ladder
[Picture by Rolf Hughes]

Notes

1 This chapter incorporates some of the writings and reflections developed while establishing a research-by-design PhD programme at the Sint-Lucas School of Architecture (now KU Leuven, Faculty of Architecture, Campus Sint Lucas), Brussels and Ghent, between 2007 and 2013, and published in the school's annual series of *Reflections*.
2 Cited by Richard Holmes (2009).
3 http://www.eurofound.europa.eu/publications/foundation-finding/2014/quality-of-life-social-policies/foundation-findings-social-situation-of-young-people-in-europe (accessed 31/3/16).
4 Karl Marx and Frederick Engels, *Collected Works*, New York 1975ff, Volume 3, p. 284. Cited by Michael Denning (2010).
5 *Communication* is here understood, after Richard Buchanan, not in accordance with semiotic or grammatical theories of communication nor dialectical theories

When will it thunder? 171

that treat communication in relation to an economic or spiritual truth but in the context of rhetoric – that is, 'the inventive and persuasive relation of speakers and audiences as they are brought together in speeches or other objects of communication' (Buchanan 1989, 91). The expanded concept of *exposition* is particularly interested in those 'other objects [and acts] of communication' (Hughes 2013).

6 The silent, solitary aspect of thinking is, of course, historically and culturally contingent. Ryle, for example, points this out while inadvertently using an already-dated analogy: 'Theorizing is an activity which most people can and normally do conduct in silence. They articulate in sentences the theories that they construct, but they do now most of the time speak these sentences out loud. They say them to themselves. Or they formulate their thoughts in diagrams and pictures, but they do not always set these out on paper. They "see them in their minds' eyes". Much of our ordinary thinking is conducted in internal monologue or silent soliloquy, usually accompanied by an internal cinematograph-show of visual imagery.' Yet Ryle also emphasises that this internal dialogue is acquired with some effort, and only after we have learned to talk intelligently aloud and heard and understood other people doing so. In a salutary reminder to those of us concerned with research communication, he adds, 'People tend to identify their minds with the "place" where they conduct their secret thoughts. They even come to suppose that there is a special mystery about how we publish our thoughts instead of realizing that we employ a special artifice to keep them to ourselves' Ryle (1949, 27–28).

7 Churchman writes, 'Knowledge is being at once at ease with a subject and deeply engrossed in it. Knowledge carries with it both a tremendous joy and a great despair – a joy at being at one with a whole area of living human activity, and a great despair at recognizing how little this oneness really is compared to what it might be' (Churchman 1971).

8 A point illustrated by Caliban's retort to Prospero: 'You taught me language; and my profit on't/Is, I know how to curse. The red plague rid you/For learning me your language!' in William Shakespeare's *The Tempest*, Act One Scene 2.

9 Biggs (2004, 8–9) writes, 'Artistic enquiry is not just artistic enquiry about the nature of the physical world but is also artistic enquiry about the artistic world. Nearly all research in Material Culture could be described in this way, and that is what makes it different from enquiries concerning the same objects in physics or engineering. Therefore the observation that questions about experience arise through the process or as a consequence of experience, is valid'.

10 Biggs (2004, 10) remarks, 'Experiential feelings do not have the same form as experiential content, i.e. experiences present themselves as experiential feelings whereas we reflect cognitively upon the content of those experiences, hence my claim that experiential feelings represent experiential content. With some experiential feelings the experiential content represented may be trivial, e.g. pain. However, other experiential feelings represent significant aspects of human experience, e.g. the aesthetic response. Thus there are both sensory and cognitive elements to experience, although I do not mean to imply that the cognitive element is necessarily synonymous with linguistic form'.

11 Originally published in *Proceedings of the Aristotelian Society, Supplementary Volume* XIX (1945).

12 Throughout this chapter, I am thinking of the special challenges of a doctoral education as it relates to the family concept of artistic research (spanning the artistic disciplines including the design disciplines, architecture, and so on with an emphasis on practice-based research). *Doctorateness* should here be understood within this particular context.

172 *Rolf Hughes*

13 Transvaluation: the dream made real
A Manifesto

The large-scale transformation of higher education – through what is commonly known as the *Bologna Process* – signalled the definitive breakthrough of "globalized" practices of teaching and research in the academic world. Ever since, the pedagogical performance of all institutions involved in this process was thoroughly measured through organized practices of evaluation. This process of formalization has now started to blur the origins of research and higher education, as well as its futures.

Research and education have long abided by the technologies of measurement. We now need to direct the evaluating practices back to their proper purpose and scope, and again take charge of the true challenge: practicing values. This is what we mean by *transvaluation* (as formulated by Nietzsche, Irigaray). Our purpose is to reconceive *politics and poetics of value*, to reorient research towards social, political, and poetical values able to manifest – or *materialize* – the worlds to come. This type of materialization, in turn, we call *worlding* (as examined by Heidegger, Nancy, Spivak): the desire to enact and transform the world as a space of poetics ("making"). Not only should these envisage the *future of materials* – crucial in an age of unrivalled technological discovery – but also the future of *intangibles*, of ideas and ideals, of dreams of a better world, of a more just society, of human equality and liberty. . . This space of poetics will be expanded by the pursuit of new transformative values that can enrich our societies, our cultures and the world itself. Institutions and disciplines might become transient "docking stations" on a journey towards cultural renovation, unleashed creativity and revitalised political ambition. In connecting the poetics and politics of value with worlding, we hope to create the conditions for a new university, the university *Bologna* once seemed to have promised.

So let us, artists, architects and philosophers involved in research, unshackle Bologna from its measurement systems by inviting students, teachers and researchers outside the routines of traditional practice and reconnecting them to speculative theory and utopian thinking. Let us call upon our competence to constantly remake, reconfigure, recompose and reinterpret complexities, through poetics and practices of value, and through the material. Let us release the creative energies needed to open up imprisoned perspectives. Let us speculate about future knowledge and future values, instead of merely evaluating existing knowledge-procedures. Let us try to invent new forms of creative knowledge and, in doing so, empower communities of common interest (instead of lingering in marketing practices such as "research by design"). To teach as well as to invent means to "learn to see the connections," as Wittgenstein once said. This illuminates the very meaning of the poetics or politics of value: to look ahead, to see what was still hidden, and to start looking where no-one has looked before.

The future university will be the site where values are forged and contested, the place where materials, energies and ideas are invented and transformed. In that sense, the future university will be a *U-topos*: the kind of space *Bologna* dreamt of, but immediately forgot upon waking. Now the story of the dream must finally be told, because the space it held *can* be realised. We, humans, are dreamers perfected. Let's use this unique evolutionary gift to start sharing our knowledge and transvaluating our world. **Transvaluation**: *the real made dream.*

Peter De Graeve – Nel Janssens – Johan Öberg – Rolf Hughes – Mattias Kärrholm – Catharina Dyrssen

Bibliography

Biggs, Michael. 2004. 'Learning from Experience: Approaches to the Experiential Component of Practice-Based Research'. In *Forskning, Reflektion, Utveckling*, edited by Henrik Karlsson, 6–21. Stockholm: Swedish Research Council.

Brewer, Garry D. 1999. 'The Challenges of Interdisciplinarity'. *Policy Sciences* 32: 327–337.

Buchanan, Richard. 1989. 'Declaration by Design: Rhetoric, Argument, and Demonstration in Design Practice'. In *Design Discourse: History, Theory, Criticism*, edited by Victor Margolin, 91–109. Chicago and London: University of Chicago Press.

Bunnin, Nicholas and Yu, Jiyuan. 2004. *The Blackwell Dictionary of Western Philosophy*. Oxford: Blackwell.

Campbell, Donald T. 1969. 'Ethnocentrism of Disciplines and the Fish-Scale Model of Omniscience'. In *Interdisciplinary Relationships in the Social Science*, edited by Muzafer Sherif and Carlolyn W. Sherif, 328–348. Chicago, IL: Aldine.

Churchman, Charles West. 1971. *The Design of Inquiring Systems: Basic Concepts of Systems and Organization*. New York: Basic Books Inc.

Denning, Michael. 2010. 'Wageless Life'. *New Left Review* 66, November–December 2010. Available online: http://newleftreview.org/II/66/michael-denning-wageless-life (accessed 12.1.15).

Frayling, Christopher, Valery Stead, Bruce Archer, Nicholas Cook, James Powel, Victor Sage, Stephen Scrivener, and Michael Tovey. 1997. *Practice-Based Doctorates in the Creative and Performing Arts and Design*. Lichfield: UK Council for Graduate Education.

Hayek, Friedrich A. 1945. 'The Use of Knowledge in Society'. *American Economic Review* 35 (4): 519–530.

Holmes, Richard. 2009. *The Age of Wonder: How the Romantic Generation Discovered the Beauty and Terror of Science*. London: Harper Press.

Hughes, Rolf. 2013. 'Exposition'. In *Exposition in Artistic Research*, edited by Henk Borgdorff and Michael Schwab, 52–64. Leiden: Leiden University Press.

Hughes, Rolf, Catharina Dyrssen, and Maria Hellström Reimer. 2011. 'Artistic Research: Today and Tomorrow'. In *Form och färdriktning: strategiska frågor för den konstnärliga forskningen* (Artistic Research Yearbook 2011), edited by Torbjörn Lind, 29–37. Stockholm: Vetenskapsrådet.

Hughes, Rolf, and John Monk, eds. 1998. *The Book of Models: Ceremonies, Metaphor, Performance*. Milton Keynes, UK and Stockholm, Sweden: Department of Telematics/Metamorphosis – Centre for Writing and Performance Research.

Hughes, Rolf, and John Monk, eds. 2003. *Hybrid Thought*. Milton Keynes: Open University.

Kuhn, Thomas. 1970. *The Structure of Scientific Revolutions*. Chicago: The University of Chicago Press.

McLaughlin, Thomas. 1996. *Street Smarts and Critical Theory: Listening to the Vernacular*. Madison: University of Wisconsin Press.

Plessner, Daphne. 2014. 'What Is a University?' *Journal for Artistic Research* 6. Available online: http://www.researchcatalogue.net/view/33909/33910/1416/0 (accessed 12.1.2015).

Ruin, Hans. 2014. 'Philosophy, Freedom, and the Task of the University'. In *The Humboldtian Tradition: Origins and Legacies*, edited by Peter Josephson, Thomas Karlsohn, and Johan Östling, 164–177. Leiden and Boston: Brill.

174 *Rolf Hughes*

Ryle, Gilbert. 1949. *The Concept of the Mind*. Chicago: University of Chicago Press.

Sclafani, Richard J. 1971. '"Art," Wittgenstein and Open-Textured Concepts'. *The Journal of Aesthetics and Art Criticism* 29 (3): 333–341.

Simons, Herbert W. 1990. 'Rhetoric of Inquiry as an Intellectual Movement'. In *The Rhetorical Turn: Invention and Persuasion in the Conduct of Inquiry*, edited by Herbert W. Simons, 1–31. Chicago and London: University of Chicago Press.

Thompson Klein, Julie. 2004. 'Interdisciplinarity and Complexity: An Evolving Relationship'. *E: CO Special Double Issue* 6 (1–2): 8.

Weitz, Morris. 1956. 'The Role of Theory in Aesthetics'. *Journal of Aesthetics and Art Criticism* 15: 27–35.

Wittgenstein, Ludwig. 1953. *Philosophical Investigations*. Oxford: Basil Blackwell.

12 Precision

The compositional accuracy of artistic judgement

Catharina Dyrssen

The intriguing aspect of judgement

Whether connected to measurable facts or various forms of value, for instance in art, judgement is still understood mainly as the logics of rhetoric and statements of priority. But what if perspectives from artistic research,[1] understood here primarily as research which is driven by imaginative modes to explore or rethink situated complexities, could also re-examine the role of judgement in research processes? Of special interest would then be how the act of 'judgement' could be enhanced as an actively constructing-composing form to explore situations and how it could operate with precision in relation to situated contexts. This would open the possibility for discussion about how the use of 'productive judgement' in an art-based and constructive sense may affect practice relevance, doctoral education and the status of knowledge creation.

What if judgement would have its outset in composition, construction and interaction with the material? Mainly from perspectives of artistic research within architecture and music, this chapter discusses how that could extensively restructure contextual agency and the range of approaches to investigation and doctoral education.

Artistic research as a maturing practice

In 2014 the Committee for Artistic Research at the Swedish Research Council completed an overview of Swedish artistic research, a work conducted with extensive contributions from higher education institutions within fine and applied arts (including architecture) and in consultation with international organisations.[2]

Parallel to developing research, the art institutions have rapidly established their research education – some still at an initial phase and in small scale, some ambitiously launching preparations at master level, some having thoroughly structured PhD education, several seeking collaborations across art disciplines. In 2015 about 100 persons had achieved a Swedish doctoral degree in the arts and are now about to enter the established mechanisms

176 *Catharina Dyrssen*

of struggles for research funding and academic positions. The potential of such an increase in new researchers, with considerably expanded and novel perspectives on how to conduct investigations, will most probably affect societal understandings of 'knowledge' and 'knowledge production'.

The survey exposed the critical-creative role of artistic research, which has outcomes that challenge parts of contemporary research discourse. It questioned remaining essentialist views in a double sense: that art and research diverge fundamentally as two separate practices and that the arts form independent disciplines, in which 'making art', as such, is synonymous with 'doing research'. Instead it was clear that research in the arts has by now developed considerable maturity and diversity, with large variations among themes, fields, conceptual frameworks and approaches.

Four tendencies can be stressed here, apparent through the overview as well as in recent funding applications: first, there is a shift of focus from reflections on the artists' creative processes to a renewed interest in art-related materiality and agency. Second, as a parallel tendency, research themes are largely driven by complex art-society issues related to capacities, possibilities and agency of artistic production and modes of investigation. Third, the art field has to large extent transgressed traditional disciplinary domains, within the arts as well as in cross- and transdisciplinary formats of academy-practice collaborations, with a range of approaches to formulate themes and develop frameworks of theory and methodology.[3] The fourth tendency exposed a strategic urge for the field to not only use theory projected from other domains such as philosophy or science but to develop theory and conceptualisation through artistic approaches and practices (Swedish Research Council 2015a, 2015b).

Hence, the overview reflected multiple ambitions both to deepen specific art-related themes and to approach collaboration with other research fields, thereby underscoring the need to assert and use artistic research approaches. Both ambitions must expand understandings of the term 'concept' from being a tool for thinking, naming and understanding into being operative for investigating, grasping and interacting in complex situations.

From Humboldt to the present

With a far-reaching history and with the rational establishment in the 19th century of the Humboldt University model, Western knowledge systems have been based on disciplinary identities, differentiated by epistemologies, objectives, modes of deduction and categorisation, and have been ordered within stable hierarchical structures. Building academic rigour and securing knowledge systems in this tradition has largely been based on the selection of observed facts and differentiated elements with characteristics that could be singled out from other qualities, be given denoting concepts, assigned essential identity and help to position unambiguous results and arguments of cause and effect in stable hierarchical structures – all serving as building

The accuracy of artistic judgement   177

blocks in an accumulative knowledge production (Liedman 2006, 205–260; Johnson 2010, 143ff). Related to the double set of systems – science and law – judgement within art was kept separate:

> In Kant's classic formulation, knowledge is a *product of conceptual synthesis* that takes the form of *propositional judgements* descriptive of the world. Consequently, aesthetic experience, which he regarded as subjective and based on feelings, lies wholly outside the realm of knowledge. Simply put, aesthetic judgements of beauty in nature and art are not cognitive (and hence not conceptual), and so they issue in no knowledge whatsoever.
>
> (Johnson 2010, 143)

An idealised image of artist and artwork contributed to drawing the line between art practice and critique, together with Kant's notion that criticism, judgement and logic were independent from sensory experience (Liedman 2006, 231–243). This notion has maintained the dichotomy between art and science in knowledge making but also between art and critique. In the institutional practices of research and critique, judgement should take clear and well-underpinned stands through reason, in which 'jumping to conclusions' would mean discreditable shortcuts. Precision has followed the same pattern: in research (and law), it has been based on selection, distinction, proof and rational logic, while art and aesthetic judgement struggle in a separate division, acting as discursively 'the other', discussing values in the knowledge production system.[4]

Still, with discursive logic spilled over to art discourses, judgement is mainly connected to distinction and argument: of right or wrong, authority and power, question and answer, judging value in the sense of clearly transferrable significance and ultimately societal use and market value. Within its appropriate limits, this kind of discernment can take a productive part in societal development (and economy) but threatens to reduce values to either measurable indicators and economic figures or 'aspects of taste'[5] (cf. PARSE 01). To enrich understanding, we must re-examine what judgement means as a shaping, constructing and modelling activity, particularly concerning artistic research practices.

These days research funding, not least for architectural research, often calls for collaboration between academia and actors in professional practice. Strong driving forces are of course private-public partnerships as significant mechanisms in knowledge-based economies. They often render a rich flow of interactive processes of learning, exchange of ideas and practice proposals, the re-examination of conditions and so on, but also of reductive forces where normative solutions for applied production and consumption are encouraged rather than 'slow reflection' and gradual change. Indicator-driven measurements and evidence-based methods increase their impact as criteria for academic rigour and evaluation and as setting standards for how

178   *Catharina Dyrssen*

research discourses are maintained, for instance as requirements in applying for research funding and jobs. They also frequently appear in media briefings to the general public or as terms for negotiating procedures in professional practice. For all these purposes, although increasingly criticised, indicator-driven conventions often dress up research as producing quantifiable results where science 'proves' something, which of course is useful for 'quick-fix' media communication, practice applications or to fulfil academic or societal (re-)action.[6]

Today we can see a generation no longer limiting knowledge to the 'masonry metaphor', adding coherent elements like building blocks to a construction. Infused with web interaction, digital imagery and symbolic production, the former dichotomy between research and art practice is extensively bridged, as more diverse, changing and expanded modes of thinking-making-communicating-financing emerge. Artistic research practices make extensive use of lateral, combinatory and non-reductive modes of experimenting and thinking. The artist/designer/architect is trained to recognise quality and interact with materiality, context and detail, for instance through worlding[7] (Janssens 2012). This implies that such approaches can address contexts as semi-contingent complexities by articulating them with the help of artistic logics instead of reducing them. This of course rapidly moves processes of knowledge making and research beyond traditional 'investigation' or 'inquiry', which needs to be discussed in a deeper sense.

Regarding architecture and music

Architecture is often referred to as practice oriented, being one of the 'making disciplines', with researching processes profoundly engaging with the material, *through the making* in specific situations (Dunin-Woyseth and Michl 2001). It is customarily regarded as transdisciplinary, bridging art, technology, humanities and social science – connecting materiality, social interaction and environment to human experience – and increasingly understood as addressing spatial-material, social-environmental, transformative and aesthetic complexities.

Music, by tradition, is often considered 'immaterial' and 'spiritual', a view rooted in Platonism and cosmic orders from antiquity and early Christianity and strongly established in the classical-romantic era. A correlated view is that music is primarily a time-related art form, as sequences of ungraspable moments (Hanslick 1918; Dahlhaus 1967; Lippman 1986). This displays polarities in music, being in one sense essentially individualistic in art production – for instance in the singular role sometimes ascribed to the composer, the 'musical genius' or the 'unique spiritual experience' – and in another sense fundamentally collective as socio-cultural phenomena of 'the audience', 'the orchestra', 'the general public' or even 'the time spirit', with musicians mediating – both in terms of status and collectivity – between the two extremes[8] (Heister 1983; Kramer 1990; Dyrssen 1995).

The accuracy of artistic judgement 179

This dichotomy between architecture and music is of course crudely simplified, but it serves as two modes by which to approach composition. So, as aspects of composition in architecture and music may shift in terms of engagement with the material-spatial-social or immaterial-timely-individual, the intention here is to examine context and detail and spatial and compositional thinking, to enrich the discussion on 'doctorateness' as a continuous and inter-subjective, constructing and shaping, learning process in academic enquiry.

The act of judgement will be considered as productive moments in the researching processes, where the researcher can grasp the investigative situations and understand them as configurations or compositions of subject-object interactions, relationships and agencies, and with variable positions in the knowledge situation. This also emphasises that the researcher, through productive judgement, holds a specific key to the creation of meaningful knowledge systems in a larger, socio-cultural-political sense.

Compositional approach 1 – music

Composer and artistic researcher Anders Hultqvist argues that context can be understood from a sensual position that cannot be conceptualised, but contains ethical positions for music and musicians that always merge the sensitive and the rational[9] (Hultqvist 2013, 31). Musical composition – usually understood as combining parameters of pitch, rhythm, timbre and articulation – has an endless amount of expressions, advanced structures and levels of complexity, that are both physical and cultural. On the one hand they are related to nature (for instance as acoustics) but on the other to contexts that provide 'cognitive glasses' (Hultqvist 2013, 39–42). Hultqvist discusses a continuous negotiation among physically, culturally and individually conditioned structures and between singular moments and time-space contexts. This means that action positions and the compositional production of meaning will always interrelate in a 'complex and labyrinthine way', making composers confident with the musical 'breathing' in the work (Hultqvist 2013, 34ff, 29–84, 2014, 47–51). Hence, music and musical composition form dynamic systems based on structural principles and related to our experience as being aesthetically acceptable. Inspired by Gregory Bateson's statement that 'information consists of differences making difference', Hultqvist tentatively understands composition as 'together the components create a potential that can be sensed as part in a message' (Hultqvist 2013, 38, my translation). Hence, to conceive and create statements of contextual meaning needs differences that can be apprehended as divergence between parts, depending on qualities, relationships, configurations and the like. If the course of events is totally random, no productive differences will appear. If similarities are too obvious then no meaningful differences are produced, and if differences become too large we do not understand how the various elements are related to one another. So together these differences create a potential that can be conceived as patterns of productive similarities and

180 *Catharina Dyrssen*

differences in a message and open for deepening and broadening the contents further.

Musical action related to the spatial – for instance bodily gestures, dance or sonic formations like 'musical gestures' – have narrative and associative aspects related to verbal language. But more importantly, they form cognitive association areas where information from several senses is merged, forming complexities or 'images of totality' (Hultqvist 2013, 67). The 'here and now' of melodic gestures may generate a feeling of closeness to which actions of counterpoint (for instance through accents, contrasts or tensions) in the musical composition can signal a distance and a 'then'. To compose audibly and musically with these different *times* can provide a sense of both architectural and narrative-processual space. There is a scale with the 'now' of *language-time* as explicitly verbalised at one end and complex and overlapping times – different experiences of past and future time through the musical-spatial experience of the composition – at the other (Hultqvist 2014, 51). Hence, with cognitive scientist Peter Gärdenfors, Hultqvist stresses the concept of 'situated cognition', implying that human awareness operates at basic level with procedural memory and spatial-material experiences of 'the real'. But experiential levels connect both to episodic memory and narrative aspects of interaction and, being socio-culturally conditioned, also at a level of more advanced social interaction and awareness where conditions can be understood and verbalised. The capacity to think with images is older than thinking with words, which implies that awareness is spatially structured and needs more cognitive processing to be transmitted into verbal form (Hultqvist 2013, 55–66). Artists often deal actively with situated cognition going beyond any simple and unspecified notion of 'creativity'. Artistic research situations frequently face multiple interconnected levels of complexities that surpass conventional promotions of distinction, abstraction and conclusion or transcend the rhetoric of argument, counterargument and synthesis. So following Hultqvist (and Gärdenfors), with the logic of an artistic approach: to convert something into verbal logics would mean a transformation which needs considerably more processing but often leads to reduction of information – or, at least, contains a considerable risk of reduction.

This of course relates to acts of judgement, which provide an opportunity to release a wider horizon of 'now' – events that together can create an experience of spatial volume and time-space relationships. Contrary to fragmentation, judgement as moments of discovery and inventions is a way to reveal multiple, interconnected layers in the artwork that can enrich and at the same time structure cognitive possibilities and insights. This can involve several modes of acting, sensing and thinking which continuously re-formulate and restructure connections between approaches. Cognitive scientist Antonio Damasio speaks here of the immediate cross-exchange among *conceptualising*, *experiencing* and *interacting* (Damasio 2006), which all occur simultaneously in human interaction with the world and its materiality.

The accuracy of artistic judgement   181

Hence, doctoral training should increasingly involve handling complex, situated conditions and relate them to actively constructing judgement. More simply, this means developing practices for imagining, finding, adapting and understanding in order to explore situated conditions, trying them out and critically rethinking relational settings, sensing what happens and undertaking possible interventions with regard to deepening and broadening the sense and logics of composition.

Compositional approach 2 – modelling and composing contexts

A compositional approach in architecture – so strongly connected to interaction with the material – enhances thinking and interacting that involves bodily engagement, awareness of social dimensions, transversal logics and formative actions. Modelling actions play key roles here as *descriptive* of spatial-material configurations – for instance by showing a building or urban space in a certain scale; as *conceptual* – enhancing the main ideas in a situation or intervention; or as *(per-)formative, prescriptive* – instructing how an architectural artefact shall be made, changed or shaped. This relates modelling closely to *simulation*, as a mode to explore or investigate situations by setting conditions and components in tentative interaction or moving them temporarily out of ordinary premises into liminal or extreme conditions, or involve narratives, to try out alternative possibilities. All these actions model existing and 'real' states as well as fictional ones ('what if?'), both playing important roles in expanding and constructing knowledge (Bunschoten 2001; Dyrssen 2010, 230ff; Janssens 2012).

Modelling also makes use of what Dana Cuff and Roger Sherman describe as the *proformative* capacity of the architectural project, 'the catalytic agency of form' which can act beyond the performative ability of the architectural project by trying out alternatives. Thus, by shaping what something may become and thereby influencing the direction that a certain development may take or open for discussing alternatives, the proformative has capacity by 'acting beforehand' (Cuff and Sherman 2011, 27f).

Urban designer and landscape theorist Ellen Braae argues that the modelling capacity conditions and expands aesthetics with a spectrum of time-related, socio-cultural, environmental, and resilience-construction perspectives, which give aesthetics a broad relevance to promote and understand changes in the contemporary urban scene. With such pragmatic perspectives on aesthetics and theory in interdisciplinary action-oriented approaches that are closely integrated with transformational practice (Braae 2015, 124), aesthetics are inscribed in cultural and environmental circumstances and can take an essential role for both professionals and users as an experiential quality of site and context linked to ethics, history, and sustainability (Braae 2015, 122–133, 142–146, 150–153). Aesthetics offer modes of thinking in which 'many types

182 *Catharina Dyrssen*

of future are offered, in which we try out new ways of forming the world we inhabit' (Braae 2015, 309), and acts as an essential capacity in the continuous alteration of contemporary urban landscapes, from several approaches: bodily and mental experiences, spatial and cultural implications and so on. Understanding aesthetics (and design) as interaction and transformation – as changing by and through what already exists – means that pre-existing contexts are decoded to grasp the logics of variety and cultivating differences and of heightening values by juxtaposing the new with the old, 'a strategy which also changes the meaning of the original' (Braae 2015, 314, also see 275–305, 308–316).

This revitalising discourse on aesthetics is, of course, relevant to judgement. Modelling activity and capacity obviously contains a productive entry to approaching composition, not unlike what Hultqvist describes in music. It shapes a constantly evolving, interactive and relational structure and the form and meaning of spatial-material-conceptual-cognitive aspects, which strongly relate to David Harvey's and Doreen Massey's dynamic understandings of space as process and non-essential, relational identity, activated as *'relational space'* (Massey 2005; Harvey 2006). It also moves the foci of understandings and knowledge from primarily demanding the production of 'truths' or 'evidence' into exploring and enriching contexts and perspectives.

Highlighting words like 'holistic' when trying to describe expanded contexts has been rightly criticised for being overly inclusive and lacking articulation. Today, largely inspired by landscape urbanism, architectural discourse increasingly refers to the concepts of 'ecologies' or 'urban ecologies' (Waldheim 2006; Cuff and Sherman 2011; Björling 2016). The concept usually takes its origin in the writings of Félix Guattari (1989), reaching back to Gregory Bateson (1973) or, with more direct socio-spatial approaches, to Rayner Banham (2001 [1971]). Björling investigates urban ecologies as *complex, productive configurations* (Björling 2016, 221–245, 308–310).

Related to artistic research, ecologies underline compositional aspects of contexts, analogous to assemblages implied for instance by DeLanda (2004, 2006) and open towards potentials in proformative approaches such as by Cuff and Sherman (2011). This needs to be explored for more fine-graded modes to articulate contexts as complex configurations or compositional processes, through spatial and musical thinking-making. And it raises the question of how details, or specific actions, can operate to change systemic conditions. Here the notion of 'acupuncture' can be transferred from architectural discourse and practice. Acupunctural interventions are precise, spatial and material projects that change both on-going spatial situations and underlying transformational processes. They can be understood as adapters that connect human, physical scale to urban context and contain potential to enrich and establish new sense-making spatial relations.[10] Acupuncture can be enacted to trigger systemic change, such as initiating improvement processes in dilapidated urban areas by making precise, incremental material-spatial changes at

The accuracy of artistic judgement 183

specific points – an improved playground, a new shortcut in the urban fabric or accessible but undefined spaces; or by social or processual alterations – for instance new participative interactions or new voices being heard.

Björling also refers to de Solà-Morales's discussion on three kinds of gazes that can be used for instance by the researcher or architect on a situation of interest to identify and form acupuncture projects: '*the strategic gaze*' searches the strategic functions and possible change of a specific site in terms of meaning, characteristics and potential; '*the compulsive gaze*' looks for over-all changes that radically affect the physical form of an urban area; '*the anxious gaze*' seeks diverse perspectives to extend the vision, include new alternatives and reflect and revalue the current situation. These alternative gazes indicate different approaches that may be transferred into other settings or interactions with matter.[11] Hence, to be aware of what kind of 'gaze' and approach to use at different stages of a researching process and within specific conditions can further develop the agency and capacity of productive artistic judgement.

Conclusions: judgement as compositional and proformative action

Understanding contexts as articulated configurations of relevance and in interaction with details or precise interventions, we can regard knowledge as evolving and shared explorations (Glissant 1997; Jullien 1999) which imply important shifts in focus and use of judgement: it moves away from the selective, categorising, evaluating aspects as found in older traditions of science and law (and art critique) – for instance demarcating abstractions, categorisations, typologies, precisely distinguished concepts, linear orders of cause and effects or defining indicators for quantitative or qualitative evaluation standards and generalisations and so forth – and instead searches precise, 'trigger' actions. This connects to Hultqvist's discussions on musical composition, and relates to Gärdenfors' emphasis on spatial thinking as complexity and to Damasio's understandings of simultaneously conceptualising-perceiving-experiencing-interacting. In artistic research, it opens for a 'proformative' (or productive) and multiple compositional approach to articulate contexts, emphasising:

1   to construct and understand *productive aspects* that can enrich – instead of reduce – conditions relevant for investigating and discussing a situation at stake. This involves the articulation of the potentials of the situation, responding to the research theme and explorative interaction but not necessarily setting these in hierarchies or a specific order.
2   to form *adaptable systems* for the situation – which can be flexible and layered to increase complexity in continuous change – and encourage working with relational components across scales, borders, categories and domains.

184   *Catharina Dyrssen*

3   *interaction with the real* – to take origin in aesthetics and art as involvement with and through the *real*, to test alteration and re-understanding, and also using fiction as a working mode oriented towards change in terms of 'becoming' and 'transforming', in systemic processes (ecology); and to test change tentatively, incrementally and radically.

4   *relational qualities* – to make visible interdependent, existing, evolving and potential configurations of conditions and elements and thereby reveal productive and interlinked possibilities.

5   *multiple communication forms* – to work with descriptions, tentative investigation, exploration, imaging and multisensory communication in various formats of dialogue and transformational processes, also to critically question conditions and enrich understandings.

6   *compositional thinking* – to act and think through context-detail relations and modelling activity. This may involve activating working formats and conceptualisations (mappings, descriptions, inter-subjective interventions and positionings of actants etc.) that give opportunities for re-configurations and new understanding, experience or action.

Compositional thinking and its related productive judgement need the capacity to connect domains and categories, unite time-space scales of past, present and future and to shift focus between detail and context, forming relational structures, links and processes. This can be done more selectively as singular actions or as multiple sweeps into situations and can shift between using focusing and broadening perspectives, being precise or ambiguous, provocative or sensitive. They use aesthetic logics, for instance with inventive spatial-musical and narrative approaches that can operate beyond 'the spectacular' or 'the utopian'. Their contexts remain as neither unspecified inclusions nor delineated domains, but set transformation, rethinking and new syntheses in focus, both in long-term perspectives and as immediate or stepwise action and increase awareness by activating knowledge creation where the system, configuration or composition shows its potential.

The acupunctural activity is a mode of judgement enacted as triggering interaction – tentative, operative and performative – with articulated, adaptive settings. It operates through active and combinatory approaches rather than selective and categorising ones and uses aesthetic logics to increase complexity. It may alter the understandings of positions, processes or configurations, enriching the situation or changing systemic relations between detail and contexts.

As acupuncture actions – or multifaceted, detail-oriented trigger actions such as 'counterpoint', accents or 'adapters' – judgement can clarify how contexts may be activated or (re-)composed. In turn, contexts can also clarify and adjust acupuncture capacities in judgement by tentatively exploring its proformative actions.

Productive artistic judgement uses the richness of multiple linkages and associative, lateral thinking and spatial awareness, criss-crossing the linear

The accuracy of artistic judgement 185

logics of observation, selection and distinction. It dwells with confidence in complex situations, recognising their relational qualities and multiple possibilities.

By pin-pointing keys to complexity, judgement serves the purpose of raising *intensity* and recognising *links* and the *quality of relations* that influence the theme at stake for exploration. Hence judging actions, whether systematic, explorative or imaginary, can 'hit the target' directly and precisely and open up situations. They can jump not to argumentative conclusions but to and through insight on possible alternatives and meaning of prospects, and trigger change, stability or depth in the complexity of relational identities and multiple contextual links.

By showing new layers and contingencies, relationships, effects and understandings, judgement can question delineations, categories and typologies as driving forces in research and knowledge. This moves the construction of meaning away from an essentialist understanding: the question is no longer of what a specific meaning *is* but how conditions, emergence and relationships can work and how they may be affected, understood, discussed and changed.

Such investigative activity transforms research topics from being objectified (and 'judged') to situations showing, adapting and affecting capacities, as acts and mechanisms of qualifying processes connected to both recognition (of the already produced or composed) and inventive thinking. At least five contextual processes are of concern here in the knowledge making of 'doctorateness' or as active parts in educational processes:

1 Knowledge as 'doxic' value systems, situated and conditioned as systems of rules within specific research domains, challenging scientific 'truth' (Rosengren 2002, 2008). This needs to be discussed not as general alternatives to the 'scientific' but as compositional systems relevant for artistic research situations and enhancements of knowledge formation.
2 The double missions often asserted for artistic research, to investigate 'how to make art' and to expand and reconfigure conditions of art practices as a dynamic relationship and embodied experience (see Biggs and Büchler 2010), should be studied more deeply as relational approaches.
3 The capacity in artistic research to work through explorative thinking-making and engagement with matter (Janssens 2012) needs to be further explored as a vital driving force in knowledge processes.
4 Assemblages as compositional mechanisms of change and interaction (DeLanda 2004) need to be refined and diversified, and proformative actions should be further developed with the purpose to investigate how they can open situations.
5 Understandings of relational space and identity in situations and discourses need to be further explored as components and actions in research compositions and to time-space-related aesthetic logics.

186 *Catharina Dyrssen*

Thus, the role of a productive judgement in artistic research is not to reduce complexity. Instead it can help to augment knowledge – as increased understanding, rethinking situations, rendering new or deeper insights, empathy or experience – to help in recognizing alternatives, atone with situations, discover possibilities and so on and enhance operative problem-solving capacity. This is a process that does not focus evaluation standards but emphasises and continuously encourages relational discourse and evolving, compositional explorative judgement and logics with accuracy and precision while making and thinking through serious-playful invention-intervention-shaping-learning processes.

Notes

1 Current paradigms for artistic research have been discussed in interesting ways by several authors, for example as (a) complexity and change, with the complex as different to the complicated (Meadows, D. 2009. *Thinking in systems*); performance + performativity (e.g. by Donna Haraway); affect, as discussed by Gilles Deleuze in *A Thousand Plateaus*; non-essential, relational identities (by Doreen Massey in *For Space*, 2005); logics in flexible configurations and assemblage systems (e.g. by Gilles Deleuze, Manuel DeLanda or Elisabeth Grosz in *Chaos, territory, art*); the socio-spatial (e.g. by Henri Lefebvre or David Harvey); the narrative and the spatial (Dyrssen 2010); the role of intuition, sensing and challenging the concept of 'knowing' (Jullien 1999; Glissant 1997); interaction with the material, worlding (Janssens 2012); doxa and research in terms of 'rethinking' (Rosengren). Also see *Yearbooks for Artistic Research* published by the Swedish Research Council, from 2004.
2 The overview of the research field was conducted by the Committee for Artistic Research as part of a large survey covering all research areas, commissioned by the Swedish Research Council and accomplished 2014–15, where I participated in the working group.
3 E.g. see Johnson (2010).
4 For a discussion on inclusions and exclusions in discourses related to space and power, see Fredriksson (2014).
5 Dilemmas of judgement and value are discussed in the first issue of PARSE (01), in which both Mick Wilson and Maria Lind touch upon the problematics of the term, but its possible productive role is not discussed.
6 The international conference *Transvaluation* was hosted by the Department of Architecture at Chalmers, Gothenburg, in 2015, with the aim to challenge the increasing indicator-driven research culture, particularly affecting artistic research practices. The conference was preceded by a doctoral course (2013–14) and workshops. A digital publication is planned 2016 – see www.chalmers.se/transvaluation.
7 The term 'worlding', emanating primarily from Martin Heidegger and Friedrich Nietzsche, has been studied from a philosophical perspective by Peter De Graeve and discussed within architecture by Nel Janssens. It was one of four themes at the Transvaluation conference (2015), where both De Graeve and Janssens were members of the main working group.
8 Social rituals related to musical performance, of course, display a large variety. Within art music, music-material-performance have been explored through artistic research e.g. by Lützow-Holm (2014).

The accuracy of artistic judgement 187

9 Hultqvist recognises several parallels between musical composition and understandings of cognitive processes, nature and synergetics and refers to books – some available in English – with strong impact on the artistic research discourse, such as *Order out of Chaos* by Ilya Prigogine and Isabelle Stengers (1985); *Märk världen* by Tor Nørretranders (1993); *Aesthetic Theory* by Theodor W. Adorno (2002, in German: *Ästhetische Theorie, Rätselcharakter, Wahrheitsgehalt, Metaphysik* 1970); *Mind and Nature: A Necessary Unit* by Gregory Bateson (1979); and several books by cognitive scientist Peter Gärdenfors.
10 Björling (2016, 67–71) refers to urban acupuncture approaches by Manuel de Solà-Morales, *The Matter of Things* (2008) and Enrique Miralles as presented in *El Croquis* (2000).
11 For instance, Raoul Bunschoten demonstrates how 'Projective Prototypes' can reveal hidden potentials and possibilities in the urban landscape. Like urban acupuncture, such prototypes can expose both physical and material conditions and underlying processes that affect and shape the urban landscape (Bunschoten 2001; Björling 2014).

Bibliography

Banham, Rayner. 2001 [1971]. *Los Angeles: The architecture of four ecologies*. Los Angeles: University of California press.

Bateson, Gregory. 1973. *Steps to an ecology of mind*. New York: Ballantine Books.

Biggs, Michael and Daniela Büchler. 2010. 'Communities, values, conventions and actions'. In *The Routledge companion to research in the arts*, edited by Michael Biggs and Henrik Karlsson, 82–98. London and New York: Routledge.

Björling, Nils. 2014. *Urbana nyckelprojekt: Planeringsverktyg för sköra stadslandskap*. Gothenburg: Chalmers University of Technology, Department of Architecture (licentiate thesis).

Björling, Nils. 2016. *Sköra stadslandskap. Planeringsmetoder för att öppna urbaniseringens rumsliga inlåsningar*. Doctoral dissertation. Gothenburg: Chalmers University of Technology, Department of Architecture.

Braae, Ellen. 2015. *Beauty redeemed: Recycling post-industrial landscapes*. Basel: Birkhäuser.

Bunschoten, Raoul. 2001. *Urban flotsam: Stirring the city*. Rotterdam: 010 Publishers.

Cuff, Dana and Roger Sherman. 2011. *Fast-forward urbanism, rethinking architecture's engagement with the city*. New York: Princeton Architectural Press.

Dahlhaus, Carl. 1967. *Musikästhetik*. Köln: Gerig.

Damasio, Antonio. 2006. *Descartes' error: Emotion, reason and the human brain*. London: Vintage.

DeLanda, Manuel. 2004. *Intensive science and virtual philosophy*. London: Continuum.

DeLanda, Manuel. 2006. *A new philosophy of society: Assemblage theory and social complexity*. London: Continuum.

Dunin-Woyseth, Halina and Jan Michl, eds. 2001. *Towards a disciplinary identity of the making professions: The Oslo millennium reader*, Vol. 4, Research Magazine. Oslo: Oslo School of Architecture.

Dyrssen, Catharina. 1995. *Musikens rum: Metaforer, ritualer, institutioner. (Musical space: Metaphors, rituals, institutions: A cultural study of architecture within and*

188   *Catharina Dyrssen*

around music). Doctoral Thesis. Gothenburg: Chalmers University of Technology, Department of Architecture.

Dyrssen, Catharina. 2010. 'Navigating in heterogeneity: Architectural thinking and art-based research'. In *The Routledge companion to research in the arts*, edited by Michael Biggs and Henrik Karlsson, 223–239. London and New York: Routledge.

Fredriksson, Julia. 2014. *Konstruktioner av en stadskärna: Den postindustriella stadens rumsliga maktrelationer.* Doctoral dissertation. Göteborg: Chalmers tekniska högskola, Institutionen för arkitektur.

Gärdenfors, Peter. 2005a. *Tankens vindlar. Om språk, minne och berättande.* Nora: Nya Doxa.

Gärdenfors, Peter. 2005b. *The dynamics of thought.* Dordrecht: Springer.

Glissant, Edouard. 1997. *Poetics of relation.* Ann Arbor: University of Michigan Press.

Guattari, Felix. 1989. 'Three ecologies'. *New Formations* (8): 131–147.

Hanslick, Eduard. 1918. *Vom Musikalisch-Schönen: Ein Beitrag zur Revision der Ästhetik der Tonkunst.* Leipzig: Breitkopf & Härtel.

Harvey, David. 2006. *Spaces of global capitalism: A theory of uneven geographical development.* London: Verso.

Heister, Hanns W. 1983. *Das Konzert: Theorie einer Kulturform I-II.* Wilhelmshafen: Heinrichhofen's Verlag.

Hultqvist, Anders. 2013. *Komposition. Trädgården – som förgrenar sig.* ArtMonitor doktorsavhandlingar och licentiatuppsatser nr 43. Doctoral dissertation. Göteborg: Göteborgs Universitet.

Hultqvist, Anders. 2014. 'Time'. In *Sound and other spaces*, edited by Catharina Dyrssen, 46–51. Gothenburg: Bo Ejeby Förlag.

Janssens, Nel. 2012. *Utopia-driven projective research: A design approach to explore the theory and practice of Meta-Urbanism.* Doctoral dissertation. Gothenburg: Department of Architecture, Chalmers University of Technology.

Johnson, Mark. 2010. 'Embodied knowing through art'. In *The Routledge companion to research in the arts*, edited by Michael Biggs and Henrik Karlsson, 141–151. London and New York: Routledge.

Jullien, Francois. 1999. *En vis är utan idé.* Gråbo: Bokförlaget Anthropos AB.

Kramer, Lawrence. 1990. *Music as cultural practice 1800–1900.* Berkeley: University of California Press.

Liedman, Sven-Eric. 2006. *Stenarna i själen: Form och materia från antiken till idag.* Stockholm: Albert Bonniers förlag.

Lippman, Edward, ed. 1986. *Musical aesthetics: A historical reader.* New York: Pendragon Press.

Lützow-Holm, Ole, Magnus Haglund, Henrik Hellstenius, Anders Hultqvist, and Anna Lindal. 2014. 'Towards an expanded field of art music'. In *Methods, process, reporting: Artistic research yearbook 2014*, edited by Torbjörn Lind, 130–155. Stockholm: The Swedish Research Council.

Massey, Doreen. 2005. *For space.* London: Sage Publications.

PARSE 01: Judgement. Spring 2015. University of Gothenburg.

PARSE 02: The value of contemporary art. Autumn 2015. University of Gothenburg.

Rosengren, Mats. 2002. *Doxologi: en essä om kunskap.* Åstorp: Rhetor.

Rosengren, Mats. 2008. 'The magma of imaginary politics'. *Art Monitor* (5) 5: 13–118.

Swedish Research Council. 2015a. *Artistic research: A subject overview*. Edited by Torbjörn Lind. Report. www.vr.se

Swedish Research Council. 2015b. 'Artistic research: A subject overview'. In *Yearbook 2015*, edited by Torbjörn Lind, 20–27, 180–202. Stockholm: Swedish Research Council.

Waldheim, Charles, ed. 2006. *The landscape urbanism reader*. New York: Princeton Architectural Press.

Index

Note: End note information is denoted with an n and note number following the page number.

actor network theory (ANT) 133, 140
ADAPT-r network/grant 73, 96
aesthetics 77, 154, 183
Agder, University of (UiA) 102–9, 112n1, 112n3
apprentice–master model 10, 52, 87, 124
architect 63, 70–2, 77, 96; as artist 52; as 'Baumeister' 52; professional title 52; role of 51, 60, 96
architectural design 26, 27, 51, 53, 58–9, 65, 66n7, 75, 150, 156, 159; definition of 66–7n7; doctoral degrees in 51, 53, 55–6, 64–6, 66n1, 73, 77; research in 69–71, 156; Simultaneous Projection 63; Swiss degrees in 51–3; Swiss schools of 51–2; Synchronous Design 63; *see also* doctorateness; doctorates/ PhDs; Ecole Polytechnique Fédérale Lausanne (EPFL); Eidgenössische Technische Hochschule Zürich (ETHZ); research; Svizzera Italiana Mendrisio, Università della (USI)
architecture 15, 51, 71, 73, 75, 89, 151, 180; and chance 75, 77; compositional approach in 153, 181, 183; of resistance 78; Swiss doctoral studies in 54; in Switzerland 52; *see also* architect; architectural design; Bartlett School of Architecture; chance; Commission for Architecture and the Built Environment (CABE); Royal Melbourne Institute of Technology (RMIT)
'architecture studio' 87
art, institutional theory of 6, 7

artistic development work 38–9; *see also* research, artistic
artistic research, institutional theory of 6, 7, 12, 15
Asia 85, 86, 88, 94
assessment process, stakeholders of 4, 6, 15, 52, 131–2, 137, 141
Australia 7, 86, 88, 94, 97, 98
authority dependence 149

Barcelona 86, 91, 94
Bartlett School of Architecture 69, 73, 75
Bauhaus 87
Bergen Academy of Art and Design (KHIB) 38
Bologna Bergen Conference 2005 37; Communiqué 45
Bologna Berlin Conference of 2003 43, 44; Communiqué 37, 147
Bologna Process 36–7, 40, 41–2, 44, 45–6, 51–2, 174n13; Bologna Declaration 35–7, 41, 43, 46, 147; Bologna Model 33–4; Joint Quality Initiative (JQI) 43, 44–5; member states 36, 39, 41, 42, 43
Bourdieu, Pierre 118
Bråthen, Elin Synnøve 109–10

chance: concept of 75; in design 77; vs. necessity 75; in perception 77; role of 83; species of 77
'clusters' *see* 'hunks'
cognition, situated 182
Commission for Architecture and the Built Environment (CABE) 85, 97, 98

communication, and artistic research
162–3, 164
community legitimization 5–6
connoisseur 17–18, 28–9, 130;
definition of 18
connoisseurship, concept of 17–19
connoisseurship model 9, 17–19
content: experiential 164, 166, 173n10
Council of Europe 41
'crit' 85, 87, 93, 97, 98
critic 28–9, 130; definition of 18
criticism, concept of 9, 17–19
Cross, Nigel 56, 65, 67n15

Damasio, Antonio 182, 183
De Groof, Jan 42, 46
Denmark 43
design computing 22, 23–4
doctoral assessment 16, 19, 26, 27–30,
45, 69, 85, 90–2, 94, 95, 107,
109, 111, 114, 124, 170; see also
doctorateness
doctoral degree 16, 35, 51, 53, 56, 65,
66n1, 102, 110, 177; meaning of 16;
see also doctorates/PhDs
doctorateness 15–16, 17, 28–9, 45,
51, 53, 56, 65–6, 69, 108, 118, 141,
147–8, 153, 158–9, 162, 166–7,
173n12, 181, 185; in architecture/
architectural design 56, 65–6, 82, 83,
95, 129–30, 140; in creative arts 6–7,
15, 114–15, 129–30, 140; definition
of 3, 29–30; differing views of 9–10;
discipline-specific aspects 7–12;
extrinsic evidence for 7–12; generic
aspects 7–12; intrinsic evidence for
7–11; as learning outcome 147;
musical/in music 114–15, 118–19;
original contribution 4, 33, 43, 93,
140; in performing arts 114–15; in
popular music 102, 107, 110, 111;
practice-based 118; standards of
40; as transferable academic value
10, 11; see also doctorates/PhDs;
research
doctorates/PhDs 44; in artistic practice
118, 169; in dance 116; definition
53; by design 69, 72–4, 77, 78, 79,
83, 169; dissertation for 54, 65,
102, 103, 115–16; higher 43; in
installation artwork 116; meaning of
147–8; in music 103–4, 115–16; in
popular music performance 104–11;

by practice 71; practice-based 35,
85–6, 91–2, 98, 114; research-
based 43, 114; research-led 114;
in performance 116; professional
(practitioner's) 43, 44; by research
35; taught 44; thesis for 54, 65; see
also doctoral degree; doctorateness;
practice-based research degrees (RDs)
drawing 20–2, 66–7n7, 70, 73, 74, 75,
77, 79, 83, 137
Dublin Descriptors 17, 19, 29, 33–4,
37–46, 130, 147; Framework for
Qualifications in 17; see also Lisbon
Recognition Convention

École des Beaux-Artes 87
Ecole Polytechnique Fédérale Lausanne
(EPFL) 51–2, 66n2
Eidgenössische Technische Hochschule
Zürich (ETHZ) 51–3, 63
England 43, 46n3, 97, 98
Enlightenment 167–8, 169
ERASMUS Network for Music,
Polifonia 39–40
Europe 7, 36, 73, 85, 86, 88, 94, 97,
118, 161
European Association of Education
Law and Policy 42
European Economic Area (EEA) 42
European Framework for Qualifications
34, 36, 130
European Higher Education Area
(EHEA) 36, 41, 45
European Qualification Framework of
Lifelong Learning (EQF) 42
European Research Council 33
European Union (EU) 36, 42, 73;
Parliament 42

Federal Administrative Court, St.
Gallen 58, 61–3, 64–5
Federation of Swiss Architects BSA
58–60, 67n10
feelings, experiential 164, 173n10
Feenberg, Andrew 139
Fichet, Johann Gottlieb 167
Flanders 129, 132, 142
Flood Strøm, Tone 43, 45, 46n1,
46n4
forms of adaptation 117
foundationalism 6; epistemic 6; social 6
Frayling, Christopher 35, 38, 162;
see also research

192 *Index*

Galileo 148
gap analysis 4, 5
Gärdenfors, Peter 182, 183, 186n9
gaze: anxious 155; compulsive 155; strategic 155
Genk 132, 134, 136, 141, 142n3
guild model/guilds 34, 87

Harvey, David 137, 139, 154
Heidegger, Martin 174n13, 186n7
Hill, Jonathan 73
Howlett, Michael 110–11
Hultqvist, Anders 154, 181–2, 183, 186n9
human–computer interaction (HCI) 132
Humboldt, Alexander von 167, 168
Humboldt University model 178
'hunks' 58–60, 64; examples of 59

identity 123–4, 178; artistic 117, 118; musical 115, 121, 126–7; national 161; personal 115; professional 115, 122; relational 154, 185
impossibility theorem 152
instruct/instruction 152–3, 155–7, 158–9
interdisciplinarity 16
interdisciplinary research 16–17, 19, 136; *see also* research
interpretative phenomenological analysis (IPA) 119
Ireland 43
Irigaray, Luce 174n13
Israel 78–9

judgement 6–8, 18–19, 35, 37, 166, 177, 179, 181–3, 184–6, 186n5; aesthetic 154, 179; artistic 155, 184; compositional 186; *see also* doctoral assessment

Kant, Immanuel 167, 168, 179
knowledge 42, 43, 72, 87, 91, 120, 147, 154, 156, 158, 159, 163, 168–9, 173n7, 174n13, 178–80, 183; academic 7, 10, 37, 82; acceleration of 34; artistic 162; building of 39, 149; for change 152; commercial exploitation of 7; as commodity 147; by design 63, 64; on design 63, 64; and doctoral degree 37, 43, 65; as 'doxic' value systems 185; as economic factor 36; experiential 164–5; explanatory 148–50; implicit

91; insider 106, 109, 112, 119; intuitive 109; making 42, 179, 180, 185; Mode 234; musical 101, 106; new 44, 65, 69, 72, 89, 91, 95–6, 148, 167; oral 106, 109, 111; *phronesis* 163–4; practice of 163–4; production/creation of 9, 15, 16–17, 34, 35, 40–1, 98, 147–8, 152–3, 167, 177–80, 184, 185; professional 94, 166; from research 56–8, 59–60, 115; situated 148, 149, 153, 156, 158, 163; stable 149, 157; systems of 181; tacit 91, 101, 109, 111; theoretical 7, 52; thirst for 121; transfer/transmission of 101, 121

learning community 87, 89, 94, 97, 98
Leeds, University of 115–16, 118, 119, 120, 126–7
Lisbon Recognition Convention 41
literature review 4, 5, 9, 27

Magna Charta Universitatum 36–7, 46
Manolopoulou, Yeoryia 74–7
Marx, Karl 161
Melbourne 85, 86
mental space 67n14, 88
methodology 74, 105, 139, 141, 178; of doctoral project 23; in humanities 11–12; research 70–1, 81; in sciences 11, 163
Middle Ages 87
mind dependence *see* authority dependence
minor activism 131–2
modelling actions 70, 133, 153–4, 159, 179, 184
music 180–2; art 101, 186n8; classical 101, 109, 111; composition 181–2, 186n9; popular 101–12, 112n1, 112n2, 112n3; Western art 101; *see also* popular music; research

Nancy, Jean-Luc 156, 174n13
neo-liberalism 169
New Public Management 33
New Zealand 98
Nietzsche, Friedrich 174n13, 186n7
NOKUT (the Norwegian Agency for Quality Assurance in Education) 105
'Nordic Model' of research, the 11–12; *see also* research
Northern Ireland 43, 46n2, 46n3

Norway 38–9, 102–5, 107–9, 112n1
Norwegian Academy of Music 38
Norwegian Artistic Development
    Fellowship Programme
    (Artistic Research Fellowship
    Programme) 38
Norwegian Law of Universities and
    University Colleges 38
Norwegian Qualification Framework 38
Nowotny, Helga 33

open-textured concept 166–7, 170
Oslo School of Architecture and Design
    (AHO) 19, 23, 26, 29–30, 38

Palestine 78–9, 82; Birzeit 79, 81–2;
    West Bank 79
Palestinian/Israeli conflict 78–9, 81;
    Israeli occupation 82; Separation
    Wall 79
paradigm shift 5, 96; vs. incompetence 5
permeable practices 18, 29
popular music: definition of 102,
    112n2; orality of 101, 106;
    performance of 103, 104, 105; tacit
    knowledge of 101
post-Fordism 131
practice-based research degrees (RDs)
    114, 118–20; in art 114; in design
    114; in music 114–15, 126–7; in
    music composition 115, 118–26; in
    music performance 115, 118–26;
    student's qualifications for 120–1;
    and student–supervisor relationship
    123–4, 126–7
Practice Research Symposium (PRS)
    87–8, 89, 90, 91, 93, 94, 95, 97, 98
practitioner-researchers, community of
    17, 18
proformative capacity 154, 155, 183,
    184, 185
protected research procedure (PRP)
    149–51, 153, 156, 158
publics, construction of 129–30, 132,
    134, 141

research 39, 54, 59, 66, 88–9, 97, 98,
    105, 168, 174n13, 179–80, 181, 185;
    academic 3, 17, 18, 41, 56, 130–1,
    140; architectural 24–6, 56, 59, 71,
    77, 83, 179, 180; architectural design
    (design research in architecture)
    69–75, 77, 81, 82–3, 93, 150, 156;
    artistic 6–7, 11–12, 17, 25, 29,

38–40, 103–4, 108, 118, 129, 131,
    141, 150, 155, 162–4, 166, 169–71,
    173n12, 177–83, 185, 186n1, 186n2,
    186n6, 186n8, 186n9; definition
    of 37–8, 40, 41, 45, 54, 107; by
    design 25, 26, 29, 56–8, 63, 64, 151,
    174n13; on design 56–8, 63, 64;
    design-based 15, 26, 130–4; design
    practice 85–7, 94–5, 99; doctoral
    3, 7, 27, 29, 64–5, 79; ethics 43,
    108; experimental forms of 122,
    127; Frayling concept of 38, 162;
    on insider knowledge 112; methods/
    methodology of 40, 71; methods
    training 90; non-observational
    149–53, 156–9; observational
    148–9, 152–3, 156–9; participatory
    design (PD) 131–4; in popular music
    performance 105, 109, 111, 112;
    practice-led (-based) 18, 25, 27–8,
    71, 85, 88, 91, 114, 117, 119–20,
    122, 139, 151, 162, 164, 169,
    173n12; practicing 41; presentation
    of 107–8; and principle of self-
    protection 149; scientific 83, 140,
    150; social constructivist approach
    of 133, 137, 139; through art and
    design 130, 133; traditional 29,
    149, 151; training 4–5, 8, 15, 159;
    transdisciplinary research 16–17,
    19; see also protected research
    procedure (PRP)
Research Excellence Framework 118
research practice: artistic 179, 180,
    186n6; structural description of 5;
    see also research
Royal Melbourne Institute of
    Technology (RMIT) University
    (previously the Royal Melbourne
    Institute of Technology) 73, 85–90,
    95, 96; RMIT model 86–95, 91–5,
    97, 98; see also Practice Research
    Symposium (PRS)

Saarinen, Eliel 71–2
Schaik, Leon van 73, 86–7, 89, 96
Schiller, Friedrich 167
scholarship: and artistic development
    work 38; doctoral 69; integrated
    88–9; modes of 89; traditional 29
science, technology and society studies
    (STS) 132–3, 134, 136, 137, 140,
    141, 142
Scotland 43, 44, 98

194 *Index*

Sharif, Yara 75, 78–2
simulation 153–4; *see also* modelling actions
Sint-Lucas/KU Leuven School of Architecture 73, 142n2, 150, 172n1
soft law 42
Spivak, Gayatri 174n13
Staufer, Astrid 63–4
Staufer & Hasler Architects 58, 62
Stockholm University of the Arts 162, 169
Svizzera Italiana Mendrisio, Università della (USI) 51–2
Sweden 38–9, 162
Swedish Law of University Colleges 39
Switzerland 51–2, 54, 55, 58–3, 66n3

Terkel, Studs 96
'The Other Market' (TOM) 133–4
transdisciplinarity 16
transgressive 5–6; vs. madness 6
transvaluation 169, 174n13
Transvaluation conference 186n6, 186n7

UK Council for Graduate Education (UKCGE) 34–5
UNESCO 42
United Kingdom 34–5, 40, 69, 75, 85, 103, 112, 117, 118, 119
university, history of 35, 167–9, 178
urban acupuncture 155, 159n1, 159n2, 184
urban ecologies 154–5
urbanisation 151

Vietnam 73, 86; Ho Chi Minh City 86

Wales 43, 46n3, 98, 110
Weisman, Friedrich 167
Westminster, University of 69, 75
Wittgenstein, Ludwig 3, 165, 166, 167, 174n13
worlding 153, 155–6, 174n13, 180, 186n1, 186n7
World Trade Organisation (WTO) 37

Zurich University of the Arts *see* Eidgenössische Technische Hochschule Zürich (ETHZ)